VIENNA—ITS MUSICAL HERITAGE

"Ja so singt man in der Stadt wo ich geboren bin"—
JOHANN STRAUSS, son

VIENNA
ITS MUSICAL HERITAGE

EGON GARTENBERG

THE PENNSYLVANIA STATE UNIVERSITY PRESS

UNIVERSITY PARK AND LONDON

to the memory of my Father
with respect
and grudging admiration

Preface

Vienna has loved all music (well, almost all), of Beethoven or Rossini, Schubert or Paganini, Johann Strauss or Offenbach, but the same thing can be said of London, Paris, or Berlin. The difference has been Vienna's influence on music. Early renaissance opera found its first home outside Italy within Vienna's walls. There it gained new vitality as the city combined two arts into a distinct style of music known today as "Vienna Baroque." The examples are countless. The symphonic efforts of Germany culminated in the Vienna of Haydn, and the miniature orchestra became his string quartet. The primitive German Singspiel, merged with Italian style by the genius of Mozart, reached its operatic pinnacle in the city just as German romanticism enjoyed its first musical bloom in Vienna with Beethoven and Schubert.

Romans, Turks, Hungarians, Germans, Habsburgs, war and peace, plague, politics, social reform, literature, fashion, wine, beer, coffee, all had a profound influence on the city and its music, and sometimes the reverse was true. In the early nineteenth century, for example, when an assembly of more than three persons in public was unlawful, Prince Metternich looked benignly on the crowds which thronged the dance halls and ball rooms. As long as they swung a leg they wouldn't swing clubs. Thus it was sixty years before the winds of the French Revolution blew through the streets of Vienna. Early in this century while official Vienna still attempted to retain the gaiety, the surface glitter of a bygone era, a new generation of composers, led by Schönberg, intuitively foresaw the inevitable collapse and holocaust and expressed it in music.

About every three hundred years, music has taken a giant step. Around the year 1000 it was the invention of musical annotation, three hundred years later the beginnings of harmony, at the beginning of the seventeenth century the emergence of opera. And at the turn of the twentieth century, Vienna was destined to be the reluctant cradle of the most recent advance. The breakdown of a worn-out social order, the hysterical excesses of worn-out tonality, demanded a new order, a new musical language. The new Viennese masters gave the musical world polytonality and the tone row. It is beyond the vision and scope of this book to venture a guess about music's future and fate three hundred years or even thirty years hence. If our world has not consumed itself by then, however, Vienna will still play a commanding musical role.

E. G.

September 1967

Acknowledgments

The author's thanks go to the following individuals and institutions:

Professor Albert van Ackere, Music Department, Vassar College, for criticism and musicological advice, particularly in the matter of baroque music.

Mrs. Janet McLean, B.M., M.M., Washington Bureau, *New York Times*, for a critical reading of the manuscript and advice on seventeenth- and eighteenth-century opera and opera performance.

Professor Rudolf Jettel, the Austrian State Academy of Music and the Vienna Philharmonic Orchestra, for advice on classical interpretation and for information on contemporary Austrian music.

Professor Helmut Wobisch, secretary of the Vienna Philharmonic Orchestra, for a copy of the complete history of the Vienna Philharmonic Orchestra.

To the late Heinrich Kralik, music critic and musicologist of Vienna, for putting at my disposal the manuscripts of his studies on "The Vienna Opera" and "The Great Orchestra" and for his kind encouragement.

Hofrat Dr. Hans Pauer, Curator of the Picture Archives and Portrait Collection of the Austrian National Library, for assistance in establishing pictorial continuity.

The Austrian State Press Service for a large selection of original photographs.

The Austrian Tourist Bureau in Vienna for advice on pictorial continuity and many photographs pertaining to Vienna's musical history.

Miss Ruby McFadden, former librarian of Wilson College in Chambersburg, Pennsylvania, for extensive bibliographic advice.

The Coyle Free Library in Chambersburg, Pennsylvania, for assistance in obtaining many sources.

Belle, my wife, for patiently and passionately sharing my hopes and dreams, defeats and despairs, triumphs and elations.

Contents

Illustrations
(pages 114/115)

Pictures marked with an asterisk are from the Bild-Archiv and Porträt-Sämm-
lung of the Österreichische Nationalbibliothek; 25 and 26 (Elizabeth and Franz
Josef in their youth) are from the collection of the Bass Museum of Art.

THE WALLED CITY

I

Birth of the City

In Vienna on May 15, 1955, representatives of the Soviet, American, British, French, and Austrian governments signed a "State Treaty" restoring Austria's full sovereignty after seven years of *Anschluss* with Germany and ten years of "Allied" occupation—the latter once compared to "four elephants in a rowboat." Vienna itself had been divided into five zones and occupied by foreign troops of four different nationalities and even more races. The Viennese were fond of relating how they had secretly listened to Allied radio broadcasts during the war: "The Soviet Union calls Austria," the announcer would intone; or "America calls Austria," or "Britain calls Austria." "We didn't call anyone," the Viennese would then explain, "but now they're all here." At the time of the State Treaty the words of the popular song weren't changed from "Wien, Wien, nur du allein" to "Wien, Wien, endlich allein"—but it may have been considered.

Other cities would have celebrated the restoration of sovereignty with parades, bunting, fireworks, feasting and dancing, but Vienna celebrated it with a nine-day music festival in the rebuilt State Opera which had been bombed out during the war. At the first performance in the new building, of Beethoven's *Fidelio*, half of the seats were occupied by distinguished foreign guests; fifteen times as many people as could be seated had applied for tickets, and thirty thousand Viennese listened over loudspeakers outside the building. The city's role as the eastern bastion of Christianity against the Turks was dusty history. Of the glories of a great empire stretching back to the Holy Roman Empire of the Middle Ages, only statues and baroque palaces remained. But Vienna still had the best claim to the title of music capital of the world.

The story began eighteen centuries earlier when the Romans occupied a Celtic settlement, Vindobona, and enlarged it into the frontier station (*castrum*) where Marcus Aurelius was to die in

A.D. 180. We can easily imagine a scene from this period: From billowing dust clouds a mounted centurion emerging into the shimmering heat of the day. Behind him a plodding legion stretching toward the horizon. Swords beating rhythmically against shin guards. Battle-dented helmets, shields, and breast-plates. Trumpets heralding the approach to Vindobona. The troops certainly weren't singing *Gaudeamus igitur*, but they were undoubtedly looking forward to a number of cups of good wine. There, on the last undulating slopes of the Alps descending toward the settlement on the Danube, legionnaires had built terraces and planted the vines they had brought from the Mediterranean. After 1,800 years these Roman vineyards still flourish. So does the wine and so does the settlement—Vienna.

In the course of turbulent centuries, Vienna grew from armed camp to fortress city to metropolis. Its history was often clouded, but its wine became clearer, to the delight of citizens, wayfarers, and poets alike. As the poet Wolfgang Schmelzer wrote in 1547,

> The deep-dug walls on every side
> Hold generous cellars, deep and wide
> Well-stocked with rich, sweet-smelling wine
> Like gold within a golden mine.

The Viennese cherish their liquid gold and praise it in poem and song, culminating in Johann Strauss's paean to "Wine, Woman and Song." Even poor vintages were used in Viennese fashion. Once, upon imperial decree of Emperor Frederick III, an especially bad vintage was brought to the cathedral of St. Stefan and mixed with the mortar that went into the building of its lofty spire. Thus Vienna and its famous beverage became inseparably linked, down to the native spelling of city and liquid, *Wien* and *Wein*. Under its exhilarating influence, aided by violin, guitar, bagpipe, or harp, tongues loosen and inhibitions vanish in that mellow Viennese state of mind known throughout the world as "Gemütlichkeit."

By the time of the Crusades, thirteenth-century Vienna had become a bustling town; two churches, a market place, shops, and artisans served the spiritual and bodily needs of Europe's feudal levies on their way to the Holy Land. The town prospered. As early as 1485 Matthias Corvinus of Hungary, who had captured the city, wrote glowingly: "The entire territory of Vienna is like an enormous garden, surrounded by orchards and vineyards." But upon his return from the Holy Land Richard the Lion-Hearted had little reason to think such thoughts about Vienna when he was arrested on the city's outskirts by the armed men of Leopold V of Austria. Legend has it that the ransom which freed him was large enough to have built Vienna's formidable walls.

When locating Vienna on the patchwork quilt of Europe, a question arises: Why did the city grow on the spot it occupies today? At first glance the location seems neither historically significant nor geographically logical. Upon closer scrutiny, however, we find the site at the foot of the Alps lying on the main north-south trade route between the Baltic and Adriatic. The location on the Danube is no less significant. Not until the Danube neared Vienna was it free from rapids, narrows, and the robber barons whose ruined castles still stare menacingly from lofty heights along the river. Thus Austria and Vienna, while firmly anchored as the West's easternmost bulwark, used the umbilical cord of the river for communication and trade with the East. With navigation a two-way street we also find unmistakable oriental mementos in the onion-shaped cupolas of Austria's churches and Vienna's love for coffee and coffee houses.

Another look at Europe's mottled map reveals the influences which shaped Vienna and which it absorbed and sublimated. There is the sentimentality of the Slavs in the north and south, the sparkle of the Magyars in the East, the language and intellect of the Germans to the West. Italian influence left its colorful marks early on the Viennese scene: from the organ grinder who roamed the streets winding his out-of-tune hurdy-gurdy to the street vendor of ices and rainbow-colored cold drinks. One *capirs* much of this from the dialect itself: "I have been *robot*ing all day," says the Viennese, as he eats *Kukuruz* (on the cob) for supper (*capiren*, "comprehend" from Italian; *Robot*, "irksome toil" from Czech; *Kukuruz*, "corn" from Hungarian). The German influence has been paramount since Austria's life and history are recorded in German. There is, moreover, another, more prosaic area of German influence, the excellence of Viennese beer. Equally as popular as wine, it is consumed in large foaming quantities together with sizeable portions of such Viennese culinary delicacies as *Schnitzel* and *Backhändel*. All these influences, slowly injected and superimposed over eighteen centuries, shaped Vienna's relaxed outlook on life.

There is perhaps no better illustration of Viennese laissez-faire than the anecdote told of famous actor-singer Alexander Girardi, the friend of Johann Strauss. A rehearsal had been called for ten o'clock in the morning, but Girardi was nowhere in sight. When he finally put in an appearance at noon, the director vented his barely disguised sarcasm:

"Mr. Girardi, if I'd been you, I wouldn't've come at all." Girardi's craggy face broke into its famous impish smile.

"Yes, You—but I have a sense of responsibility."

This relaxed attitude and ostrich-like behaviour did not desert the Viennese even in times of danger. Rumor has it that during World War I the German General Staff considered a certain military situation "serious but not hopeless" while their Austrian counterparts saw it as "hopeless but not serious."

Mellowness in peace and war was further abetted by the gradual expansion of the Austrian Empire to include many tongues and religions and racial characteristics, mainly through marriage rather than conquest. "Austria lost its wars but won its marriages." Famous exceptions only tend to prove the basic truth of this bon mot. Austria did repulse the Turks twice before the walls of Vienna and did hand Napoleon his first defeat at Aspern. Nor were all Habsburg marriages happy or heaven-blessed. Observe the fate of Empress Maria Theresia's daughter Marie Antoinette on the guillotine, or of Empress Elizabeth at the hands of an assassin. Nevertheless over the centuries the house of Habsburg ruled and grew through marriage so successfully that its marital fortunes became proverbial throughout Europe: "Tu, felix Austria, nube."* All those migrations and invasions, acquisitions and marriages, made Vienna, the capital of an empire, a commercial, political, scientific, and artistic center. It resulted in that unique blend of Viennese sentimentality, pessimism, penchant for the good life, intellect, and lively charm.

---

* The much quoted second line of a poem:

Bella gerant alii!	Let others make war!
Tu, felix Austria, nube.	Thou, happy Austria, wed.
Nam quae Mars aliis	For Venus gives thee those realms
Dat tibi regna Venus.	Which on others Mars bestows.

II

The Emperors' Dance

The seed of genius needs fertile soil, and the artistic atmosphere of Vienna irresistibly attracted musicians and composers. Already in the thirteenth century, Walter von der Vogelweide, an Austrian of the lesser nobility and one of the great minnesingers exclaimed, "In Österreich lernt ich singen und sagen" (In Austria I learned to sing and poetize). By the seventeenth century one traveller remarked, "There are so many musicians in Vienna, one would be hard pressed to meet more of them anywhere else."

Credit for the cultural influx goes to a succession of Habsburg rulers who wished to enhance the splendor of the court with famous poets, musicians, painters, and builders. The founder of the dynasty, Rudolf of Habsburg, was a man of great capacity, valiant and chivalric in war, fortunate in battle, and much feared. Through valor and perseverance he rose from petty count to emperor and acquired the Duchy of Austria for himself. Shortly after his death, work was started on the cathedral whose entire front shows the influence of Rudolf's romanesque period. Maximilian I was one of Rudolf's early successors. Although Machiavelli described him as a weathervane moved by whims of the moment, he was a man of intellectual brilliance, high artistic appreciations, and personal charm which foretokened Vienna's lighthearted gaiety. In his youth he was a figure fairy tales are made from. When he rode into Ghent on a large chestnut horse to take Mary of Burgundy for his bride, he was clad in silver armor with his head bare and his flowing hair confined by a circlet of pearls and gems—the very picture of youth, manliness, bravery, and promise.

Most Habsburgs became omnivorous lovers of music and collectors of art. The famous imperial museums were founded by Ferdinand I in 1540 and were enriched by successive Habsburgs until they rank today with the most famous anywhere. Duke Albert of Saxony, who married Maria Christine, Empress Maria Theresia's favorite daughter, founded the Albertina in which he placed a wealth of drawings by

Rembrandt, Rubens and Dürer. They had been collected mostly through the zeal of mad Rudolf II, one of the greatest art lovers among the Habsburgs. It was he who ordered Dürer's "Feast of the Rosary" carried from Venice to Prague on the shoulders of four men, in order not to expose it to the joltings of a carriage. Not all Habsburgs, however, were so artistically sensitive. Emperor Josef II had the same picture auctioned in 1782 together with "some other old trash," among it a picture described as "a naked female bitten by a mad goose" which turned out to be Titian's "Leda and the Swan."

Under the impact of the Reformation, the Papal court in Rome lost some of its magnetic attraction and influence, and the court of Habsburg rose to the forefront among patrons of the arts. Thus an era started in which by day mighty emperors signed treaties which changed the face of the earth and conducted their own compositions with their own orchestras and opera companies at night; when princes and archdukes sang and danced with professional ease, great field marshals acted in plays which outdid in splendor anything ever produced; when every member of the imperial household was expected to be an active musician or actor. It was that love of music, that understanding, which nurtured Vienna into musical prominence and produced a stream of musical expression unequalled anywhere in its constant flow and flower throughout three centuries.

Surprisingly, a lasting artistic influence came through another Roman invasion, fifteen hundred years after Emperor Marcus Aurelius wrote his *Meditations* in Vindobona. This time it was not legions of unnamed Roman soldiers but the poetic and musical flower of Italy whose proud names and melodious art left their mark. The second Roman invasion of Austria began when the first Italian opera troupe reached Salzburg in 1618. One year later Salzburg boasted its own opera stage, and Vienna established one shortly thereafter. In 1619 Emperor Ferdinand II brought his private orchestra from Graz to Vienna and merged its sixty musicians with the court orchestra. Barely twenty years later Vienna witnessed the operatic masterpieces of Monteverdi, Cavalli, Sances, and Bertali, the foremost composers of their day, who took up residence at the imperial court as musical advisers to the emperor.

Italian music, a late-comer among the arts of the Renaissance, by that time had conquered Europe. It had created opera, cantata, chamber music, and concerto and had become the highest expression of musical art. Vienna became an Italian city in the musical sense.

It absorbed and sublimated Italian influences which had started with the marriages of Ferdinand II and Ferdinand III to Italian and Spanish princesses.

Who were the other musical masters who flocked to Vienna? Beginning with the court conductor Giovanni Valentini in 1629, they were predominantly Italian and the influence of Marcantonio Cesti, Antonio Draghi, and Antonio Caldara ranged into the classical period of Haydn and Mozart. The few German and Austrian composers among them were strongly infused with the Italian idiom. Yet Johann Jacob Froberger's compositions were important enough to be studied by the great Bach. The compositions of this eminent keyboard virtuoso reveal the first ideas of the future Viennese school, as did those of Wolfgang Ebner whose most famous work was a set of thirty-six variations on a theme by Emperor Ferdinand III, the number of variations representing the age of the monarch. Beyond any doubt Johann Heinrich Schmelzer was the most prominent native composer of his time and the first Austrian violinist of world renown. He was among the first to incorporate Austrian folk and dance tunes into his compositions. It was that native contribution, superimposed upon the Spanish-speaking court and the Italian musical idiom, which fused all these influences into a unique baroque art form to be known as the "Vienna style." The imperial court, surprisingly, recognized and rewarded that trend, and among the multitude of Italians Schmelzer was elevated to the post of Imperial Court Kapellmeister in 1679, the first German-speaking composer to be so honored, only to be cut down by the plague one year later.

The high mark of Italian influence was reached under four emperors who ruled between 1640 and 1740 and who were musicians, composers, dancers and conductors in their own right (Ferdinand III, 1637–57; Leopold I, 1657–1705; Josef I, 1705–11; Charles VI, 1711–40). During their reign Vienna grew politically and musically into a supranational city. It balanced the polyphonic fervor of the north with the sensuous operatic flow of the south and synthesized them into a high point of European musical culture. By then the great artists of Europe vied for the honor of serving at the Austrian court, not only for the large fees offered but because of the artistic rapport which had been established between sovereign and artist. For the wedding in 1631 of Ferdinand III to Maria Anna of Spain, the first of his three wives, none other than the Spanish poet Calderón de la Barca wrote a comedy. Historians of the time considered

Ferdinand unequalled: "Er stützte sein Szepter mit Leier und Schwert" (He supported his throne with lyre and sword) was said of the monarch who was statesman, poet, sculptor, composer, and patron of the arts.

His son, Leopold I, who succeeded Ferdinand at the age of seventeen, was equally the image of the devout imperial Maecenas. During his 48-year reign he heard three Masses daily, two sermons on Sunday, one in German and one in Italian, kneeling throughout, his eyes on the prayer book spread before him on the stone floor. Although threatened by the Turks, he found time and money for sumptuous operatic productions. Estimates of the cost of maintaining his orchestra, reputed to have been the finest in Europe, ranged up to 60,000 florins. Four hundred operas were performed during his reign, and he himself composed operas and sacred and secular songs. He composed a requiem on the death of his first wife, Empress Margarita, composed a lament on the death of his second wife, Claudia Felicitas, which was also sung at the grave of his third wife as well as his own funeral. His love of music did not desert him even in the hour of death. As it approached he ordered his court musicians assembled in the antechamber, there to play his favorite music while he lay dying. His body, dressed in Spanish court attire, complete with plumed hat, cloak, and sword, lay in state for three days in the Knights' Hall of the Imperial Palace. Then his heart was deposited at the Loretto Chapel, his vitals in St. Stefan's. The body was borne in the dead of night, in silent stately procession to the imperial burial vault, the Capuchin crypt, while the populace of Vienna, all clad in black, their heads bared, lined the streets and lighted the silent path with innumerable tapers and torches.

Leopold's interest in music was so all-consuming that he started a collection of the musical masterpieces of his time which still exists and which contains original scores of Carrisimi, Stradella, Tenaglia, and Pasquini. Leopold's brilliant mind enabled him to correspond with the philosopher Leibnitz. His most lasting contribution, however, lay not in the musical field, but in introducing the "equestrian" or "horse ballet." Until this day Vienna remains the only city in the world which still perpetuates the spectacle and tradition of the equestrian ballet in its Spanish Riding School. Shortly after World War II, its famous snow-white Lipizzan stallions were saved from extinction by U.S. General Patton who had them removed from the city.

Hans von Francolin, in his "Book of Tournaments," tells of the splendid tournaments, the forerunners of the horse ballet, held in the inner courtyard of the imperial palace of Ferdinand I, in honor of his son-in-law Albrecht of Bavaria in 1560. A sham fortress had been erected and the king's knights proceeded to storm it. They fought on foot, armour, shields and weapons gleaming, knightly plumes waving gaily amidst the breaking of spears, until the citadel was taken. The knights, whose numbers were three times as great as that of the defenders to insure success, wore gold ornaments, chains and spurs. Among them, the court jesters, in bright red costumes, rode backwards on asses, much to the delight of the highborn ladies assembled.

The most famous horse ballet of Leopold's reign was the ballet tournament "La Contesa dell' aria e del' aqua" (The contest between air and water), a musical collaboration of Bertali and Schmelzer, produced with unbelievable pomp. Carlo Pasetti, Italy's foremost scenarist was called from Ferrara to supervise the staging. For the inner courtyard of the imperial palace, he designed a temple of Diana in marble, bronze, and lapis lazuli. A brass fanfare opened the spectacle, followed by an aria of the allegorical figure of "Fame," ushered upon the scene by Jason's ship, the *Argo*. The horse ballet which followed was in the form of a joust, arranged by the Florentine nobleman Carduzzi, also brought to Vienna for the occasion. The production reached its apex with the appearance, on stage, of the emperor. Attired as Roman Imperator, complete with gold laurel wreath and gold breastplate studded with diamonds and topazes, he rode a black stallion whose bridle was encrusted with precious stones. He was followed by an array of Austria's nobles whose robes also were adorned with innumerable precious stones while their horses shimmered in gold cloth and gold-tooled leather. The majestic procession closed with the emperor's colorful mounted guard and a group of riders on "saltatori," dancing horses which performed in Spanish gait.

All those performances, however, were overshadowed by the most famous production of the century: Marcantonio Cesti's *Il Pomo d'Oro* (The Golden Apple), according to a member of the audience, a performance such "as had never been seen before and, as long as the world will stand, won't be seen again." That spectacle in five acts and sixty-seven scenes unfolded in a lavish five-hour performance with technical equipment and scenic changes to impress even a modern audience. A special three-tiered theatre, seating 1,500 people, had been built for the occasion. The stage depicted a Greek temple adorned with the Habsburg double eagle. The emperor and his Spanish bride, Margarita Teresa, were seated in the center of the theatre on a raised platform, surrounded by the imperial halberd bearers. The court and nobility who had come from the far corners of the empire to witness the spectacle, filled the galleries.

In the prelude to the opera, the might of Austria was depicted by an equestrian statue of the emperor surrounded by his predecessors. Above it, on clouds, "Austria's Glory" rode on Pegasus, and on stage stood the allegorical figures of Austria's possessions, Italy, Sardinia, Spain, Hungary, Bohemia—and America. After the prelude the sixty-seven scenes, designed by Ludovico Burnacini, the most sought after stage designer of his day, presented spectacles never seen before anywhere. Scenes from heaven and earth, with rain and hail, lightning and thunder; scenes in temples and forests, palaces and caves, at sea and in harbors, vied with the Furies' defeat and wailing flight to Hades. Venus and Neptune, driven in sumptuous chariots bedecked with flowers and surrounded by denizens of the seas, were followed by Jason's ship in a hostile sea and sea battles so realistic that they caused the death of one singer. In the triumphant finale the entire house of Habsburg, beginning with Rudolf I (now dead four hundred years) appeared on clouds while the chorus jubilantly predicted a great future for the newlyweds and their royal offspring.

Shortly thereafter the star of another Italian, Antonio Draghi, rose in Vienna. His importance is borne out by the fact that Haydn, a century later, conducted Draghi's opera *Penelope* for Prince Esterhazy. So enamoured was the emperor with Draghi's music that he not only conducted his works but appeared as a dancer on stage in the performance of his opera *King Gelidor.*

While it is difficult today to visualize one of the great rulers of the earth dancing on stage, it was common practice in baroque Vienna. Leopold's daughters were required to study singing and dancing, sang repeatedly in court cantatas, and danced in opera ballets. Aristocracy staged its equestrian ballets, and in the intimate atmosphere of the court theatre performances the entire entourage took part, including the pages. In later years Empress Maria Theresia was to call herself jocularly the oldest virtuoso in Europe because her father, Charles VI, had made her sing on stage at the age of five, sharing it with the famed castrato Senesino. On another occasion Charles himself accompanied the castrato Farinelli on the harpsichord and presided over the rehearsals. It was he who enticed

Metastasio, the most famous opera librettist of his time, to join the Vienna artistic entourage.

Those performances were not indulgently dismissed as the fatuous efforts of highborn amateurs. Apostolo Zeno, imperial court poet at the Vienna court, reported to friends in Italy:

> I could not begin to describe to you the applause with which my drama was received, which was performed, to the marvel of all only by chevaliers and their ladies, who also danced, played, with the imperial Highness at the head of the orchestra, with the greatest and most skilled mastery of a professor. . . . The three ladies who sang the solos were simply magnificent, and if they were musicians by profession and had to make their living with their singing, they could easily rank with the best, even in Italy.

Music permeated the life of Vienna to such an extent that even servants were pressed into musical service. As late as 1789 a want ad appeared in the Wiener Zeitung: "Wanted by nobleman a servant of good repute who plays the violin well and is able to accompany difficult piano sonatas."

It was in Draghi's time that another "Spectacular," half play, half ball, took place in 1689 on the occasion of Czar Peter's visit to Vienna. Its title was "Die Wirtschaft" (The Inn), and the Emperor and Empress of Austria appeared as the "Innkeepers of the Double Eagle." Servants roles were filled by princes of the realm and chimney sweeps by Austrian counts. The Czar appeared as a Friesland peasant amid a multitude of soldiers, slaves, hunters, gardeners, shepherds, gypsies, and pilgrims, costumed as Greeks, Romans, Chinese, Germans, Venetians, Egyptians, Turks, Indians, Tartars, Moors, Poles, and Swiss, all played by Austrian noblemen.

Josef I continued in the footsteps of his father. Himself a composer (three of his compositions are still preserved) he made the Vienna court more than the meeting place of the musical great. Composers Giovanni Bononcini, Alessandro Scarlatti, and Caldara were his personal friends. His reign witnessed another sensational production, Bononcini's *Camilla, regina di Volsci* in 1697. Eye witnesses reported that the Viennese "have absorbed music so completely, so perfect are their operas in poetic and musical composition, so magnificent their ballets and scenery, so lavish their costumes, that Vienna . . . now even outdoes the lavishness of *Il Pomo d'Oro*." Eventually the Josephinic opera houses proved inadequate for mounting such colossal operatic pageants. In 1708 a new opera house was built, the Kärntnerthor Theatre, famed forerunner of Vienna's imperial opera.

The era of Josef I was given added luster by the emergence of the most prominent figure of the Vienna baroque, Johann Josef Fux. His rise from peasant boy and lowly organist to Imperial Kapellmeister in 1715 is one of the Horatio Alger stories of Vienna. Although his musical creations were legion, he is chiefly remembered for his textbook on polyphony, *Gradus ad Parnassum*, which earned him the title of "Austrian Palestrina." *Gradus* attained such fame that Fux's pupil and patron, Emperor Charles VI, had the volume printed and published at his own expense. Its original Latin text was translated into German, French, Italian, and English and served as an indispensable textbook for Haydn, Mozart, Cherubini, Beethoven and generations of music students.

Actually Fux was a historic anomaly. At a time when sensuous Italian opera was making ever greater inroads into baroque music and actually rose to perfection in Vienna, Fux was a polyphonic island in its surging stream. Yet at the height of his fame he was better known than Bach whose *Well-tempered Clavichord* was published the same year as *Gradus*. The mere fact, however, that the polyphony of Fux and the operas of Caldara, Porpora, and Lotti flourished side by side in Vienna and cross-pollinated each other indicates the musical stature Vienna had attained. Its power of absorbing and fusing these vari-colored influences into a homogeneous *one* was to produce in time the unique "Vienna Style."

Meanwhile Charles VI had succeeded to the throne after his brother had succumbed to the dreaded smallpox. At his court, the music pulse continued strong. Himself a musician and composer, the emperor accompanied Caldara's opera *Euristes*, with his daughters Maria Theresia and Maria Anna singing the solo parts on stage. He founded Vienna's world-famous Academy of Music and was accompanied on his travels by his entire orchestra of 140 musicians. By modern standards, however, the musician's lot was not an enviable one. Contemporaries reported that "the poor musicians are required to perform chamber music, tafel Musik (dinner music), oratorios and operas more than eight-hundred [!] times a year, not counting rehearsals."

The splendor of Vienna had become proverbial throughout Europe. Travellers gazed in wonder at the five-story palaces of gleaming marble in the narrow, and surprisingly clean, medieval streets, the gilded doors, the princely furnishings, tapestries, huge mirrors in hand-wrought silver or exquisite china frames, delicate porcelain figurines, crystal chandeliers, gallery upon gallery of paintings by the world's greatest painters, the unending stream of liveried servants, canopied chaises and luxurious carriages. And, above all, the much sung-about beauty and natural charm of the women of Vienna, all uniting with music to create a high point of European culture. Thus Vienna, at the opening of the eighteenth century, was a city where the musical great of the world congregated, a city of which Montesquieu remarked to Prince Eugene of Savoy: "Alas, one only dies in Vienna, but one does not grow old there."

III

Coffee with Cream

What of the people of this ant-hill metropolis, teeming on narrow cobblestone streets within the straitjacket of its walls? The Viennese lived merrily and miserably. Death and taxes were equally rampant, but wine and music always sustained the people. The streets swarmed with soldiers, peasants, liveried servants, carriages, artisans, peddlers, travellers and all the nationalities of the empire: Hungarians, their boots fitting like gloves, splendid in their embroidered dolman vests and their braided black hair, and short jacket and cap of otter skin; Poles with their circular-cut hair and short redingotes; Wallachians in their embroidered breeches; Serbs in short, tightly-fitted jackets, open across the chest, faithful dagger conspicuously displayed in the belt; Jews in high silken hats and black caftans, long beards and side locks; Turks in soft shoes with pointed-up toes, red breeches and fezzes of many hues; Moravian tinkers loaded with bowls, pans, buckets, and mouse traps; Bohemian beggar "Musikanten" with fiddle, accordion or bagpipe, wandering from one house court to another, enticing young and old to come to the windows to listen to love songs which would dreamily make them throw down some coins. Intermingled with this multitude, the swarthy faces of proud Venetians and Spaniards, all enjoying life in relaxed fashion except when dodging the prancing horses of the aristocrats in the narrow, crowded streets. Not so evident but far more important were the clannish men of the guilds in their appointed quarters: the goldsmiths in the Goldschmidgasse (Goldsmith Street), the clothweavers in the Tuchlauben (Cloth Arcade), the wool merchant in the Wollzeile (Wool Lane), the butchers at the Fleischmarkt (Meat Market), the bakers at Bäckerstrasse (Baker Street).

Wandering among this bustling humanity were Vienna's indispensable street singers who sang doggerels and played their tunes, in the streets by day, in the inns by night. Their singing to the tune of viol, lute, or bagpipe provided the Viennese with music for births, weddings, dances and after-funeral feastings. And at a time of generally poor communications made poorer by wars and highwaymen,

16

theirs was an important service beyond mere entertainment: providing information and news.

One of them—Mark Augustin—attained world fame of sorts. His songs were a shade above the rest, his services much in demand, and his trade-mark, "Ach, du lieber Augustin," a "must." One wintry night, after his favorite hang-out, the Griechenbeisel (Greek's Inn), had closed, he was shambling home through dark, icy streets when the ground suddenly gave way beneath him. He felt himself fall into a deep hole. Too drunk to care, he simply adjusted himself to the contours of his dark surroundings and fell asleep. Early next morning a shocked burial party saw him climb from a pest hole, a mass grave, hurriedly dug to receive the victims of the plague. His body, saturated with spirits, had withstood both cold and plague, and there was Augustin, the only man ever to fall into a pest hole and live to tell the tale.

Thus the Viennese lived merrily, miserably, and devoutly in a crammed world of their own, apart from court and court music, enjoying their own gay and sentimental entertainment which was to win fame in decades and centuries to come. By then a new stimulating brew—coffee—was adding to Vienna's zest for living and was to rival the popularity of wine. It came about in a circuitous way.

Emperor Leopold I had been exasperated with his obdurate, proud Hungarian subjects. Uprisings, followed by repression, followed by rebellion opened a vicious cycle. Finally, the aroused Magyars, forgetting their common Catholic heritage with the Austrians, called on the Turks for help. The Turks came under the command of Grand Vizier Kara Mustapha. Ugly rumors of captured villages and towns running red with blood, of captives skinned alive, preceded them. The Magyars, and the Austrians, now had second thoughts. Although the Protestants had been bad enough, there had remained the slenderest of Christian bonds, but the Turks were something else again. But it was too late: On July 14, 1683 the Turks arrived before the walls of Vienna, 200,000 strong.*

The emperor fled the city, ostensibly to seek help from the Electors of Saxony and Bavaria and John Sobieski, King of Poland. The aristocracy and anybody who had any means of escape left at the same time. The rest filled the churches to overflowing, hoping to find solace and shelter in prayers and in numbers while refugees

---

* This was the second Turkish siege of Vienna, the first one having taken place in 1529.

from the suburbs streamed into Vienna seeking protection within its strong walls. The defence of the city was left to Charles of Lorraine and Vienna's stalwart governor, Count Rüdiger von Starhemberg, who set out to repair the walls, two-and-a-half miles long but now in disrepair, armed and drilled students and citizens, took control of all food and set up make-shift first-aid stations. The Duke of Lorraine left 8,000 troops in the city and, after scorching the suburbs, withdrew with the rest of his 20,000 troops, biding his time for future battle.

While the Viennese scanned the horizon in vain for relief, the Turks bombarded the city incessantly for sixty days and attempted fifty assaults against its walls. Count Starhemberg manfully held out against overwhelming odds, even after the enemy had overrun the outer fortifications. No roof remained unscathed under the constant bombardment. The refugee-filled city fought bravely but was threatened by pestilence, famine, and lack of water, compounded by thousands of wounded citizens and soldiers. Urgent messages to the Duke of Lorraine, the emperor, and King Sobieski were intercepted and the messengers hanged in full view of the helpless defenders. One day Georg Kolschitzki (Kulczycki), a lad of twenty-three, appeared before Count Starhemberg and volunteered, despite the obvious risks, to either get a message through the enemy lines or gain useful information through espionage. He let himself be taken prisoner within the enemy camp, posing as a merchant from Belgrade wishing to do business with the Turkish army. Chance comments, informally dropped, gave evidence of Turkish fears of impending imperial attack. Kolschitzki was able to relate these rumors to Vienna's sentries and eventually managed to escape from the Turkish camp and report to Count Starhemberg in person.

Meanwhile the Electors of Saxony and Bavaria had heeded the urgent appeals for help against the infidels as had the King of Poland. The German armies began to assemble on the Kahlenberg, one of the last Alpine foothills overlooking the city. Only Sobieski's troops were late. But the view from the Kahlenberg was ominous: As far as the eye could reach, the five-mile plain between the hills and the city was filled with the white tents of the Turks. The smoke of their guns and the answering fire of the defenders at times obscured completely the view of the city with only the cathedral spire visible. Although hit by innumerable Turkish missiles it had withstood all punishment which was taken as a good omen for the final victory of the Christian cause.

Finally the relief armies were assembled on the heights of the

Kahlenberg and the Duke of Lorraine decided that they must attack soon, even without Sobieski's army, if Vienna was to be saved. The decision made, a last Mass was heard at the hilltop monastery before the historic descent. Within the beleaguered city, its commander-in-chief, Count Starhemberg, had spent most of his days and nights on an outer balcony of the cathedral spire, high above the city. From there the white sea of Turkish tents and the Turkish sentries patrolling the conquered outer bastions could be observed, as well as the ranks of weary defenders facing them from the battered walls. The morning of September 12 dawned, gray, silvery. A sunbeam speared the clouds as the count scanned the horizon for relief. Suddenly he stood transfixed, the next moment he leaped excitedly to the balcony ledge. There, ringed by the silver band of the Danube on the slopes of the Kahlenberg, the early sun shone on fluttering standards, gleaming armour, helmets, horses, massing, moving. The governor's exhaustion vanished with the night. He drew his sword and bellowed with stentorian voice that echoed among the winding streets and ramparts below: "To arms, to arms, we are saved."

A gun salvo was the signal for the Christian armies to descend the slopes. The Turkish commander, Kara Mustapha, took part of his army to meet the threat. Cannon fired in advance of the attacking troops, opening huge wedges in the Turkish lines. Duke Charles ordered the flanks to attack, closing pincers about the Turkish main body. This was a calculated risk which left the Christian army's center open to counter thrusts. The Turkish leaders were unaware that this was a weak unprotected center since Sobieski's troops had not reached the field at the prearranged time. Two hours passed in bitter, deadly struggle with both wings engaging the enemy and the Duke of Lorraine fearing a concerted Turkish drive against his center which would split the Christian armies in half. The Turks, on the other hand, were at a similar disadvantage: They were forced to keep an eye over their shoulders lest they be caught between the relief armies and possible sorties by the Vienna defenders, now in their rear. Suddenly, martial trumpets. Out from the cover of the Vienna Woods galloped Sobieski's Polish cavalry with banners flying, armour shining, plumes waving, long lances pointed straight at the enemy. A thundering avalanche fell upon the Turkish center.

The charge was decisive. By sundown the battle was over, all resistance broken. The Turks fled, abandoning 180 cannons, thousands of tents, food, armour, all the spoils of war they had amassed on their westward march to Vienna. Grand Vizier Kara Mustapha escaped on horseback without body guards or trappings and did not stop until he had put sixty weary miles between himself and Vienna—and his sumptuous tent boasting bathrooms with scented water, precious rugs, chandeliers, lavish bedding, treasures of gold and silver, tapestries, delicacies for his educated palate, and a huge hoard of nearly a million ducats. An adjoining tent disclosed a gory sight, the beheaded bodies of two of the vizier's wives, killed to prevent their falling into Christian hands. And Kara Mustapha met the same fate when he reached Belgrade; his head was brought to the sultan on a silver platter.

The entry of King Sobieski and Duke Charles into liberated Vienna was greeted with wild enthusiasm. Emperor Leopold's reception, since he had fled the city, was considerably cooler. To pacify the populace, he was forced to make a public gesture of humility by walking on foot to St. Stefan's cathedral to give thanks for deliverance.

At this point one of Austria's future grand figures enters upon the scene. Prince Eugene of Savoy, who had distinguished himself in the fighting, was then a young man, only twenty years old. Born in Paris in 1663, the ugly, frail, misshapen child was destined for the monastery, but from earliest youth preferred Caesar to censer. Trumpets not church bells became his favorite sounds. He toughened his frail body with strenuous exercises, slept on the ground wrapped only in a soldier's cloak. Eventually he approached King Louis XIV, asking for a military commission. Refused, he turned to Austria and future glory. His fortunes rose rapidly in the imperial service. First command of a regiment, then an army, next field marshal, finally commander-in-chief of all Austrian armies. He met the Turkish army again and cut it to ribbons in 1697. But not until decisively beaten by Prince Eugene at Belgrade in 1717 was the Turkish threat to Vienna and the Western world finally broken. There can be no doubt that the strong-willed ugly little man was the greatest military mind Austria ever possessed.

Prince Eugene and Vienna took to each other immediately. The Viennese, he wrote, "are of an extraordinary easygoing nature and let everything run its own course." Such an attitude apparently complemented the character of the hard-driving warrior, and he engaged one of the greatest architects of the time, the Austrian Fischer von Erlach, to build his sumptuous summer palace—the Belvedere—at the outskirts of the city. Fischer von Erlach eventually built the imperial library, the Karlskirche in memory of Charles VI, and the Pest column on the Graben. Together with another famous architect, Lucas von Hildebrandt, he gave Vienna the baroque flavor it still retains.

Prince Eugene quickly became a Viennese. When not directing Austrian military destinies, he spent his days at his palace and in his sumptuous library, reputed to have been one of the most elaborate in the realm. The philosopher Leibnitz was as fascinated by the princely library as he was by the prince's company: "I am convinced that no man will advance the cause of science to a greater degree than Prince Eugene." And as he scanned the thousands of books, Rousseau exclaimed:

> The astounding fact is that there is hardly a book which the prince has not read before sending it to be bound. It is hardly believable that a man who carries on his shoulders the burden of almost all the affairs of Europe, that the highest commander of the Empire and the Emperor's first Minister should find as much time to read. His judgment is extra-ordinarily accurate and his conduct of the most endearing simplicity.

That "endearing simplicity" did not extend to Eugene's taste in architecture, and the Belvedere is one of the classical examples of baroque in Europe.

Unless matters of state kept him away from the capital, Prince Eugene spent many of his evenings with his charming and devoted lady friend, Countess Battiany. Vienna knew well the prince's splendid cream-colored horses and carriage, complete with pink harnesses. The horses, in turn, knew Vienna equally well. So well, in fact, that they would find that Countess' palatial home without guidance and would stop at the lady's doorstep on their own accord with the prince and his driver and footman often fast asleep.

Unbelievable as it may seem, Turkomania overtook Vienna in the wake of its ordeal. Everything Turkish became stylish. Turkish fashions for ladies became the rage as did robes for men. Turkish pipes and tobacco appeared in Vienna as did Turkish drums and cymbals and candy. Pictures of languorous odalisques appeared in Vienna coffee houses, reclining on mountains of cushions, their scantily-clad bodies and come-hither eyes enticing the beholder. In a manner of speaking, Turkish swords became pruning hooks. Turkish guns were melted down and recast into the largest bell for the cathedral. First named the "Josephine" after Emperor Josef I, it was later renamed the "Pummerin" because its solemn, deep-throated tolling was so powerful that it could be heard a hundred miles away.

But coffee made the most lasting impression. The daring young man—Georg Kolschitzki—who brought beleaguered Vienna its first news of impending relief, did not go unrewarded. When the Turks fled they also left before the walls hundreds of sacks of coffee. Coffee, although not unknown in Europe, having been introduced in England earlier, was not generally popular. It was a thick, syrupy beverage, brewed in tiny copper containers over charcoal fires. Kolschitzki received, as a reward of his own choosing, these hundreds of bags of coffee. He proceeded to roast the beans and grind them finely. Then he brewed them in a huge kettle over a roaring fire in the fireplace of his own home and eventually extracted a pungent blackish brew which he peddled from door to door. Its exhilarating effects made it an immediate success. Georg soon abandoned peddling and opened a room with the shingle "Zur Blauen Flasche" (At the Blue Bottle). The first Vienna coffee house was born. There, for the first time in history, coffee was served mixed with milk or cream. Soon young and old, low-born and exalted, drank "Kaffee," sometimes to counteract the adverse effects of that other favorite, wine.

The coffee house became a symbol of the city. Its relaxed, smoke-filled atmosphere was perfect for Vienna's idea of a rest period of indeterminate length, and it became the preferred meeting place of all strata of society. There, over a cup of coffee, newspapers were read, politics argued, revolts planned and regimes toppled, business transacted, cards, billiards, and chess played, friends greeted, and babies diapered. The imagination of the Viennese devised an endless variety of coffee houses. There was the small, low-ceilinged café in whose quiet atmosphere the habitué would slowly sip his coffee over a number of hours while perusing innumerable newspapers and magazines; there was the society pleasure dome with salon orchestra or the outdoor café which featured a large orchestra or even a military band. There were coffee houses for the horseman, the newspaper man, the chess player, the bureaucrat, the aristocrat, the writer, the musician. And whoever was served a *Schale Gold* (cup of gold), a cup of that pungent brew topped by a crown of *Schlag* (whipped cream), knew that the word "diet" had not been invented in Vienna.

IV

Il Divino Boemo

At the height of baroque opera there began a constant ebb and flow of decay and reform. Opera then consisted of three elements—the literary, the musical, and the spectacular. First the literary and musical chores were neatly divided. The recitativo, explaining the action to the dainty plucking of the harpsichord, was the domain of the poet, while the composer highlighted the action with the aria. The third ingredient, the spectacular aspect, however, abetted by outside influences, constantly chipped away at both the literary and musical expression. Under the reign of Austria's emperor-composers, the spectacular soon tended to overpower the other elements, due to two influences, one natural, one freakish.

Although conceived originally as court entertainment, opera eventually became the entertainment of the masses with Venice alone boasting no less than sixteen opera houses. Such a trend tended to lower artistic standards, because it was the spectacular in either voice or stage production which attracted the man in the street. This led increasingly to stage tricks and voice embellishments, to the detriment of literary and musical values.

The other influence which aided such degradation of art came from the castrati who stood to gain by it. The existence and rise of the castrati stemmed largely from the enthusiasm of the church of Rome for opera, whose vocal splendor it sought to add to the church service. The exclusion of women from active participation according to church law—*mulier tacet in ecclesia* (women are silent in church)— presented a formidable obstacle. To surmount it, boy sopranos were sought. They proved undependable, and their voices were of short duration and lacked the warmth and sensuality of female voices. Finally the castration of boy sopranos and altos was introduced so that through arrest of their vocal growth their beautiful high voices would not be impaired but would gain warmth with maturity.

The history of the castrati is closely allied with the Sistine Chapel where they were first heard in 1562. Opinion was divided as to their merit. Their admirers declared that "they touched the soul" while detractors sneeringly referred to their singing as "capon's laughter."

The practice of castration to insure male sopranos and contraltos was not fulminated against until the eighteenth century and was finally outlawed as "barbarous" only during the second half of the nineteenth century. The tonal purity and range of the castrati, coupled with their stupendous perfection of vocal agility, makes it almost impossible today to present operatic masterpieces of that era, all of which were composed with the range and virtuosity of the castrati in mind.

With their growing popularity it became inevitable that all major roles of opera were sung by these eunuchs, and audiences were treated to the fantastic spectacle of Achilles, Caesar or Alexander the Great being portrayed by soprano or alto voices. Soon all opera became subject to the whims of the castrati. Men (?) like Senesino or Farinelli,* acclaimed as the greatest castrato of the century, reigned supreme, and their temperamental escapades only added to their fame. The public encouraged the outrageous behaviour and demands of the castrati, some of whom insisted on singing a specific aria in every opera, regardless of whether it fitted the action or not, simply because it contained an applause-getting cadenza. These monstrous mountains of flesh, dressed in fantastic costumes of their own design, thought nothing of wearing the trappings of an Indian maharaja although the action was laid in ancient Rome or Egypt. In such an aura of artistic decay, the composer, who had been called upon to highlight the spoken word, was degraded to the menial task of merely annotating an outline of music with the singers making up their embellishments, in total disregard for story, action, and continuity. (But the composers eventually rebelled; Verdi threatened to sue anyone who changed a note without his consent.)

During the ensuing conflict between development and reform on the one hand and decay and mutilation on the other, there arrived in Vienna in 1736, by post stage from Prague, Christoph Willibald Gluck, a young man of twenty-two, raw-boned of figure and wit, who soon joined the household of one of Vienna's greatest musical patrons, Prince Lobkowitz. The great moments of Vienna's musical history lay still in the future. Fux and Caldara led the musical literati; later pre-classicists, Wagenseil and Monn, were at the beginning of their careers, Haydn was a mere child of four. The Italian musical idiom was all-pervading.

The main influences of Gluck's early musical life undoubtedly were Giambatista Sammartini, his Milan teacher, and Handel whose

---

* Francesco Bernardi (1680–1750) and Carlo Broschi: (1705–82), respectively.

music he heard while travelling with Prince Lobkowitz to London. Handel became his favorite. Nonetheless he began to grind out operas in the prevailing Italian style in which he became moderately successful. Upon returning to Vienna he married Marriane Pergin in 1750, over her father's strenuous objections. The father's attitude was understandable since Gluck had neither steady income nor position and lived on chance engagements—and his wife's dowry. Besides, his roving eye had already begun to set Italian and Viennese tongues wagging.

Yet the fact that his marriage removed the cloud of financial insecurity may have contributed to Gluck's first major success two years later when his opera *La Clemenza di Tito* was performed in Naples. The success was doubly remarkable because of the first sparks of what the Italians considered Gluck's "German Style." The main role was cast for a tenor, a major dramatic innovation, while the other male parts remained castrati. Even old composer Francesco Durante, when queried about Gluck's innovations, was moved to reply: "I do not know whether this passage conforms to the rule of composition or not but I can say to you, that we should all be proud, myself included, had we conceived or written it."

News of the success of "Il Divino Boemo," as the Italians nicknamed Gluck, soon reached Vienna, with pleasant consequences. Gluck received his first permanent position, and soon thereafter Empress Maria Theresia invited him to write an opera for her. He chose Metastasio's libretto to *Le Cinesi* because the story was familiar to the empress who had sung it some twenty years earlier in a musical setting by Reuter senior. Maria Theresia was delighted and reciprocated with the appointment of Gluck as Imperial Kapellmeister. Luck had it that at the same time Count Giacomo Durazzo, a liberal, cultured lover of the arts was appointed Court theatre intendant. There developed between Gluck and the count, and later with the poet Calzabigi, an artistic collaboration which was to bear rich fruit. Adding to Gluck's climb was another sensational success, of his opera *Antigono* in Rome, which earned him the order of Cavalier of the Golden Spur. Despite the promiscuity with which that particular decoration was handed out (Mozart also received it but wore it only once), Gluck, upon his insistence, was to be known henceforth as Ritter von Gluck (Chevalier de Gluck in France). While his friends remained unimpressed, the title proved its worth with the easier dazzled distaff side.

At this point Gluck found himself prominent and financially successful but artistically a respected mediocrity. He was writing

for immediate consumption, and his operas were unabashed tours de
force in the coloratura style of the day, lavishly produced but often
musically barren. Despite his age of forty-two he had created nothing
to insure his lasting fame. He could have continued in his comfortable rut, composing for the palate of his musical contemporaries by
day, and enjoying the company of female admirers at night. Yet the
turn of genius is inexplicable. Gluck's opera *Orfeo* is generally regarded as the turning point of opera and his career, yet his music to
Angiolini's ballet *Don Juan* already harbors the seeds of the great
upheaval. The often striking resemblance to Mozart's work clearly
marks him as a forerunner of that great classicist as well as of Weber
and Wagner. Gluck's *Don Juan*, says Martin Cooper, "is comparable
only to Mozart, as great as Mozart in its greatest moment and never
unworthy of comparison with him." In comparing the two works
of the same title, one cannot escape the thought that Mozart was
acquainted with and inspired by the work of the older master.

In 1761 Ranieri Calzabigi appeared in Vienna after an unsuccessful
financial venture in Paris. His friend Casanova says that he moved in
aristocratic circles early in life. Like his libidinous compatriot, Calzabigi was a cultured libertine, part-time poet, atheist, and fortune
hunter. In Vienna he soon moved among aristocrats again and met
Count Durazzo.

> Count Durazzo—to whom I read my "Orfeo"—contracted me
> to have it performed at the theatre. I accepted on the con-
> dition that the music be composed to suit my taste. He sent
> me to Monsieur Gluck who, he added, was ready to put him-
> self at my disposal . . . Gluck was not then considered among
> the great composers of the day . . . I indicated all the nuances,
> the tempi and begged the composer to banish the long runs, the
> cadenzas and the ritornelli and all that was Gothic, barbarous
> and extravagant. M. Gluck readily entered into my views.

One is astounded, in retrospect, at the arrogance of Calzabigi. But
even if he made all these suggestions to Gluck, it is one thing to make
suggestions and another to have the genius to carry them into practice. Yet there ensued a close artistic cooperation between the two
men who proceeded to create two masterpieces that stood Vienna
and the world on its ear, despite the "old school" opposition of court
poet Metastasio and composer Georg Reuter.

On October 5, 1762, after much intrigue, the first performance of
Orfeo took place in the presence of the empress and her court. While
the armies of Maria Theresia and Frederick the Great made history
on the battlefield, Vienna made history of a different nature. From
the moment the curtain rose, from the first chant of the Furies, from

the first perfect note of the castrato Guadagni, Vienna was presented with another "first" in its musical history. The static action, the disappearance of the separation between aria and recitative, the full accompaniment of the orchestra, the piercing sounds, all were new and disconcerting. But regardless of whether the Viennese understood or approved, Gluck, now forty-eight, had "arrived."

Gluck adjusted himself with surprising ease to increased wealth and fame. With *Orfeo* successful even in Italy (twenty-seven performances in critical Parma alone), he moved to a larger home, the same house in which Weber later was to write his opera *Euryanthe*. Yet, while working on his second important opera *Alceste* in which his ideas of reform were carried even farther, we find him tossing off *Il Parnasso Confuso* for performance by the imperial family. Coming between *Orfeo* and *Alceste*, two milestones in operatic history, this frothy nonentity, a mixture of French humor and German music, has some justification. Beyond the easy added income offered to shrewd Gluck, it also catered to the artistic limitations of the imperial family and, perhaps most important, offered needed relief from the task of creation.

Calzabigi prepared the text for *Alceste* from the Euripides original, and Gluck now carried through all the reforms he had planned. The 1767 score carried a preface, almost a manifesto, outlining the composer's intentions. The only conventional feature in the first—Italian—version was the castrato for the role of Admetus. Vienna, too deeply steeped in the Italian model, could offer only respect but no enthusiasm. Nonetheless Gluck's fame grew. He was the leading musical personality of the day, and his robust figure could be seen in the company and the boudoirs of all leading prima donnas. At his private musicales, musical and high society mingled in profusion.

Two events of that time had considerable impact on Gluck's future. In the home of Calzabigi he met talented young Antonio Salieri, and at the residence of Lord Stormont, the British Ambassador to Austria, he was introduced to Bailly du Roullet, French attaché and enthusiastic music lover. Salieri became Gluck's only pupil. Eventually, with the help of Gluck and Metastasio, he became Imperial Court Kapellmeister. It was from that influential position that Salieri in later years intrigued against the threatening genius of Mozart.

Gluck was tiring of Vienna. The significance of his reforms had escaped the Viennese, and his operas had not met with the success they deserved. Also, certain female attachments had become too cloying for comfort. When his great friend and protector, Count Durazzo, resigned his position to become ambassador to Venice,

Gluck lent a sympathetic ear to an invitation by the dauphiness, Marie Antoinette, to move to Paris and to du Roullet who suggested collaboration on Racine's *Iphigénie en Aulide*. In the autumn of 1773 Gluck left Vienna for Paris with the complete score of *Iphigénie* in his pocket. Vienna had lost him for years to come.

If Vienna had been indifferent, Paris could be expected to be hostile because it had become mired in the staid concept of the operas of Lully and Rameau which dominated the scene. Their original order and dignity had deteriorated into empty formality and pompous posturing, a condition which applied, in a wider sense, to the court and its ruling circles. Filth and disease were rampant among nobility who appeared in elaborate silk and lace and with lice in their perukes, who pursued their intrigues and orgies in the dim, drafty halls of the king's palace where wine froze at the table in winter. There was total disregard and ignorance of basic hygienic observances. Madame Pompadour was as dirty as she was beautiful. Perfume was a matter of necessity rather than a luxury, and the highest princes of the realm thought nothing of interrupting a court dance to relieve themselves against the tapestried marble walls.

Conditions at the Paris opera proved equally intolerable. Rehearsals consumed six months and were constantly aggravated by incidents ranging from petty complaints to open sabotage. With Marie Antoinette sponsoring him, Gluck took things in stride. When the leading soprano threatened open revolt, Gluck addressed her calmly: "Mademoiselle, I am here to present Iphigenie; if you care to sing, fine, if you do not care to sing, suit yourself. I will then see the Queen and will tell her 'It is impossible for me to present my opera here!' Thereupon I will get into my carriage and return to Vienna." The rehearsals continued without further incidents. Finally, on April 19, 1774 *Iphigénie* was presented to a curious Paris and, despite innovations, was a tremendous success. Even lethargic Vienna was impressed and Maria Theresia sent word through her ambassador that she had elevated the composer to the position of "Kammer Kompositeur" at a salary of two thousand florins.

Dismayed but not defeated, the adherents of Italian *opera seria* in Paris contrived a shabby competition. Quiet, retiring Niccola Piccini, who for several years had rested on his modest laurels in Naples, was lured from retirement to Paris and commissioned to write an opera on the same theme on which Gluck was working. When Gluck heard of the plot he furiously tore up the finished parts of *Roland* and concentrated on *Armide* instead. But fortune eluded him for the moment. While his *Armide* was abused and criticized, Piccini's *Roland* proved a huge success. Gluck was undismayed. Leisurely he bade goodbye to his amours and departed for Vienna where he spent the winter composing *Iphigénie en Tauride*.

By leaving Paris when he did, Gluck missed the unfortunate young Mozart who arrived in March of 1778. The musical public and the ruling cliques, completely embroiled in the Gluck-Piccini feud, shunted the young Austrian ignominiously to the side lines. While Mozart cooled his heels and froze his fingers in the antechambers of French nobility, Gluck's music carried the day. When Gluck eventually heard *Entführung aus dem Serail* (Abduction from the Seraglio) in Vienna, however, he praised it and twice invited the younger man and his wife to be his dinner guests.

Iphigénie en Tauride became another Gluck *succès éclatant*. Having again taken five months in rehearsal and offering the innovation of no overture, it had been eagerly expected and was enthusiastically received. Baron Grimm, who lent only halfhearted assistance to Mozart's efforts to establish himself in the French capital, waxed enthusiastic about Gluck's new opus: "I do not know whether this is melody but perhaps it is something better. When I hear Iphigenie I forget that I am at the opera. I seem to be listening to Greek tragedy."

Despite his Parisian triumph with *Iphigénie* which he considered the crowning glory of his life, Gluck grew tired of Paris. Now sixty-five years old, he decided to return to Vienna permanently. He was now sufficiently wealthy to live in the grand manner and felt secure enough in his fame to palm off as his own Salieri's opera *Les Danaides*, claiming, despite Calzabigi's sarcastic protest, that he had written the first two acts and Salieri the third. Wealth and dissipation went hand in hand with inactivity to undermine his health. Vienna's light wines were replaced by imported brandy; intemperance and irascibility, formerly diffused by feverish activity, increased. Repeated fits of apoplexy, a result of the debauchery of younger years, now limited his creativity to the unimportant music to Klopstock's odes. His health, despite urgent doctor's warnings, declined rapidly: His wife succeeded in keeping alcohol away from him for weeks at a time. But one day a friend came to dinner. After dinner coffee was served and liquor placed on the table. The temptation was too great. Before his wife could stop him, Gluck seized the bottle of brandy and drained its contents. That night he collapsed in a final fit of apoplexy.

If his body was wasting away, his keen mind and razor wit remained unimpaired. When Salieri queried him as to whether the part of Jesus in his oratorio *The Last Judgement* should be sung by a tenor or a bass, Gluck, with a twinkle in his eye, replied: "If you wait a little longer I should be able to advise you from personal experience."

V

Poets and Peasants

November 1749. The chill of winter filled the crooked streets, clung to the stoop-shouldered houses around the cathedral. The boy shivered in his threadbare suit. Standing on a windy corner in the failing light of day young Josef Haydn was undecided as to what to do.

"Sepperl, what are you doing out so late? Why aren't you at the singing school?"

Haydn turned, surprised to face Johann Michael Spangler, a music teacher and church singer who had befriended him.

"I'm no longer at the school."

"So they finally kicked you out of St. Stefan's church choir. What was it this time, again one of your pranks?" Haydn hesitated in reply. "Well, out with it, boy."

"It wasn't so much the prank, Mr. Spangler . . . I've lost my voice."* Spangler's attitude visibly changed from indignation to pity.

"So you're not a boy soprano any longer; well, it had to happen some time. What are you going to do?"

"I don't know."

"Where are you going to sleep tonight?"

"I don't know that either."

"Well, no use standing here and catching your death of cold. You might as well come to my house for the night."

Haydn stayed with the Spanglers for a while, sharing a tiny room with their baby, barely subsisting on money earned from playing in churches, at dances, weddings and serenades. Despite hardships, naive good humor never deserted the boy, and as his manly tenor developed he put it to such good use that his talents came to the attention of Anton Buchholz, a minor judiciary official. Buchholz had sufficient confidence in the boy to subsidize him with 150 gulden for the continuation of his studies.†

---

* Haydn could have remained had he followed the callous advice of his teacher, Georg Reuter, Jr., and joined the ranks of the castrati to retain his ringing soprano voice. His father quickly vetoed the idea. Thus Haydn's expulsion became inevitable.

† In his will Haydn left 150 florins to Buchholz' daughter, making it a point to state that it was a gesture of his gratitude to her father because the original loan had been repaid some fifty years earlier.

Thus enriched young Haydn made his first significant move, renting a room of his own. It was a miserable hole on the sixth floor of the Michaelerhaus, a staid stern building occupied by poets, painters, and musicians. His room was without heat, water had to be carried up the six flights of stairs, and candles were his sole night time illumination. He didn't care; he had a room of his own and, joy of joys, a broken-down clavier in it. His eager enthusiasm knew no bounds. Many years later he told his friend Rochlitz:

> I never had any proper teachers. I always started right away with the practical side, first in singing and playing instruments, later in composition. I listened more than I studied but I heard the finest music in all forms that was to be heard in my time, and of that there was much in Vienna, oh so much. I listened attentively and tried to turn to good account that which impressed me most. Thus, little by little knowledge and ability were developed.

There was indeed much music to be heard in Vienna. The famed British musicologist, Dr. Charles Burney, reported in 1772: "Vienna is so rich in composers and encloses within its walls such a number of musicians of superior merit, that it is just to allow it to be, among German cities, the imperial seat of music."

Haydn's drive could not be stopped. His first composition, a serenade, so impressed Kurz Bernardon, a local impressario, that he commissioned Haydn's first opera *Der krumme Teufel* (The Crooked Devil). As luck would have it, in the same Michaelerhaus, six flights below Haydn but in much more comfortable circumstances, lived famed old Metastasio, court poet and the greatest opera librettist of his day. He might have heard the rickety clavier sounds emanating from six flights above him in the early morning or late evening hours when Haydn diligently worked on his lessons and compositions. Suffice it that Metastasio was sufficiently impressed to recommend the boy to famed Niccolo Porpora, one of the foremost baroque composers and singing teachers in Vienna.

Haydn shrewdly recognized the rare opportunity. Porpora could teach him more than all the books he had studied. To insure Porpora's help Haydn offered himself to the crotchety old composer in the dual capacity of accompanist and valet. He described Porpora's treatment as "impossible, rude and overly demanding" but gladly submitted to the "impossible" for a chance to have his exercises and compositions corrected by one of the foremost musicians of the day and, at the same time, meet such famous composers as Gluck and Georg Wagenseil.

Meanwhile Josef's younger brother, Michael Haydn, who had

outshone him at the boys' choir of St. Stefan, forged ahead again. At the age of twenty he assumed the impressive position of Kapellmeister to Bishop Count Firmian of Grosswardein in Hungary. But in the game of tortoise and hare, tortoise Josef, impressed but undaunted, moved ahead relentlessly. Countess Thun happened upon a Haydn sonata, was impressed, began clavier and singing lessons with him, and introduced him to her circle of the nobility. A new world opened for Haydn. Count Karl von Fürnberg commissioned his first quartet and recommended him in 1759 as music director to Count Ferdinand von Morzin at whose castle Haydn composed and performed his first symphony. Despite the rapid transition from hovel to palace, Haydn's luck held, because Prince Paul Anton von Esterhazy was among those listening at Morzin's castle.

Prince Esterhazy lost no time in enticing the promising young musician away from Count Morzin and in a carefully detailed contract dated May 1, 1761, offered him the position of Vice Kapellmeister. Actually Haydn was required to be conductor, arranger, composer, teacher, administrator, councillor and mediator. It bespeaks his level-headed, extra-musical talents that he handled all tasks with skill and efficiency. If his position was no more than that of a well-paid liveried artistic lackey, as befitted eighteenth-century standards, Haydn nonetheless enjoyed wearing the richly silver-embroidered light blue frock-coat and knee breeches of the princely house of Esterhazy. And his father considered it one of the proudest days of his peasant life when he visited his son and watched him conduct the twenty-two piece orchestra in the livery of so famous a prince of the realm.

On February 9, 1756, at eight o'clock in the evening, a son was born to Leopold and Maria Mozart. He was baptized Johannes Chrysostomus Wolfgang Teophilus Mozart. The father occupied the position of violinist at the court of Prince-Archbishop von Schrattenbach of Salzburg and was the author of one of the foremost violin study books of his time. The boy's surname, Teophilus, would change in time to Gottlieb and again to Amadeus, all meaning "God's Beloved."

Mozart showed the first bloom of uncanny musical inclination at the age of three when he climbed upon a chair and began to pick out melodies and chords on the clavier. From that moment on he had only one teacher, his father, who for twenty years, for better or worse, guided his son's destinies as teacher, adviser and impresario. Mozart's actual career began at the age of six when his father decided that the world should share, admire, and reward the precocious genius of his child. A journey to the court of Munich in 1762 caused a sensation. News spread wildly, and in September of the same year Leopold Mozart presented his two talented children, Wolfgang and his older sister Nannerl, at the court of Vienna. Empress Maria Theresia and her court were enchanted. Confided Mozart senior to a Salzburg friend:

> At present I have no time to say more than that we were so graciously received by both their majesties that my relation would be held a fable. Wolferl sprang onto the lap of the Empress, took her around the neck and kissed her very heartily. We were there from three to six o'clock and the Emperor himself came into the antechamber to fetch me in to hear the child play the violin. Yesterday, Theresa's day, the Empress sent us, through her private treasurer, who drove up in his stage before the door of our dwelling, two robes, one for the boy one for the girl. The private treasurer always fetches them to court.

Aside from the second-hand clothes two hundred gulden were also transmitted to the proudly boastful father of the delightfully unspoiled child whose play and manners had delighted the imperial pair. Once, after he had fallen on the slippery floor and had been helped to his feet by Princess Marie Antoinette, Wolfgang promptly declared that he would marry the princess.

After the death of Prince Anton Esterhazy, Prince Nicolas, "The Magnificent," became Haydn's new patron, the second of four Esterhazys in whose employ Haydn was to create for thirty years. History records no major changes in Haydn's life during the reign of that generous and vivacious prince whose estate, Esterhaza, boasted an art gallery and opera house and who was an understanding patron and lover of the arts:

> My prince was always satisfied with my works. Not only did I have the encouragement and constant approval but as a conductor of an orchestra I could experiment, observe what produced an effect and what weakened it and was thus in a position to improve, alter . . . and to be as bold as I pleased. I was cut off from the world; there was nobody to confuse or torment me and I was forced to be original [Haydn to Rochlitz].

Eventually, in 1766, Haydn became First Kapellmeister of his finely honed group of musicians. Despite the magnificence of the palace, however, living conditions for the musicians were typically eighteenth-century, pitiable and inadequate, with four men living in one room and completely separated from their families. Haydn was one of the few exceptions with three rooms at his disposal. He demonstrated his ingenuity and his selfless devotion to the others' plight, however, when he tactfully, through music (his *Farewell Symphony*), pointed up the misery of his co-workers separated from their kin. The understanding prince thereupon immediately ordered the company to depart for Vienna and reunion.

While Haydn's fame was slowly seeping beyond the confines of Esterhaza, Vienna's reaction ranged from disinterest to dislike. Emperor Josef II called his music "tricks and nonsense." When Haydn composed the opera *La Vera Constanza* for Vienna, intrigues against its performance became so vicious that Haydn withdrew the work in disgust.

The death of amiable Archbishop von Schrattenbach brought narrow-minded, tight-fisted Hieronymus Count Colloredo to the Archbishopric of Salzburg in 1772. Both Mozart father and son were by then holding positions with the archbishop's musical household, Leopold Mozart as Vice Kapellmeister, Wolfgang as organist. With Mozart Sr., bent on exploiting his "Wunderkind," however, the Mozarts were seldom in their seats in the archbishop's orchestra. It was inevitable that their frequent absences from Salzburg, with father and son travelling hither and yon through Italy, Germany, and France, should build tension between the Mozarts and their employer. Sooner than expected and feared, young Wolfgang's position at Salzburg court became untenable.

What made the situation doubly difficult, although neither father nor son was aware of it, was that young Mozart was historically called upon to bridge the gap between Haydn's pleasant and accepted servitude and Beethoven's proud independence. Unconsciously at first, but giving rein to ever stronger impulses, Mozart began to detest the yoke of servitude and the shabby treatment of a master who, at best, was indifferent to the genius among his servants. After only one day in Vienna with the archbishop's retinue, Wolfgang sarcastically reported to his father in Salzburg:

> Dinner was served at half-past eleven in the forenoon . . . and there sat down to it the two valets in attendance, the controller, the confectioneer, two cooks and my littleness. The two valets sat at the head of the table and I had the honor to be placed at least above the cooks . . . There is no meal in the evening but each has three ducats, with which you know one may do a great deal! Our excellent Archbishop glorifies himself with his people,

receives their services and pays them nothing in return . . . Yesterday we had music at four o'clock, and there were about twenty persons of the highest rank present . . . We go to Prince Gallitzin today, who was one of the party yesterday. I shall now wait to see if I get anything; if not I shall go at once to the Archbishop and tell him without reservations that, if he will not allow me to earn anything, he must pay me, for I cannot live on my own money.

Time and time again Wolfgang, with the assistance of his father, by distasteful, fawning, scraping methods, sought an appointment at some court only to be rebuffed. There exists no more telling example of his plight than the letter of Empress Maria Theresia to her son, Archduke Ferdinand, age nineteen, Governor of Lombardy, concerning Mozart's employment:

> You ask me about taking into your services the young Salzburg musician. I do not know in what capacity, believing that you have no need for a composer or for useless people. If, however, it would give you pleasure I do not wish to prevent you. What I say is intended only to urge you not to burden yourself with useless people and not to give such people permission to represent themselves as belonging to your services. It gives one's service a bad name when such people run about like beggars.

Mozart, unaware of his "uselessness," continued his frantic efforts to escape provincial Salzburg's slings and the archbishop's arrows. In 1777 he could endure these abuses no longer. After a final furious scene in which the archbishop used foul language, Wolfgang asked for dismissal from the services of his Salzburg patron. He was not to be granted even such small satisfaction. The audience ended unceremoniously with Mozart being kicked out the door by the archbishop's chamberlain, Count Arco. Nonetheless Mozart was jubilant over his newly won freedom and one month later set out to tour Mannheim and Paris which, he hoped, would bring fame and fortune at last. To mollify the annoyed archbishop and preserve his own precarious position in Salzburg, Leopold Mozart stayed behind, and Mozart's mother, for the first and last time, accompanied the twenty-two year old Wolfgang as chaperon.

Even the shrewdest of men such as no-nonsense Haydn was not safe from grave mistakes. One such mistake was to last Haydn a lifetime. Young Therese Keller whom he had ardently courted, inexplicably decided one day to enter a convent. In a moment of weakness quite alien to his character, young Haydn let her wily father

talk him into marrying shrewish daughter Marie Anna, Haydn's
senior by three years. As a wife she proved wasteful, quarrelsome
and unable to bear him children. As a companion she was jealous,
inartistic, and totally unaware of her husband's budding genius. In
1779 Haydn's securely settled routine, regulated to the point of dull-
ness, was to be severely jolted by the addition to Prince Esterhazy's
musical entourage of Antonio Polzelli, a consumptive third-rate violinist, and his wife Luigia, a second-rate mezzo soprano. In surroundings totally devoid of female companionship save that of his shrewish
wife, Luigia's modest but ever-present physical charms were an inescapable attraction for Haydn. What at first had seemed like another
routine addition destined to barely ruffle the Kapellmeister's routine
soon became "l'affair Polzelli," as the nineteen-year old Luigia,
Haydn's junior by twenty-eight years, began to strike sparks in the
emotion-starved composer.

A delicate situation arose with the apparent knowledge of all, from
the prince and Haydn's wife to the lowliest scullery maid. It presented a fait accompli and a tacit challenge against which neither the
prince's authority nor Marie Anna's jealousy could prevail. Although
the Polzelli's musical services proved wholly inadequate, they remained on the Esterhazy payroll. If the prince wished to retain his
prominent music director he had no choice but to ignore the awk-
ward situation and to keep the two mediocre musicians on his staff.

In January 1779 Mozart returned from his journey to Mannheim
and Paris. Begun with high hopes, it ended dismally, without position
or commission, with dreams shattered and his mother dead and buried
in distant Paris. On his way to Paris Mozart had stopped to hear the
Mannheim orchestra, undoubtedly the finest of its day. There he met
the Weber family whose fortunes were to be fatefully entwined with
his. There was Fridolin Weber, a distant relative of the famous opera
composer, dominated by his strong-willed wife Cecilia; there was
Josefa, Mozart's future "Queen of the Night"; flirtatious, musically
talented Aloysia; easy-going, warm-hearted Constanzia; and bovine
Sophie. It was love at first sight between the young genius and the
blossoming Aloysia. She knew his arias by heart, sang them with
pleasing voice and flirtatious eyes. When Wolfgang, reluctantly and
upon his father's strict written orders, left for Paris, it was amid
mutual vows of eternal love. The distress of his stay in Paris was only
relieved by dreams of reunion with Aloysia who had meanwhile
moved to Munich and was singing at the Munich opera. Little did
Mozart realize what the absence of replies to his ardent letters indi-

cated: that the pleasing voice of a seventeen-year old, talented but inexperienced girl was hardly enough to make her a member of the Munich opera and secure her as influential a sponsor as Count Hadik, the Bavarian Minister of War. Mozart can be forgiven for the vulgar doggerel he flung into Aloysia's face when confronted with the shattering facts upon his return.

Travelling without his knowledgeable father for the first time, Mozart was unprepared for and unequal to the beady-eyed, ruthless intrigue of the Paris salons. The young composer and virtuoso, who had long outgrown the kudos he had received as a "Wunderkind," expected nonetheless a measure of recognition. To his consternation he was completely ignored in the artificial heat of the Gluck-Piccini controversy. With each failing attempt, Mozart's heart filled more with distaste which turned to agony at his mother's death and finally to hatred of everything French.

With the exception of his last days on earth, the Paris experience became the low ebb of his life. Paris aristocracy would either let him wait or ignore his letters of recommendation. Le Gross, the director of the Concerts Spirituels would commission a symphony from him but forget to have it copied, performed, or paid for, although he had praised it as "the best symphony ever written for the Paris orchestra." Finally even Mozart's Paris guardian, Baron Grimm, a friend of the family, despaired of the dour young man in mourning clothes and sent him home on an inexpensive slow coach. Nothing points up the Paris conditions and Mozart's state as the baron's final letter to Leopold Mozart:

> He is too sincere, not active enough, too easily taken in, too little aware of the means of achieving success. Here, in order to succeed, one must be crafty, enterprising and bold. For the sake of his fortunes I would wish that he had only half as much talent but twice as much ability to handle people and I would be less worried about him—The greater part of the French public does not know him; but here everything is given to recognized names ... You see, my dear Sir, why in a country where all mediocre and detestable musicians have made immense fortunes, your son could not succeed at all.

Leopold Mozart also had no illusions about his son:

> On the whole I should feel quite easy in my mind, were it not that I have detected in my son an outstanding fault, which is that he is far too patient, or rather easy going, too indolent, perhaps even too proud, in short that he is the sum total of all these traits which render a man inactive. On the other hand, he is too

impatient, too hasty, and will not bide his time. Two opposing elements rule his nature. I mean, there is either too much or too little, never a happy medium. If he is not actually in want he is very satisfied and becomes indolent and lazy. If he has to bestir himself then he realizes his worth and wants to make his fortune at once. Nothing must stand in his way; yet it is unfortunately the most capable people and those who possess outstanding genius who have the greatest obstacles to face. [To Baroness Wald- stetten in 1782.]

Between the lines, the letter also reveals a father's frustration while watching his son slip from his sphere of influence; because in 1781 Wolfgang had decided to leave stifling Salzburg for the last time and settle in Vienna.

The entire musical world became aware of Haydn and began to pay him homage. In 1781 King Charles III of Spain presented him with a gift. England asked permission to publish his works. The Concerts de la Loge Olympique in Paris invited Haydn to write six symphonies. Boccherini admiringly and admittedly imitated his style. The King of Naples commissioned several works for his favorite instrument, the lira organizzata. Frederick William II of Prussia, an accomplished cellist and later patron of Mozart and Beethoven, sent a personal letter and valuable diamond ring which Haydn cherished to the end of his days. (In contrast, Vienna continued to exhibit only contempt for his music, and the Vienna Tonkünstler Sozietät—Tone Artists Society—had the effrontery to refuse his petition for mem- bership.) The honors from far beyond the Esterhazy confines had a curious and not unexpected double effect on Haydn: he felt honored and began to feel hemmed in.

Monsieur Le Gross [the same Le Gross who treated Mozart so shabbily] wrote me a great many nice things about my Stabat Mater which had been given four times with great applause . . . [he is] much surprised that my compositions for voice are so pleasing. If they could only hear my opera "L'Isola Disabilitata" . . . I assure you that no such work has yet been heard in Paris or perhaps in Vienna either. My great misfortune is that I live in the country. [Haydn to his publisher Artaria in 1781.]

Mozart followed his irresistible urge to move to Vienna despite the advice of others. Count Arco had warned him:

Believe me you allow yourself to be far too easily dazzled by
Vienna. A man's reputation here lasts a very short time. At first,
it is true, you are overwhelmed with praises and make a great
deal of money . . . but how long does that last? After a few
months the Viennese want something new.

Nor was he willing to heed his father's opinion:

The Viennese public . . . cannot even understand what seriousness
means and their theatres furnish abundant proof that nothing but
utter trash such as dances, burlesques, harlequinades, ghost tricks
and devils antics will go with them.

Nothing could change Mozart's opinion of Vienna:

My special line is too popular not to enable me to support myself. Vienna certainly is the Clavierland! And, even assuming that
they get tired of me, they will not do so for a few years . . . in
the meantime I shall have gained both honor and money.

Events seemed to prove him right, and between 1781 and 1785 the
sun of success shone brightly. His "Akademien" were fully sub-
scribed. The publisher Artaria paid one hundred ducats for his six
"Haydn" quartets. His life was a busy round of composing, giving
concerts, and visiting with friends.

The two men who had long been kindred spirits—Haydn and
Mozart—finally met in Vienna. It was a great day for music. Despite
the difference in age, Mozart twenty-five, Haydn forty-nine, there
ensued an enduring friendship, broken only by Mozart's death. Few
contemporaries could sense the significance of the meeting:

Mozart and Haydn, whom I knew well, were men, who showed,
in their personal association with others, no other outstanding
spiritual force and practically no learning or higher culture. An
everyday turn of mind, insipid jokes, and, as regards the former
composer, a thoughtless way of life, were all they displayed in
their association . . . and yet, what depths, what world of fantasy,
harmony and melody and emotion lay concealed beneath these
unprepossessing exteriors. [Memoirs of Karoline Pichler, in
whose home Mozart's last quartets were played.]

It may have been the dissimilarity of their character which, besides music, attracted the two men to each other. Mozart, the mercurial artist, Haydn the even-tempered, calmly reasoning creator.
Mozart, the dramatist and man of the stage, the virtuoso and show-

man, Haydn, the inconspicuous conductor with limited ability as a
soloist. Mozart, the overly protected, helpless creature, unable to cope
with life, money, time, and health, Haydn, the rugged individualist
of strong personal habits and shrewd thinking. There were other
traits that attracted them to each other, such as the complete absence
of professional jealousy, rare at any time. But most of all it was the
respect each had for the other's art and, beginning with 1781, their
cross influence. Mozart acknowledged his debt to the older man by
dedicating six quartets to his "beloved friend Haydn," and each defended the other's work to the point of self-depreciation. When
someone criticized Mozart's harmonic daring Haydn opined: "If
Mozart wrote it he must have had good reason for it." Mozart cut
Kozeluch, a Viennese court composer, down to size when the latter
criticized Haydn with the deprecating phrase: "I would have never
written that." Replied Mozart: "Nor would I. And do you know
why? Because neither of us would have had such an excellent idea."
"If they melted us both together there would still not be enough
stuff to make one Haydn." Companionship, understanding, and the
feeling of being part of the musical main stream were the ingredients
Haydn missed in Esterhaza and cherished in Vienna. It was on one of
those happy musical occasions, made happier by the presence of
Leopold Mozart in Vienna, that Haydn admiringly told the proud
old man: "I tell you before God and as an honest man that your son
is the greatest composer known to me either in person or by reputation."

Through close acquaintance with Mozart's work, Haydn inevitably
became aware of his own limitations. In 1781 he had still felt that his
operas could vie with those of any composer. However, after Mozart
had created *The Marriage of Figaro*, *Cosi fan Tutte*, and *Don Giovanni*, Haydn reviewed his own efforts and acknowledged Mozart's
superiority: "You wish me to write an opera buffa for you," he wrote
an admirer in Prague in December 1787.

> Most willingly if you are desirous of having a vocal composition
> of mine for yourself alone; but if it is with the idea of producing
> it on the Prague stage I cannot comply with your wish. All my
> operas are too closely connected with our personal [Esterhazy]
> circle so that they could never produce the proper effect which
> I have calculated in accordance with the locality. It would be
> different if I had the incalculable privilege of composing a new
> opera for your theatre. But even then I should be taking a great
> risk, for scarcely any man could stand comparison with the great
> Mozart.

Among Haydn's joys in Vienna were the chamber-music sessions with Mozart, either in Mozart's flat or in the house of Prince Ester-hazy's personal physician and Haydn's friend, Peter von Genzinger. There he also had the sympathetic ear of Marianne von Genzinger, the doctor's charming spouse and Haydn's ever-understanding con-fidante. Those chamber-music sessions, with prominent composers Dittersdorf and Vanhall rounding out the quartet, were exquisite music-making occasions, usually attended by a small, select audience including the composer Paesiello, the poet Casti, and the music-loving merchant Michael Puchberg who was to carve his own niche in Mozart's life. When their hunger for music-making was momentarily stilled, the company would repair to another room for physical refreshments and a game of billiards in which the accomplished Mozart took equal pride.

Enter the evil spirit in Mozart's life: Maria Cecilia Weber, the scheming mother whom Mozart had known in Mannheim and whose daughter had jilted him in the past. After father Fridolin's death, mother and daughters had settled in Vienna. Mozart, eager for com-panionship, renewed his friendship with the Webers and in May 1782 moved in with them when the mother decided to take in roomers. His innocent romance with the younger daughter, Constanzia, was aided and abetted by the mother who connived to trap the promising young man into marriage. Here efforts were crowned with success after three months. Although now twenty-six years old, Mozart was still tied closely enough to his father's authority to request his consent to the marriage. Disregarding his father's earnest but distant objec-tions from Salzburg, he married Constanzia on August 4, 1782.

Mozart was happy. He lived in the city he loved, he had a wife, he was composing, he was successful. His opera *Die Entführung aus dem Serail* (The Abduction from the Seraglio) had been performed in Vienna with fair success. Gluck had attended two performances, praised the composer and invited him to dinner. The emperor had vague objections—"Too fine for our ears, my dear Mozart, and too many notes," but Mozart was not fazed—"Exactly as many as needed, Your Majesty."

The success of *Entführung* did not bring about the hoped-for court appointment because all available positions were filled by Gluck, Bono, Salieri, and Kozeluch, and the emperor was not in-clined to create another post to tie the genius Mozart to his court.

The undisguised distress of the musical nobility over the emperor's indifference did little to fill Mozart's pockets. He composed "at breakneck speed"; his mind was overflowing, his pen swift, his taste unerring, he stood at the threshold of immortality. The world was at his feet and neither Salieri's calumnies, the court's indifference, nor his mounting debts could stifle the joyful pace. It was then that two men who were to have lasting impact appeared on the Vienna musical scene.

Baron Gottfried van Swieten, diplomat, administrator, and wealthy music patron, was a man of many contradictions. Miserly and lavish, narrow-minded and inspired in turn, he either failed miserably or achieved splendidly in his appointed task. His was a broad intellect, and his musical taste was to have wide influence. Early in life he had decided not to follow in the footsteps of his famous father, court physician to Empress Maria Theresia, but embarked on a diplomatic career which took him to the Prussian Court of Frederick the Great and to the Court of St. James. Upon his return to Vienna he became director of the Imperial Library and president of the Imperial Education Commission. His narrow, pedantic attitude was ill-suited to either task, and due to the ludicrous standards applied by him, many irreplaceable volumes in the library were destroyed.

His influence on the musical life of Vienna was more favorable. Although as a dilettante and amateur composer, his music was as stiff as his bearing, he was passionately devoted to music and his name is forever linked with those of Mozart, Haydn, and Beethoven. His Sunday morning musicales for a selected few were a focal point of music in Vienna and the well of many historic developments. Frederick the Great drew van Swieten's attention to the music of Bach and Bach's sons; later in England he became acquainted with Handel's oratorios. Van Swieten realized the greatness of these masterpieces and upon his return set out to acquaint musical Vienna with the music of these two giants. It is reported that his was the only copy in Vienna of Bach's *Well-tempered Clavier*. His commissions to Mozart for transcriptions of Bach and Handel scores and his collaboration with Haydn show his musical perception.

Lorenzo da Ponte was a genius of a different order. Born in 1749 in the ghetto of Ceneda, Italy, as Emanuele Coneglia, he, his brothers, and widowed father were baptized in 1763 by the Bishop of Ceneda and took the name da Ponte. The bishop realized the boy's potential and assumed responsibility for Lorenzo's education. It was a stroke of luck for the boy, since his virile father remarried shortly thereafter, and his second wife bore him a dozen children.

Lorenzo took the lower order of abbé and moved to Venice where he eked out a living as a schoolmaster. In due time his extracurricular activities with the damsels of the city became so notorious that no less a personage than the Empress Maria Theresia had him banished from Venice, a fate similar to that of his good friend Casanova. Da Ponte's circuitous travels eventually landed him in Vienna, the city to which all artistic roads led, armed with a letter of recommendation to Salieri. Although the court still looked askance on the adventurer-teacher-poet, in view of the previous banishment, so strong was Salieri's influence and the resurgence of Italian opera, that Emperor Josef II granted da Ponte an appointment as court poet while still denying Mozart an equal position. To reciprocate da Ponte wrote his first libretto for Salieri. He also promised one to Mozart who voiced skepticism at ever receiving it.

Fortunately that first libretto, set to music by Salieri, was a total failure, overshadowed by an opera by Paesiello with a libretto by da Ponte's rival, Casti. Salieri promptly parted company with da Ponte which left him free to prepare the promised work for Mozart. The collaboration of the two, each a master in his field, gave the world such masterpieces as *The Marriage of Figaro*, *Cosi fan Tutte*, and *Don Giovanni*. So closely attuned were the minds of the two artists, that Mozart wrote the music to *Figaro* as the words flowed from da Ponte's quill.

If Mozart felt compelled to return to his beloved Vienna which neglected him while Prague received him jubilantly, da Ponte was cut from a different cloth. With the death of Emperor Josef II, da Ponte's tenuous ties to the court were abruptly cut. Hostility against him was again given full vent. He fled to Trieste and thence to London where he became poet to the Italian opera company. And June 4, 1805 found him arriving at Philadelphia to escape his London creditors. There he made several unsuccessful business ventures before moving on to New York. The rest of his career was equally checkered, ranging from grocer to first professor of Columbia's Italian department. After writing his memoirs, the doddering but still suave and flamboyant name-dropper died ingloriously as an impoverished merchant. His body, placed in a crypt before burial, somehow vanished into an unmarked grave. Even in death the two masters of the opera, Mozart and da Ponte, were akin.

Mozart's pen raced on, barely keeping pace with the flow of his invention but falling behind his mounting debts. The populace and nobility still attended his "Akademien," and he was touched and more than ever convinced of Vienna's understanding and taste when his audience demanded the repeat of the powerfully pathetic movement of his "Concerto in E Flat." Yet, after five years of exposure the magnetism was becoming weak. *Figaro*, the first joint creation of Mozart and da Ponte, was by no means assured of success. There was Beaumarchais' story to be considered which had been banned by the Vienna court as offensive and revolutionary. But wily da Ponte rewrote, cajoled, and adapted to suit the censors until he finally wheedled their permission for Mozart to proceed. But trouble was only beginning. Wrote Leopold Mozart to his daughter in 1785: "The first rehearsal for 'Figaro' will take place on the 28th. It will be a miracle if the opera succeeds for I know that there are immensely strong intrigues against it. Salieri and all his tribe will move heaven and earth to keep it off the stage." And despite the enthusiastic reception of the opera in rehearsal, where Mozart received ovations from orchestra and singers alike, intrigue against the work mounted to such fever pitch that at the night of the first performance, at the close of the first act, a number of singers refused to return to the stage. Mozart, on the verge of despair rushed to the emperor's box and in great agitation explained the situation. For once the monarch rose to the occasion. He sent orders backstage that there be no disobeying. The performance proceeded.

Figaro's lukewarm reception in Vienna was totally overshadowed by its triumph in Prague. "The enthusiasm was without precedent," the composer wrote a friend. "People never got tired of hearing it. Figaro's songs resounded in the streets." Mozart, hard pressed by mounting debts, gladly accepted an invitation to Prague by the impressario Bondini, to witness the triumph of the opera and earn one thousand gulden through opera and concerts. So fired was Mozart's imagination by the experience that he wrote a symphony especially for Prague. Thus during January and February 1787 he witnessed the triumphs of both opera and symphony in an atmosphere of adulation so rare in his success-starved life. Bondini, who stood to make a fortune, immediately commissioned another work for Prague. Composer and poet set to work.

Il Convitato di Pietra (The Stone Guest) by Giovanni Bertati was the splendid choice of da Ponte for his libretto of *Don Giovanni*. In addition da Ponte sought the advice of his friend Casanova whom he met in Prague. Again the magic of Mozart transformed an often used plot into a masterpiece. The overture had to wait until the early morning hours of the day of the performance as Mozart unerringly flung it on paper during the night. But the following night witnessed again a wildly enthusiastic reception by music- and Mozart-loving Prague. "Die Prager verstehen mich" (The people of Prague understand me). Mozart, surrounded by friends, embraced by strangers, overwhelmed with offers to stay, was happier than he had been in years. Finally the recognition he deserved and craved was his in Prague. Yet back to Vienna he went.

What demon drove Mozart back? We are reminded of the story by Bruno Frank in which a singer on stage desperately sings with all his virtuosity in order to impress a seemingly impassive listener only to discover too late that the listener is deaf. With few exceptions it was for Vienna that Mozart wrote his masterpieces, yet Vienna turned a deaf ear and, after listening to the early exhibitions of the prodigy and the young virtuoso, shunted him aside to listen to the likes of Salieri.

Mozart was not blind to these developments. It must have been his unyielding determination to prove to Vienna that his was a mastery above all that drove him relentlessly back to the city he loved best. And he did little to improve the deteriorating situation by ruthlessly expressing his incorruptible musical standards and opinions:

> About the Clementi Sonatas. They are valueless as compositions as everyone who plays or hears them will recognize. Clementi is a charlatan like all Italians . . . what he does well are passages in thirds . . . apart from this he has nothing, absolutely nothing, not the least inspiration or taste and still less feeling.

or describing his pupil Josepha Auernhammer:

> If a painter wanted to paint the devil from life he would find him in such a face. She is fat as a peasant, sweats so as to make you sick . . . one is punished enough for the whole day if one's eyes have unluckily fallen upon her . . . she is hideous, dirty and horrible.

Third, Mozart's vacillation between patronage and free lancing contributed to his downward path in inescapable sequence. When the foot of Count Arco propelled him from the narrow security of the archbishop's protection, he left a world built on patronage and entered the desert of the independent artist where only the strongest, like a Beethoven, would survive. Yet Mozart was intuitively right. It would be unthinkable to find him in the role of court conductor, his genius stifled, subject to an insensitive sovereign's whim. Thus he unwittingly prepared the ground for Beethoven by addressing his final symphonic trilogy to the world at large.

Devoted Haydn was concerned over his friend's worsening plight.

Oh, if I only could explain to every musical friend and to the leading men in particular [wrote he to his impresario] the inimitable art of Mozart, its depth, the greatness of its emotion and its musical concept as I myself feel and understand it; nations then would vie with each other to possess so great a jewel within their borders. Prague should not merely try to retain this precious man but also remunerate him; for without this support the history of any great genius is sad indeed, and gives little encouragement to others to adopt a musical career, and for lack of this support many promising talents are lost to the world. It enrages me to think that the unequalled Mozart has not yet been engaged by some imperial or royal court. Do forgive this outburst but I love the man so much.

But the good news had preceded Mozart to Vienna. Informed of Mozart's Prague triumphs and of the disapproval of imperial inaction, the emperor relented. Three weeks after Gluck's death, Mozart was appointed to his position, Royal and Imperial Court Composer. Yet the reluctant sovereign acted shabbily even while granting the position. Where Gluck had received two thousand gulden, Mozart had to be satisfied with a pittance of eight hundred. Sighed he: "Too much for what I do; too little for what I can do."

Haydn felt confined by Esterhaza's provincial atmosphere:

Here I sit in my wilderness [he confided to Marianne von Genzinger in 1790], forsaken like some poor orphan, almost without human company, melancholically dwelling on the memory of the past glorious days [of a Vienna visit]. Yes, past, alas! And who can tell when those happy days will return, those charmed meetings where the entire circle was but one heart and soul—all those delightful musical evenings which can only be remembered and not described. All gone, gone forever. [Upon my return] I did not know for three days whether I was Kapellmaster or Kapellservant. Nothing could console me . . . I am doomed to stay at home. It is indeed sad to be a slave.

Then, in September 1790 Prince Nicolas died. Haydn's gilded cage was about to open. Prince Anton who succeeded Nicolas had no musical ambitions. The famed orchestra was disbanded. Haydn was kept on for reasons of prestige but was free to go wherever and whenever he pleased. Free at last! He rushed to Vienna, to friends, to society, to music—and was promptly showered with foreign offers.

But for the moment he was too happy in the enjoyment of friends and freedom to consider any offer.

Mozart grew cold with loneliness and despair. The symphonies of Kozeluch, the operas of Salieri won acclaim while *Don Giovanni* earned the adjectives "vainglorious," "eccentric," "wasteful." The thieves and leeches began to gnaw on his entrails. Instead of composing he had to waste time in finding money lenders, usurers, choosing "the most Christian among those unchristian people." Yet he, the neediest of men, lent the hard-earned hundred ducats sent to him by the King of Prussia to "a friend I could not refuse." Mozart's "dear friend," Anton Stadtler, for whom he had written the glorious clarinet concerto and clarinet quintet, repaid him by stealing the pawn tickets for Mozart's silverware. When Mozart was reproached for not bringing Stadtler to justice, he shrugged: "He plays such a beautiful clarinet."

His friends, pupils, patrons, boon companions of happier days, had all vanished. When he made a last attempt to arrange for a subscription concert to obtain desperately needed funds, the messenger returned with the subscription list empty save for one name—Swieten. Only one man, the merchant Puchberg, a fellow Freemason, remained Mozart's friend to the end, and to him Mozart turned repeatedly with pitiful requests for funds.

> My God! I am in a position I should not wish my worst enemy to be in and if you, my best friend and brother, forsake me, then I, together with my poor sick wife and child am blamelessly and lucklessly lost.

> If you would be so kind, so friendly, as to lend me the sum of one or two thousand Gulden, for a period of one or two years, at suitable interest, you would be doing me a great favor. You will no doubt realize and acknowledge that it is inconvenient even impossible to live from one installment of income to another. Without a certain necessary capital sum, it is impossible to keep one's house in order. Nothing can be done with nothing.

Thirteen such letters to Puchberg alone . . . Be it said in honor of Mozart's friend that he responded with payments totalling over nine hundred gulden.

True to his father's earlier predictions, Mozart, in distress, desperately continued to seek new avenues to bolster his dwindling revenues:

> I should long since have sent a specimen of my poor work to
> his Highness the Prince (to whom I beg you will say in my name
> that I lay myself at his feet and thank him most humbly for
> the present he has sent me) . . . I place at the end of my letter
> a list of my latest-born children of my fancy, amongst which
> his Highness has but to chose that I may serve him . . . If his
> Highness would be so gracious as to commission me, year by
> year, with a certain number of symphonies, quartets, concertos
> for different instruments or other pieces according to his choice,
> his Highness would be well and punctually served, and I should
> be able to work with a more collected mind, being sure of having
> work to do. [1786, letter to the Chamberlain of Count Fürstenberg.]

Thus one of Vienna's greatest minds begged, crawled, fawned and
humbled himself to keep from starving. Miraculously, the engulfing
financial catastrophe did not impair his creative powers. During the
summer of 1788 we find him busy finishing his last three symphonies
within the incredible span of six weeks and starting on the opera
Cosi fan Tutte which the emperor had commissioned.

One day in the autumn of 1790, a stranger, his German accented
with English, presented himself at Haydn's lodgings.

"My name is Salomon. I have come from London for you, we
shall conclude our accord tomorrow."

Thus, within the seconds it took to speak the words, the life and
world of Haydn was changed. Johann Salomon was a man of many
talents. Born in Bonn where his family shared a house with the
Beethovens, he emigrated to London where he won great acclaim
as a violinist. He was equally successful as impresario. Having admired and championed Haydn's music, he now wanted to bring the
master to London. While travelling in Germany he heard of Prince
Esterhazy's death and immediately changed his itinerary to see
Haydn in Vienna. It bespeaks Salomon's managerial ability that, when
he confronted Haydn so bluntly, he had already worked out all
arrangements in detail. It was not an easy decision for Haydn to
make. He had been pining too long for Vienna to leave it so quickly
again. But so convincing were Salomon's arguments, so glowing the
prospects, so enticing the picture the impresario painted, that Haydn,
although now nearing sixty, was unable to resist the invitation.

His friends were naturally worried about the fate and future in a strange land of a man who had been confined to one provincial estate for over thirty years. Mozart, who cherished the friendship of the older man, exclaimed in his usual brusque manner: "Oh Papa, you have had no education for the wide world, and you speak so few languages." But Haydn exuded strength and confidence: "My language is understood all over the world." After having spent the last day in Vienna with his friend Mozart, Haydn left Vienna with Salomon on December 15, 1790. When shaking Haydn's hand in farewell, Mozart, in tears, said prophetically: "I am afraid, Papa, this will be our last farewell."

Despite the language barrier, Haydn was overwhelmed by the kindness of distinguished Londoners whom he had previously met in Vienna. Salomon, as good as his word, had arranged for lodgings, sightseeing, and rehearsals, all leading up to the expectantly awaited first appearance on March 11, 1791 when Haydn's newly composed symphony, No. 93, was to be the pièce de résistance.

It seemed like all London had turned out for the gala event, complete with lavish gowns, full dress uniforms, bemedalled chests, and swords. Salomon had seen to it that the orchestra was of high caliber, numbering forty players, almost twice the size of the Esterhazy ensemble. Salomon personally led the string section, playing a Stradivarius once owned by Corelli, Haydn conducted from the harpsichord with unusual vigor. Doctor Burney, who had greeted the composer with a poem of welcome, described the effect of Haydn's personality as "electrifying" and the audience's reaction as "enthusiasm bordering on frenzy." Overnight Haydn had become the toast of London. Usually restrained Britishers waxed enthusiastic. The entire concert series was an immediate sell-out, carrying the composer to unheard of triumphs and heights of enthusiasm.

Mozart had first met the actor and impresario Emanuel Schikaneder ten years earlier in Salzburg when he and his troupe had performed there on tour. When the actor settled in Vienna in 1789 to act in and direct a suburban theatre in a Singspiel repertoire, they renewed their acquaintance. It was therefore not surprising that Schikaneder should approach Mozart and suggest that he compose a "magic opera" so popular in Vienna. The libretto, by Schikaneder, was a concoction of phantastic trappings and magic tricks immensely enjoyed by the escapist Viennese. Only Mozart's music elevated it into the realm of art, a fact which, together with Mozart's pointed references to Freemasonry, completely escaped the audience. The *Magic Flute* nevertheless was a milestone in opera, elevating the trite German Singspiel and the ancient "machine play" into the realm of true German opera. Yet the first performance at the historic Theatre an der Wien was Schikaneder's, not Mozart's success. (The program read: "An opera by Mr. Schikaneder"—and below in small print, "music by Mr. Mozart.")

While Mozart was working on the *Magic Flute*, a laconic black-clad messenger arrived at his lodgings with a curious commission. His patron, who wished to remain anonymous, wanted Mozart to compose a Requiem Mass. Mozart gratefully accepted the unexpected commission, but a cloud of foreboding assailed him concerning it. He could not forget the mysterious, uncommunicative messenger. Later it became known that the messenger was the steward of Count Franz von Walsegg Stuppach, an amateur musician who palmed off the works of unknown or distressed composers as his own. But Mozart had already developed a fixation—the black messenger was death himself who had ordered his—Mozart's—own requiem.

Responding to the enthusiasm of London, Haydn reached his creative peak and composed his first six "London" symphonies. They clearly reflected the growth of his inventiveness due to his association with Mozart. It was typical of Haydn that although he basked in freedom and British adulation his humble, unassuming friendliness never deserted him. This endeared him to all and particularly to the widow of music master Johann Samuel Schroeter of whom he became very fond. That his feelings were warmly reciprocated added to Haydn's London joys.

In July 1791 he was accorded the crowning honor of his London venture. Upon the recommendation of Dr. Burney, he was invited to attend the Oxford Commemoration and receive the honorary degree of Doctor of Music. The son of the humble Rohrau wheelwright had arrived. And his future music was deeply influenced when he attended the second Handel Festival in Westminster Abbey. Haydn was deeply moved by the performances. "He is the master of us all . . . No music has ever moved me so much in my life."

While working on the Requiem, Mozart, ill and weakened (it was rumored in Vienna that he was being poisoned by Salieri), received from ever-loyal Prague a commission to write an opera to be performed on the occasion of the coronation of Leopold II, successor to Josef II, as King of Bohemia. Mozart used *La Clemenza di Tito*, a libretto by Metastasio repeatedly set to music by Scarlatti, Jomelli, Caldara and Gluck. It did not find favor. Its lack of success in the city of his greatest triumphs only served to deepen his depression and hallucinations of impending death, particularly when he heard that the empress had contemptuously pronounced his work "una porcheria tedesca" (German rubbish). He returned from Prague to Vienna looking wan, weakened, feverish.

Physically exhausted and racked by dizziness, vomiting, and fainting spells, but mentally inspired, he feverishly continued on the Requiem: "I cannot remove from my eyes the image of the stranger. I see him constantly. He begs me, exhorts me, commands me to work. I continue, because composition fatigues me less than rest. I have finished before I could enjoy my talent . . . I must finish my funeral song, I must not leave it incomplete."

Haydn to Marianne von Genzinger: "The Prince of Wales is having my portrait painted."

Mozart to his sister-in-law Sophie: "You must stay with me tonight and see me die . . . I already have the taste of death on my tongue."

In London Haydn heard about the death of his friend, but disbelieved it until it was verified upon his return to the continent. He was beside himself for some time. Equally deep grief was to shadow his life two years later. His dear friend and confidante, Marianne von Genzinger, a woman of charm and grace died in the bloom of womanhood at age thirty-eight. With two of his dearest friends gone and musical Vienna as unreceptive as ever, it is not surprising that, on January 14, 1794, we find Haydn and his friend and valet Elssler (father of future famed dancer Fanny Elssler) in Baron van Swieten's carriage, heading toward London again. London's esteem for him was undiminished. According to a contemporary press account, it was truly wonderful what sublime and angust thoughts this master weaves into his works. Passages occur that render it impossible to listen without getting excited. We are altogether carried away by admiration and forced to applaud . . . [Haydn] conducts himself in the most modest manner. He is indeed a good-hearted, candid man, esteemed and beloved by all.

Admiration increased, ties were strengthened, friendship closer. When Haydn's noble friends introduced him at court, an honor which the monarch of his native land had never accorded him, Haydn's and England's future seemed inextricably entwined. Yet when approached by his noble friends to take up permanent residence in England, Haydn reluctantly declined in favor of Vienna. This despite an invitation by the queen to take up summer residence at Windsor Castle, an invitation cordially seconded by the king.

Why would Haydn wish to leave England where he was famous and feted to return to Vienna where his best friends were no more, where he was neglected by public, press, and potentate? Why would he leave behind an assured and considerable income in exchange for a social and musical position which was anything but secure? It could not have been attachment to his estranged wife nor his faded ardor for Luigia. Unlike Mozart who returned to defy the fates, Haydn's return was prompted by his advancing years. To be the idol of London was one thing, to be forced to compose and conduct at a constant, feverish pace another. Haydn felt that Vienna's relaxed atmosphere would be more conducive to his creative efforts and, since he had arrived at a station in life where he was master of his fate, he reluctantly decided to leave. We can see how difficult the decision must have been. Although his last concerts took place in May, he lingered until August before he waved a final farewell to English shores.

Nominally still attached to the Esterhazy court, Haydn was pleased to learn that the prince preferred Vienna to his estate. Haydn went about reorganizing the prince's musical household and eventually conducted a brilliant performance of Draghi's opera *Penelope*. Fortunately Prince Nicolas II was not pleased with the creations of his famed music director. Crude, autocratic, his petrified musical tastes harking back to another century, he only kept Haydn attached to his household for prestige reasons. But he did not realize that he was dealing with a changed man. When he once arrogated unto himself musical criticism during a rehearsal, Haydn, to the consternation of all, retorted: "Your Highness it is *my* duty to decide this."

What had further contributed to the estrangement between prince and composer was Haydn's London-inspired interest in one of music's gigantic forms, the oratorio. He had brought with him an English text on the *Creation* which none other than Baron van Swieten translated into German for him. Swieten actually went further than translation. He prepared the bilingual libretto and thought nothing of advising Haydn on how to compose the oratorio, such as suggesting that the passage "And the Lord said: Let there be light and there was light" should be sung only once for greatest effect. Surprisingly, neither Haydn nor Mozart, or Beethoven later, resented Swieten's advice. Swieten went even farther than libretto and advice. He rallied a group of musically-inspired Vienna noblemen who underwrote the expenses for the first momentous performance of the *Creation*.

Haydn had given fully of his profound musical knowledge and deep religious feelings. "Never was I so devout as when composing The Creation. I knelt down every day and prayed to God to strengthen me for my task . . . and when I felt my inspiration ebbing I rose from the piano and prayed." The premiere of the *Creation* on April 29, 1798 was to vindicate Haydn and Vienna; on that day full recognition belatedly came to him in the imperial city. Word had spread and a special detachment of police had to restrain the crowds who thronged to watch the intellectual, musical, and aristocratic elite of Vienna enter the Schwarzenberg Palace. Inside prevailed a hushed, reverent atmosphere. The orchestra was one of the largest ever assembled in Vienna, the violins alone numbering seventy-two and the soloists were of the highest caliber. Haydn conducted with a baton as was customary at religious performances and Salieri was at the harpsichord. "The effect of the performance was overwhelming . . . Three days have gone by since that enchanting evening and still the music sounds in my ears and my heart; still the memory of all the flood of emotion then experienced constricts my chest" (Vienna newspaper report). The audience was enraptured. Suddenly Haydn found himself Vienna's man of the hour, "our Haydn." To sweeten the triumph, van Swieten, in a gesture of innate grandeur, presented the composer not only with his stipulated fee but with the total receipts from the opening performance.

As a prelude to the superhuman effort of the *Creation*, Haydn, then sixty-five, had composed the work dearest to the hearts of his countrymen, the melody which was to become the most treasured of all, the "Kaiserlied," the Austrian national anthem. It was first solemnly sung throughout Austria on February 12, 1797, the emperor's birthday. With Austria at war with France, the proud melody immediately took hold. The emperor was pleased and as a token sent Haydn a gold box. A trinket to one of the world's greatest composers for a great patriotic act. Somehow it never occured to the monarch to present Haydn with a decoration, official recognition. Mozart, on the other hand, who had needed money desperately, had been incongruously rewarded with a medal.

A tidal wave of Austrian and foreign recognition now threatened to overwhelm Haydn. The snobbish Vienna Tonkünstler Sozietät belatedly made him an honorary member. Sweden nominated him to its Royal Academy. Paris, despite the war with Austria, invited Haydn to conduct his works in France. In 1800 the *Creation* was performed in Paris. Napoleon attended and had Haydn presented with a medal (!) to commemorate the event.

Despite failing health, Haydn continued to work. Neither his wife's death nor Luigia's marriage to an Italian singer caused a ripple in his well-ordered life in relaxed Vienna. At a rapid pace he composed the "Nelson" Mass, the "Theresia Mass," and the string quartets for Prince Lobkowitz. As if all that was not sufficient, these efforts were overshadowed by another gigantic oratorio. Again all social and concert preparations were in the knowing hands of van Swieten. The orchestra for the *Seasons* was even bigger than that for the *Creation* and included three timpani parts. The premiere on April 24, 1801 was another Haydn triumph. Official recognition came when the empress arranged for command performances of the two oratorios at court and personally sang the soprano solos with much taste and expression but a small voice.

Although almost drained of physical strength, Haydn nevertheless collaborated with Beethoven in a concert for the war-wounded and, in Eisenstadt, near his native village, composed the "Creation" Mass. Weary he then retired to his suburban home in Vienna for two major tasks still remaining: a thematic catalog of his compositions and his last will and testament. The stillness of his solitude was broken by new honors arriving from the Netherlands and again from France. A visit by the composer Luigi Cherubini was especially pleasing to the frail old composer who spent many happy hours with the younger man. But the crowning moment of Haydn's full life was yet to come, a performance of the *Creation* at the University of Vienna on March 27, 1808. Again military guards had to be called out to restrain the crowds. Austrian nobility mingled with such distinguished musical greats as Beethoven, Hummel, and Salieri. Haydn, now too weak to walk any great distance, was carried into the great hall of the university in an armchair amidst trumpet and

drum flourishes and shouts "Long Live Haydn"—and was seated as
an equal among nobility. Salieri conducted and Franz Clement, to
whom Beethoven was to dedicate his violin concerto, led the violins.
At the passage "And there was Light" the audience broke into
tumultuous applause, and Haydn tearfully raised his hand and eyes
heavenward: "Not from me, from Him cometh All."

His weakness did not permit him to sit through the entire performance. Great emotion filled the hall as the honored, gentle, frail
man left the festive gathering at intermission. Never-ending applause
mingled with shouts welled through the hall, innumerable handkerchiefs waved in tearful farewell. Beethoven knelt before the old
master and kissed his hands. Everybody sensed the inevitable—it was
Haydn's last public appearance.

When the French occupied Vienna, Napoleon personally ordered
an honor guard posted at Haydn's home. A French officer whom
Haydn befriended sang to him and "gave him much pleasure." That
same day Haydn played the piano for the last time. Significantly it
was the Austrian anthem, his anthem. His friend's—Mozart's—requiem was sung at the funeral as French and Austrian officers
mounted a guard of honor.

And how had Haydn's dear friend and fellow genius—Mozart—
fared in death? Baron Swieten, the same nobleman who acted so
magnanimously on Haydn's behalf, advised Constanzia Mozart—for
reasons of economy—to arrange for the cheapest, third-class funeral.
When the brief church service at a side chapel of St. Stefan's had
ended and the crude pine coffin was carried outside, rain mixed with
snow had begun to fall. The few who had attended hurriedly sought
shelter. Slowly the horse-drawn hearse continued in the driving rain
to the St. Marx cemetery where Mozart's emaciated remains vanished into a pauper's grave together with twenty other bodies. From
four thousand miles away, in a deserted New York cemetery, the
adventurous spirit of da Ponte must have laughed wryly from
another unmarked grave. It was left to Salieri, Mozart's lifelong
enemy, to grant grudging tribute to the man whose mere shadow had
threatened Salieri's place in the imperial sun. Said he upon hearing
of Mozart's death: "Good riddance, . . . otherwise we all would
have been breadless in a short time."

Ironically, Mozart and Haydn also met different posthumous
political fates. Haydn's "Kaiserlied" remained the Austrian national

anthem until after World War I when the First Austrian Republic adopted a new "Staatshymne" by the Austrian composer Wilhelm Kienzl with words by Karl Renner. Haydn's melody was used again from 1934 until 1938, however, with new words by Ottokar Kernstock. But in 1946 the Second Republic adopted the final choral of Mozart's "Masonic Cantata" as the official "Bundeshymne." The words, by Paula Preradovic, were selected in a nation-wide contest. In Germany, however, the third verse of the "Deutschlandlied" (*Deutschland, Deutschland über Alles* . . .), adapted to Haydn's melody by Hoffmann von Fallersleben in 1841, still remains the national anthem.

VI

The Lion

"Dear Beethoven: You are travelling to Vienna in fulfillment of your long-cherished wish. The tutelary genius of Mozart is still weeping and bewailing the death of her favorite. With the inexhaustible Haydn she has found refuge, but not occupation, and she is now waiting to leave him and associate herself with someone else. Labor devotedly and receive Mozart's spirit from the hands of Haydn." This prophetic letter by Count Waldstein, which carried with it the vision and the muted fanfare of future triumphs, accompanied a stocky youth, somber of mien, wild of hair, from Bonn to Vienna. It was to prove the key in Ludwig van Beethoven's drive for recognition. Together with others by Stephen von Breuning, it opened for Beethoven the doors of the salons of the mighty.

The journey in 1792 was not Beethoven's first visit to Vienna. He had come there as a lad of seventeen, five years earlier, to play for Mozart. That meeting had opened inauspiciously with both men occupied by their own thoughts: Mozart lamenting the death of his father, Beethoven worried about his mother's sickness. After listening distractedly to the sullen young man with the pockmarked face, Mozart wished to test his visitor's powers of improvisation. Young Beethoven passed the test so impressively that Mozart listened with fascination. At the end of the improvisation he turned to his assembled friends: "Watch him, he will make a great noise in the world." A prophecy antedating that of Count Waldstein.

If Beethoven had hoped to study with Mozart, it was not to be. Shortly after his arrival he was recalled to Bonn to the bedside of his mother who died shortly thereafter. When Beethoven returned to Vienna Mozart was dead and he began to study with Haydn. There was discord between the two men from the outset. Haydn, at the peak of fame, was impatient with the dour young man, whose lisp, gait, dress, and accent marked him as the German provincial. Nor could he summon the patience to cope with the unruly ideas which constantly cropped up in the youngster's mind: "head-strong, self-willed, learning from bitter experience rather than from lessons."

Beethoven was equally impatient with the set ways, the tried-and-true formulae of Haydn. When the composer Johann Schenk pointed out to the young student that Haydn had not bothered to properly correct Beethoven's exercises, he turned against the master: "Haydn never taught me anything." He secretly began to take lessons from Schenk. When Haydn left on his second London journey he turned Beethoven over to fellow composer Albrechtsberger. The coldness Beethoven felt for Haydn was transferred to Albrechtsberger while, on the other hand, he was charming to Schenk, and could even be humble to others if he felt so inclined. Years later, the proud composer of the "Eroica" and *Fidelio* would leave a note at Salieri's door: "The pupil Beethoven was here."

The keys of Waldstein and Breuning fitted well in the princely locks of Vienna, and Beethoven's improvisatory powers on the keyboard opened the doors further. The athletic shoulders of his five-foot-three frame, the wild black mane and dark face with the lion's nostrils became a common sight in the high-ceilinged salons of Vienna. That picture of "strength personified," of "Herculean energy," coupled with his powerful imagination at the keyboard soon made him the darling of a fickle crowd of admirers and supporters. He was attractive to all, from women of high rank to chambermaids, all of whom admired his "sensitive mouth," "dazzling teeth," "beautiful eyes," or his personality which was, in turn, described as "gracious, wild, agreeable, angry, menacing." According to his pupil, Ries, Beethoven

> was fond of the company of women, especially if they had young and pretty faces, and generally, when we passed a pretty girl he would turn and gaze keenly at her through his glasses . . . he was frequently in love but generally only for a short time. Once when I twitted him about the conquest of a pretty woman he admitted that she had held him in the strongest bonds for the longest time—fully seven months.

While his musical genius took wing, Beethoven remained earth-bound in other matters. He tried in vain to learn how to dance, a must in Vienna. Beethoven, the master of music, could not hold to a simple dance rhythm. Surprisingly, his sense of tone was also deficient; he could never sing in tune, and his pianos were always out of tune.

If Vienna's princely crowd had envisaged using Beethoven for their diversion, to push him aside when tiring of him, they were to have a rude awakening. What separated Mozart and Beethoven was the French Revolution. Where Haydn had labored in willing servitude and Mozart in unsuccessful revolt, where Gluck had achieved an artful blend of impertinence and diffidence, Beethoven faced his benefactors with contempt and insult. Through a miraculous blend of personality, genius and historic change, Beethoven thus became the chosen instrument to bridge music from rococo classicism to Romanticism.

Revolt came naturally with Beethoven—revolt against nocturnal piano lessons supervised by a drunken father, against the princely system of patronage. Revolt rang in his ears at the age of six when the Liberty Bell pealed from Independence Hall in Philadelphia and at eighteen when the cry "A bas la Bastille" echoed from Paris. Revolt blazed in the "storm and stress" of Goethe's *Werther* and *Götz von Berlichingen*, Lessing's *Minna von Barnhelm*, Schiller's *Die Räuber* and *Don Carlos*. The father of his friends, the Brunswick sisters, was an outspoken champion of America's revolt against England. Said Therese von Brunswick, "I was brought up with the names of George Washington and Benjamin Franklin."

Despite handicaps of appearance, speech, and behavior, Beethoven made fast progress. Almost overnight he moved from attic hovel to Prince Lichnowsky's palace. Such was the prince's care for his guest that Beethoven joked: "The prince would like to enclose me in a glass ball so that neither the unworthy nor their breath would touch me." Beethoven held court in Vienna's palaces. Many of these nobles—Lichnowsky, Lobkowitz, Esterhazy, Brunswick, Kinsky— were accomplished musicians as was natural in Vienna. They had succeeded in making servants of Haydn and Mozart, but they gladly served Beethoven whose genius was interwoven with strength, charm, and rowdy vulgarity. Even his most illustrious pupil, Arch-duke Rudolf of Austria, was not above Beethoven's rebuke when he kept the composer waiting.

Inevitably Beethoven could not content himself with pianistics and improvisation: 1795 saw the first performance of his Opus No. 1, the trios for violin, cello, and piano. An incident throws into relief Beethoven's continued mixture of respect and distrust for Haydn. Beethoven played the three chamber works privately for the older man who praised the first two but counseled against publication of the third. Beethoven immediately suspected that jealousy had prompted the advice, not stopping to think that Haydn, famous and conservative, had recommended caution only because he had been unable to gauge the progress in his former pupil's work and felt that the public would be equally uncomprehensive. But when the trio was performed in London, composer-pianist Cramer exclaimed: "This is the man who will console us for the loss of Mozart."

The fledgling Beethoven had left the ground. In his opus two, again a mixture of pride and respect: It was dedicated to "M. Joseph Haydn, Docteur en Musique," but when Haydn requested that the composer designate himself as Haydn's pupil, Beethoven refused. But the deep-seated respect for Haydn never deserted the younger man. When the old master praised his "Prometheus" music, he graciously countered with a compliment of double-meaning: "But it's a long way from being a Creation." Nor did he ever fail to bow before the towering achievements of the man for whom he had first played in Vienna. Upon hearing Mozart's C-Minor Concerto he exclaimed: "I will never be able to create the like of it."

Superimposed upon early triumph was the first shadow of future pain and sorrow—the terrifying signs of oncoming deafness which began to add a poignant note to his music but at the same time roused him to defiance:

> I must go out and lustily knock about the world. There is no greater joy for me than to pursue and produce my art . . . oh if I were only rid of this affliction I could embrace the world! I feel my youth is just beginning. . . Every day I approach nearer the goal which I feel but cannot describe . . . No thought of peace. No! I cannot endure it! I will seize fate by the throat; most assuredly it shall not get me wholly down—oh, it is so beautiful to live life a thousand-fold.

Yet before he could make peace with his fate he had to wring from his soul that document of despair known as the "Heiligenstadt Testament," that pained bleeding of mind and cleansing of mental toxins. Beethoven, proud, famed, refused to accept his fate, not knowing that deafness was to aid his development, driving him from virtuosity, even human contact, and toward creation, leaving interpretation to others.

As if drawing strength from earth and art, Beethoven rose stronger from affliction and at the age of thirty made a first attempt at a symphony: The critics sneered: "Confused explosions of the over-weening conceit of a clever young man." "A caricature of Haydn pushed to absurdity." But the public took the work to heart and the "experts" followed. Five years later the *Allgemeine musikalische Zeitung* described a Vienna performance: "A glorious production, showing extraordinary wealth of lovely ideas, with perfect con-nection, order and lucidity." Even Carl Maria von Weber, often a virulent critic of Beethoven's work called the work "feurig strömend" (fiery streaming). Beethoven, once started, progressed in several directions as was always his wont. Emperor Franz had ended the custom of wearing wigs officially, Beethoven had done so in music. While he acknowledged that "the septet was written by Mozart," he was nevertheless strongly attracted to the ideal vehicle for pure music, the string quartet, resulting in the six "Lobkowitz" quartets. Progress was swift and awe inspiring. History was made with the "Pathetique" Sonata which established the "cyclic idea," and the music critic Rellstab did his bit in publicizing Sonata Op. 27, No. 2 by dubbing it the "Moonlight" Sonata. A return to a larger work with his Second Symphony added new touches to the established form.

"I am not at all satisfied with my work so far," he remarked one day to his friend Krumpholz, "and I intend to take a new road from today on." Nobody, perhaps not even Beethoven, realized the significance of that decision which was to reveal itself with the emergence of the "Eroica" Symphony in 1804, the "Waldstein" Sonata, and the "Leonore" opera sketches. In what biographer Schauffler calls "the battle ground of the sketchbooks" and in a state of inspiration which Romain Rolland describes as "controlled ecstasy," Beethoven filled the period of little more than a year with elemental developments ranging from Promethean fire to firefly caprice, from cyclopean power to gossamer fragility. Exclaimed admiring pupil Carl Czerny, "With him every sound, every motion became music and rhythm."

But the Viennese raged at the charming finale of his Second Symphony as a "repulsive monster, a wounded dragon, throwing its unwieldy body about and lashing wildly with the tail as it stiffens in its agony of death." At the public premiere of the "Eroica," one young "connoisseur" was heard to remark, "I'd give a kreutzer for this to end," and the critics, who suddenly found the first two symphonies marvels of classic order, considered the "Eroica" "Wearisome, interminable, ill-knit," and advised the composer to "go back to the first symphony . . . Let him take his earlier works as models."

Beethoven, racing against time and handicap, could not be denied. His hunger for knowledge became insatiable. Swieten had introduced him to Goethe and Homer. He knew Shakespeare (in German translation) and Schiller by heart. In contrast to Haydn and Mozart who had continued their creations in the same mold which gave them satisfaction, Beethoven reached a new height in expression and form with his "Appassionata" sonata. According to the trustworthy Czerny he considered the "Appassionata" and the "Eroica" among his favorite compositions.

Meanwhile he had embarked on the project which was to exalt and depress him more than any other. The first sketches of the opera *Leonore* appeared shortly after "Eroica" and the "Waldstein" sonata. Beethoven had ventured into the realm of opera despite the warnings of the composer Luigi Cherubini, despite his ignorance of the stage and the intrigue connected with every operatic production in Vienna. During the ten-year labor, his only opera, finally called *Fidelio*, was re-written three times, was supplied with four overtures, and was, according to Beethoven's conception, never completed. "Of all my children, this is the one that gave me the worst birth pains, the one that brought me the greatest sorrow, and for that reason it is the one most dear to me. Before all others I hold it worthy of being preserved and used in the science of art." "The Science of Art"—in itself a remarkable expression in Beethoven's time. It was a labor which would have overwhelmed a lesser spirit, a work where one single aria opening was sketched eighteen times, where twenty-two lines of vocal music occupy sixteen pages of sketch books.

The first Vienna performance on November 20, 1805 was a dismal failure. The work was withdrawn after three performances. During the Napoleonic wars, Vienna's spirit somehow was not raised by the spectacle of victory over an oppressor. Beethoven's princely friends nonetheless endeavored to save the work. In a gloomy post-mortem at Lichnowsky's palace, they entreated the composer to make changes, but Beethoven, wrapped in icy withdrawal, could not be moved. Finally Princess Lichnowsky, on her knees, begged the composer to reconsider, and in the face of her entreaty Beethoven relented.

Despite the magnificent *Leonore* No. 3 overture written especially for the second attempt at performance, the mutilated opera, now re-named *Fidelio*, survived only two performances. The critics tore it to shreds:

> All impartial connoisseurs are fully agreed that there never has been composed anything so ill-knit, so unpleasant, so confused, so revolting to the ear. The most acid modulations succeed each other in a truly horrible cacophony.
>
> ... shattering din, paltry ideas ...
>
> ... obstinate art which has neither beauty, natural feeling or facility ...

One critical expert went so far as to refer to the triumphant off-stage trumpet solo heralding liberation as "the solo for postilion's horn." Final vindication in Vienna would have to wait fully eight years.

"The great distinction of a superior man: steadfastness under grievous misfortune." Beethoven fully lived up to his own maxim. Undaunted by threatening deafness or operatic failure he busily engaged himself with the "Rasumovsky" Quartets and the G-major Piano Concerto. But great men may be brought to their knees. Beethoven had kept his increasing deafness a secret, even from his friends. But one day he and his student Ries had been walking in the fields when Ries remarked on the sweet sound of a flute being played. Beethoven had not heard. Worse, Ries now knew that the master was deaf. They continued in embarrassed silence from which no words of comfort could rouse the stricken composer. Thoughts of suicide overcame him. Yet the defeat by nature served only to rouse him to defiance. "Let deafness be a secret no more."

What helped Beethoven greatly in the struggle to regain equilibrium in a world growing silent about him was the friendship of the Brunswick family and the Brunswick sisters in particular. The stormy petrel from the Rhine and the wild flowers from the *puszta* understood each other by instinct. Beethoven was immensely grateful for the warmth, intimacy, and understanding of the family; Therese Brunswick could play Beethoven's sonatas to perfection. Franz Brunswick received the "Rasumovsky" Quartet manuscripts with the ink barely dry, and the "Appassionata" is dedicated to him. As to the finale of that sonata, Ries relates an instance of the workings of genius:

> One day Beethoven said: "Come Ries, let us take a little walk." [during the walk] . . . he had all the time been humming and sometimes roaring to himself, high and low, without actually singing any notes. When I asked him what all this meant, he said: "I have just thought of a theme for the last movement of the sonata." As soon as we reached his room he stormed to the pianoforte without even taking off his hat. I sat down in a corner and he forgot about me at once. For an hour or so he raged through the glorious new finale of the sonata. When at length he rose he was astonished to see me and said: "I can't give you a lesson today. I must go on with this."

Beethoven all but became part of the Brunswick family. "Farewell, dear brother, be it to me, I have none I would care to call such." This ending of a letter to Franz Brunswick shows a closer kinship than to any member of his own family.

To their everlasting glory, the musical nobles of Vienna gave Beethoven support no other composer had ever enjoyed. In 1805 Beethoven was to add the most illustrious name yet to his list of sponsors, Archduke Rudolf of Austria who proved a talented pupil and generous patron. But no amount of generosity and forebearance on the part of his patrons could soften the truculent spirit of the master. When in 1806 Prince Lichnowsky requested Beethoven to play before French officers quartered on his estate, Beethoven refused indignantly. He first locked himself in his room, then left in the dark of night and walked a mile to the stage depot to return to Vienna rather than play for the hated French invaders. Upon arrival at his abode he promptly smashed the prince's plaster bust. History will remember these true Viennese noblemen who acted kindly and generously in the face of Beethoven's undisguised contempt. It is a curious reversal that they are only remembered today because they placed themselves at the disposal of genius. No other document reveals the change of the times more than the note of Beethoven to his runner-of-errands, Count Ignaz von Gleichenstein:

> You lost a great deal, not by missing my music, but you might have met a charming talented prince, and, as a friend of your friend, you would certainly not have been made painfully conscious of the height of his rank. Forgive this small expression of pride. It comes more from the pleasure of knowing that those I love are instantly lent distinction, than from petty vanity.

The letter refers to an invitation Beethoven had obtained for the count to a musical gathering at the palace of the Archduke. What a total reversal—the artist benevolently extending to the aristocrat the lustre of his name.

As Beethoven's ability to communicate decreased, his feelings of insecurity and distrust increased apace and so did his miserliness and avarice. He meddled in the affairs of his brothers, questioned the smallest expenditures of his housekeepers, and entered into shady practices with his publishers. Only on rare occasions in the past had that feeling of unsureness crept into his attitude as when he had handed Prince Esterhazy his first Mass: "May I say that I turn over the Mass to you with great misgivings since you are used to hearing the inimitable masterpieces of the great Haydn performed for you." When the musically reactionary Esterhazy made a derisive comment on the work to Beethoven in the presence of Johann Hummel, his music director, Beethoven felt ridiculed. Nothing could keep him at a place where his work had been so misunderstood, and he left Eisenstadt the same day.

Yet the rude, abrupt Beethoven could be most tender and understanding. When Baroness Dorothea von Ertmann lost her child, he invited her to call, and when she came he sat down at the pianoforte, saying simply, "now we will talk to one another in music." For more than an hour he played without stopping and, as she remarked, "told me everything and at last brought me comfort."

Only in retrospect can the concert of Thursday, December 22, 1808, be considered a historic moment in music and Vienna, because circumstances conspired to bring about disaster. The program contained Beethoven's Fifth and Sixth Symphonies, the G-major Piano Concerto, the Piano Fantasy with orchestra, plus the aria "Ah Perfido," selections from his C-major Mass and the Choral Fantasy in C minor for piano, chorus and orchestra. All in one concert! All performed for the first time! All done without rehearsal and performed in an unheated hall! To make matters worse, the piano performances, which marked Beethoven's last appearance as a virtuoso, were the low point of the evening. Nor did he help matters by quarrelling with the soprano and publicly insulting members of the orchestra. Vienna was totally oblivious of the evening's significance. The box office was a disaster. The doubly unhappy result was that Beethoven became even more withdrawn. His obsession of persecution increased markedly. His neglected clothes became so shabby that he was arrested for vagrancy. Eventually, by tacit agreement, his friends looked after his clothes and replaced them regularly. Beethoven, too absorbed with matters musical, never noticed.

On November 1, 1808, however, a message which demanded attention had arrived at his abode. Jerome Bonaparte, King of Westphalia, offered Beethoven a wage of six hundred gold ducats. Again Vienna's aristocracy rose to the challenge. Upon receiving secret information of the offer, Countess Erdödy persuaded Archduke Rudolf and princes Lobkowitz and Kinsky to retain the composer in Vienna by subsidizing him at four hundred florins per year for life. Their generous gesture remains undiminished by the fact that Lobkowitz' bankruptcy, Kinsky's death, and inflation in the wake of the Napoleonic wars eventually reduced the subsidy to a mere pittance.

In 1810 ended an unbelievably fertile ten-year period which saw the birth of six symphonies, fifteen piano sonatas, the Septet, the Quintet, two trios, five concertos, six overtures, an oratorio, a ballet and a Mass. Two years of creative aridity followed until 1812 when the Seventh and Eighth Symphonies and the G-major Violin Sonata sprang forth. That period of musical hibernation also marked Beethoven's one-sided love affair with Therese Malfatti, the fifteen-year-old niece of his physician. While music languished Beethoven preened, only to be gently rejected by Therese, twenty-five years his junior. When Beethoven met Bettina Brentano, the sister of his friend, however, all other loves momentarily paled. To the surprise of his friends, Beethoven emerged from his shell. There was undisguised mutual attraction, trust, and warmth between kindred spirits. There was understanding and inspiration in Bettina's company and the joining of emotions. No one described his greatness better than did Bettina to Goethe: "There was a simultaneous fermentation of his pride and genius. When he is in such a state of exaltation his spirit begets the incomprehensible and his fingers accomplish the impossible."

Through Bettina, Goethe became acquainted with Beethoven. In the beginning their admiration was mutual. The composer expressed "deepest reverence and admiration" for the poet and Goethe reciprocated. But their feelings soon cooled. In 1812 when Goethe and Beethoven were walking arm in arm through the spa of Teplitz, the empress and her retinue approached. Beethoven pressed Goethe's arm and growled: "Stay where you are, they must make way for us, not we for them." The court poet was shocked. He stepped aside and, hat in hand, let the imperial party pass while Beethoven stoically proceeded. To Goethe's surprise the imperial ranks opened for Beethoven. The composer afterwards chided the poet for his deference, and their regard for each other underwent a decided and permanent change: "Goethe is too fond of the atmosphere of the court, more so than is becoming to a poet." Beethoven is "an utterly untamed personality."

Such truculence did not prevent Beethoven from expressing the most tender thoughts when the occasion or the subject elicited them:

> My Angel, my all, my very self . . . my thoughts press on to you, my immortal beloved . . . Life is possible only wholly with you or not at all . . . Wherever I am, you are there with me . . . is not our love a truly celestial abode, but also immovable as the firmament."

Who was Beethoven's "Immortal Beloved"? Volumes have been written on the subject, but it seems that the true holder of the title will forever remain the unsolved secret of Beethoven's life.

His music of that period holds no such riddles. Remarks friend and biographer Schindler of the "Archduke" Trio: "I hold the Andante to be the most beautiful ideal of holiness and divinity . . . words can be of no avail here; they are wretched servants of the divine word delivered by music."

Not all his creations were divine, however. Sublime thoughts stand side by side with such uninspired works as the incidental music to "King Stephan" and "The Ruins of Athens," both commissioned for a newly opened theatre in Budapest and dedicated to the Empress of Russia. Later Beethoven compounded the musical felony. When the London Philharmonic commissioned three overtures from him, he palmed off on them the two overtures plus the equally inferior C-major Overture, opus 115. London felt insulted, and Beethoven's act only tended to lower his prestige there.

The coarseness of jocular manner and speech so often in Beethoven were also woven into his music and duly outraged his pigmy contemporaries. Beethoven, however, had intended just such grandly untamed music in the finale of his Seventh Symphony on which he remarked to Bettina: "I am the Bacchus who presses out for mankind this glorious wine and intoxicates their souls." Such continued unbridled humor, although now typical with the composer, caused never-ending furor among his foes and consternation among his friends. "Incomprehensible, diffuse, over-complicated," were the acid comments of Weber, and even Beethoven's friend, the composer Louis Spohr, found the symphony "too long drawn out."

Unfortunately also, Beethoven's humor was a one-way street. While nobody was safe from his heavy-handed humor, biting tongue, and practical jokes, he would go into a rage if the same were inflicted upon him. He did receive his comeuppance once from Abbé Stadler whom he asked for a blessing. The priest raised his eyes towards heaven with a wry smile and, while making the sign of the cross, murmured: "Hilft's net, schad's net" (If it won't help, it won't harm).

Beethoven's financial embarrassment, brought on by Lobkowitz' bankruptcy, inflation, and Kinsky's death, proved more severe than he had anticipated. The situation deteriorated to such an extent that he had to go into self-imposed confinement at his lodgings because his one pair of shoes fell apart and he did not own a shirt without holes. Financial necessity may have forced him to stoop again to inferior composition. The result was "Wellington's Victory" or "The Battle Symphony," composed for Mälzel's Panharmonicon, a forerunner of the player piano. Its flag-waving platitudes even grind "God Save the King" through a furious *fugato*, suggesting the jubilation of the King's subjects. It bespeaks the taste of the Viennese of 1813 that the "Battle Symphony" became Beethoven's key to success. At charity concerts for war widows and orphans, Vienna flocked to hear it together with the Seventh Symphony plus marches by Pleyel and Dussek. Everybody who was anybody in musical Vienna participated. Spohr fiddled, Moscheles smashed the cymbals, Salieri commanded the guns offstage, Hummel pounded the bass drum together with a musical aspirant, Meyerbeer by name, who could not keep time and was mercilessly flayed by Beethoven. Young Schuppanzigh, Beethoven's favorite quartet player, was among the violins, and Dragonetti, the famous string bass player who played Beethoven's cello sonatas on the bass, much to the composer's delight, led his section. Schubert, twenty and unknown, was in the audience.

There was, however, a beneficial side to Beethoven's low-end triumphs aside from the charity aspects. He was suddenly popular in Vienna and his much maligned *Fidelio* rose to its first success on the coat tails of the "Battle Symphony." Beethoven could either not resist the lure of easy income or was forced to continue to mine that low-grade lode to improve his still precarious financial condition. Because shortly thereafter we find him occupied with an equally inferior product, "The Glorious Moment" for the Congress of Vienna.

Napoleon had captured Vienna twice, in 1805 and 1809. After a brief bombardment of the venerable walls, the city surrendered. During the bombardment Beethoven had fled across-town to the house of a friend in whose cellar he sat out the cannonade with a pillow pressed against his ears. The surrender completed, Beethoven returned to his own abode and Napoleon ensconced himself in the imperial summer palace of Schönbrunn. After his banishment to Elba in 1813, Vienna was restored to its old splendour. For a brief moment it became the political center of the world when the Congress of Vienna, called by Britain, Prussia, Austria, and Russia, convened within its walls.

Beethoven's coffers began to refill. Three more concerts followed the premiere of his "Battle Symphony." To balance this commercial trend, he began a complete revision of *Fidelio*. Vienna actually knew two Beethovens. One—the composer of exalted masterpieces, the companion of princes, the other—the man walking the hills and fields, lonely and alone, his hearing disintegrating and with it his contacts with life. People began to call him "The Crazy Musician." As distrust and misanthropy increased with his handicap, so did his steadfastness in the face of adversity. A footnote at the bottom of his *Fidelio* manuscript attests to his faith. After the words "With God's Help" he added his own credo, "Man Help Thyself." The spring of 1814 witnessed the last public performance by the composer, in the piano part of his "Archduke Trio." Deafness and poor technique due to lack of practice forbade further public playing. "In forte passages," recalled the composer Spohr, "the poor deaf man pounded the keys until the strings jangled and in the piano passages he played so softly that entire tone groups were inaudible."

Despite all their faults, their reluctance to face facts, their tolerant sloppiness, none had truer affection for and understanding of beauty in its many manifestations than the Viennese. In the post-Napoleonic years, music was popular not only for its own beauty, but for its fleeting qualities which eluded Metternich's spies and censors. The Viennese, seeing an escape from the despotism of Franz I, threw themselves into music making and dancing with a good-natured, carefree zest which often bordered on frenzy. Dancing, singing, eating and drinking, and a good and glorious time went hand in hand with typhoid, tuberculosis, and venereal disease. Conditions within the cramped city walls became intolerable and compelled aristocracy and burghers alike to spill out into suburbs and vineyards. Maria Theresia and Josef II encouraged that trend. Vintners and their vines aided and abetted everything that was gay, easygoing and lightly responsible in the Viennese.

The bare stretch of land before the walls was now used for parades, drills, fairs, circuses, or just promenading. There, on balmy summer evenings, one would observe the gay Viennese streaming through the twelve city gates. The men in tight waist coats with dark velvet collars, set off by brightly flowered vests, flowing artist's ties, and stovepipe hats, the trousers tightly fitting; the laughing Viennese girls in their immense hoop skirts reaching to the ground, offset by daringly deep-cut bodices and enormous bonnets with "walking gardens" on top. There were smartly uniformed officers in dark blue tunics and light blue trousers piped in red, one arm around the waist of one of the proverbially saucy Viennese washerwomen, whose dark hair was crowned with the polka-dot kerchief and its enormous bow knot, their trade-mark.

There on the glacis, they walked and talked and gawked at the carriages drawn by prancing horses, the ladies with enormous hats shielding delicate complexions, sheltered in turn by tiny parasols. The dandies at their sides in bright velvets, matching stovepipes and bright brocade vests, flicking imaginary dust specks from their sleeves or stealing ardent glances at one and all. The main occupation of all promenaders was to flirt or watch the hawkers, puppeteers, itinerant musicians, singers, jugglers who, together with innumerable beggars, mingled with the crowd.

If they could tear glances from each other or from their immediate surroundings to look up, they would wave to friends promenading atop the wide, six-mile long city walls to catch the cool breezes wafting towards the city from the Vienna Woods, or walking their Pekingese or Spitz which had become a status symbol among the burghers of Vienna. When bringing their produce in oxen-drawn carts through the city gates in the early morning hours, farmers could observe Beethoven walking rapidly on those ramparts, rain or shine, a lonely figure against the early dawn, clothes unbuttoned, untamed mane snaking in the breeze, a gawky figure, singing, shouting, gesticulating, creating. Robert Schumann painted a word panorama of an even wider scene:

> This Vienna, with memories of the great German masters, must be a fertile field for a musician's imagination. Often, when I looked down upon it from the mountain tops, it occured to me how frequently the eyes of Beethoven must have restlessly roamed over the distant Alpine chain; how Mozart may have dreamily followed the flow of the Danube which always seems to swim in forests; and how Papa Haydn may have peered up to St. Stefan's tower, shaking his head at such dizzying height. Put together the pictures of Danube, St. Stefan's and the far mountain ranges, cover them with the faint scent of Catholic incense and you have a portrait of Vienna. And when the charming landscape comes wholly alive for us, strings may be heard that otherwise might never have sounded within us. At the touch of Schubert's Symphony and the clear blossoming life in it, the city rises more clearly than ever before us, and most plainly I can see again how such works can be born in just such a setting.

Beethoven, storming along the city ramparts, saw little of this, because he was caught in the turbulence of his own tornado, a storm without a calm center. Those who knew him have described the composer of this period:

> His eyes are full of turbulent energy. His hair, which seems to have remained for years beyond the touch of comb and scissors, shades the broad brow in an abundance and disorder with which only the snakes on Gorgon's head can be compared . . . friendliness and affability do not lie in his character except when in the circle of close intimates . . . even his oldest friends must always obey his will . . . It was interesting to note how music translated itself from the man's soul to his features . . . his facial muscles tightened and his veins stood out; his wild eyes rolled in frenzy, the mouth twitched, and Beethoven looked like a sorcerer who feels himself overpowered by the very spirits he had conjured up. [Sir John Russell]

> From the first ray of the sun till dinner time, the entire morning is dedicated to mechanical toil, namely writing his music down. The rest of the day was given to thought and putting his ideas in order. The last mouthful had barely touched his lips . . . when he began his usual promenade . . . running in double time a couple of times around the city as though he were being stung.

Whether it rained, snowed or hailed, whether the thermometer showed 16° of cold, whether the north wind puffed its cheeks, whether thunder roared or the sun's heat directly fell on his head—what difference did it all make to the consecrated one who carried his God in his own heart and for whose spirit, perhaps, in the very might of the elements' upheaval, the mild springtide of paradise was blooming. [Seyfried]

In 1818 Beethoven received from England a Broadwood piano inscribed with the names of England's foremost pianists. The Austrian government, in a rare bow to genius, admitted the instrument duty-free. The piano actually meant little to Beethoven except for the honor implied, because he was now totally deaf. A visiting friend found him furiously hitting a bootjack against a piano leg in a vain test to hear any sound at all. There were constant complaints of rheumatism, ear pain, colic, of thieving housekeepers. Aside from matters musical, he was utterly helpless and without common sense in matters of everyday life. His persecution complex was further deepened by the fickle Viennese' preference for Rossini's lilting music. All this contributed to the inevitable downward path of the lonely, ailing, unloved, suspicious deaf man.

It is chilling to consider the exalted music side by side with the incredible picture of gross avarice which Beethoven now presented. The *Missa Solemnis*, that sublime musical cathedral, was offered by the composer to four publishers at the same time and finally given to none of them in a flagrant display of questionable ethics. While doing so he also offered the Mass in private subscription to those long-suffering patrons whom he considered "princely rabble," and again at the same time also to the Berlin Sing-Akademie. To leave no stone unturned, he also contacted Goethe in Weimar, banking on their earlier friendship, and asked for assistance in subscription at the Weimar court. Goethe ignored him.

From the first youthful inspiration to the final note, it took Beethoven nearly thirty years to complete his Ninth Symphony. Its monumental themes parallel Beethoven's spiritual motto, "Per aspera ad astra." The premiere of the Ninth at the historic Kärthnerthor Theatre on May 7, 1824 was a historic occasion. The program announced: " 'Consecration of the House'—Overture / 'Kyrie, Credo and Agnus Dei' from Missa Solemnis / 'IX Symphony.' " The significance of the occasion had not been lost on musical Vienna, and applause interrupted "that miracle of repetition without monotony," the famous scherzo with its humorously bouncing timpani beat. Vienna's finest artists again helped to make the evening a success. Beethoven, totally deaf, also "participated" but seemed remarkably unemotional. With only two rehearsals the performance of the giant work was far from adequate, yet its emotional impact on those assembled was obviously great. Beethoven continued to beat time, stony-faced. Only by chance did the solo soprano realize that the deaf master was unaware of the reaction. It was necessary to tug at the composer's sleeve and to turn him around to make him aware of the tumultuous applause. When the audience, in turn, realized that it was not indifference or rudeness but his affliction which had kept him from acknowledging the tribute, there followed a scene rarely equalled in the musical history of Vienna. Women broke into tears, handkerchiefs were waved, men shouted themselves hoarse to give vent to their feelings which went far beyond artistic appreciation.

Yet Beethoven's split personality asserted itself again. After promising London sole performance rights for eighteen months for which he received the stipulated fee, he broke the promise with a Vienna performance. To add insult, he dedicated the symphony to the King of Prussia who reciprocated with a fake diamond ring.

Like Prince Rasumovsky and Prince Lobkowitz before him, Prince Gallitzin, in 1822, engraved his name in the annals of music when he commissioned a number of string quartets from Beethoven. In the utter silence of his world, the composer created his loftiest and most remote musical landscapes, beyond any attempt at popular acceptance. Nonetheless, these quartets (the last one surprisingly subtitled "La Gaiete") were avidly sought by publishers. Despite such flattering recognition, Beethoven felt more neglected by the Viennese than ever and declared himself impoverished, although both assertions were unfounded.

In 1825 he moved for the last time—to the "Schwarzspanierhaus" (Black Spaniard House), incidentally an apt description of the swarthy, dark-haired Beethoven. There the sketches of a Tenth Symphony were found after his death. Despite his deteriorating condition, Beethoven made desperate attempts to escape from his silent shell and communicate with the world around him. He went so far as to visit his brother Johann about whom everything irritated him, including the name of the town where he lived—Gneixendorf. But the town's beautiful surroundings filled him with renewed vigor and inspiration, although "the mad man" elicited from others sentiments ranging from giggling laughter to impotent rage. One of Johann's servants who acted as Beethoven's valet left a vivid picture:

> At half past five he was up and at his table, beating time with hands and feet, singing, humming, writing. At half past seven was

the family breakfast and promptly after it he hurried outside and wandered about the fields, calling out, waving his hands, going now slowly, now very fast, and then suddenly standing still and writing in a kind of notebook. At half past twelve he would come into the house for dinner and after dinner he went to his room till three or so, then again into the fields till about sunset. At half past seven he came to supper and then went to his room, wrote till ten and then to bed.

Thus Beethoven's last complete work, the Quartet in F major, opus 135, came into being in October 1826. Unwittingly a simple servant left a picture of a genius drawing inspiration from the earth while annoying men and terrifying beasts.

Late in December Beethoven returned to Vienna. The open coach was cold and drafty. To complicate the vexatious journey, he was forced to spend the night en route in an unheated inn. He arrived with a high fever and took to bed. Poor care, stubborness, and ignorance worsened his condition until a doctor had to be called. He immediately diagnosed pneumonia. Improvement seemed well under way when an outburst of typical Beethoven rage brought about "summer cholera," jaundice, and dropsy. The latter made four tappings necessary, but Beethoven had not lost his sense of humor: "Better water from my belly than from my pen."

Because of medical ignorance and the impossible living conditions in the vermin infested quarters, Beethoven's condition worsened rapidly. Breuning visited him and presented him with the complete works of Händel, and Beethoven, as always, uttered words of admiration for the pre-classic giant. Despite his desperate condition he discussed the future recognition of his late quartets. His strength was ebbing, however, and while writing his last will in a failing hand he was supported by his brother Johann and Breuning. Informed of a present of Rhine wine from the music publisher Schott, he could only murmur, "Pity, pity, too late." Beethoven's last moments were true to form. Roused during a storm by a flash of lightning and roaring thunder, he raised himself from the pillow, shook a fist towards the skies in farewell defiance, and fell back, his eyes open.

His relatives who, despite his protestations, had always suspected he was wealthy, started an intense scavenger hunt after his death. A secret drawer yielded seven bank shares, the picture of Therese von Brunswick, and the unmailed letter to the "Immortal Beloved." A recent gift of one hundred pounds to Beethoven from England was also found. Like Schott's wine, it had arrived too late to be either consumed or concealed.

VII

The Singer of Songs

An eleven-year-old boy was totally unaware of the historic event of December 22, 1808 which gave Vienna and the world Beethoven's Fifth and Sixth Symphonies. His name was Franz Schubert, and he wore the shabby uniform of the Convikt, a Catholic school for boys which provided much of the music for the court. The school orchestra in which he played second violin was his only diversion from the harsh rule and drab existence of the cloistered institution. Overtures and symphonies by Méhul, Cherubini, Kozeluch, Haydn, and Mozart were the musical menu, with the young players standing at their music desks while playing. There the boy met his first life-long friend, Josef Spaun, nine years his senior, who soon noticed that a short, stocky boy with a friendly round face

> far surpassed me in rhythmical surety. This aroused my interest and made me realize with what animation the lad, who otherwise seemed quiet and indifferent, gave himself to his impression of the beautiful symphonies which we played. Once I came upon him alone in the music room, sitting at the piano which his tiny hands could already play very passably . . . Under my friendly encouragement he played me a minuet of his own invention. He was shy and red with embarrassment; but my approval made him happy. The lad confided to me that he often secretly wrote his thoughts down; but father mustn't know about it; he was dead set against his son's devoting himself to music. After that I sometimes slipped him music paper.

In recognition of obvious talent, young Franz was soon promoted to first violin. His musical horizon was also widened when he began to sing the great Masses in the imperial court choir. But despite all promising signs, father Schubert remained unrelentingly opposed to Franz's entering the "breadless" musical profession. Finally the father issued a cruel ultimatum: "Either stop your musical activities or stop your visits at home." Franz chose music and remained at the Convikt which he now called his prison. Only at his mother's death of typhus a year later did father and son reunite at the funeral. Less than a year after his wife's death, father Schubert married a young lady twenty years his junior. She was to bear him five more children but always professed a fondness for her stepson.

In 1812 Schubert began to study counterpoint with Salieri who was impressed but too busy and too self-inflated to give the boy more than careless supervision and instruction. Antonio Salieri was an anachronistic holdover, bypassed by the music of the Vienna classic masters whom he openly despised—"Music ceased with Gluck's death." Historian Rochlitz recalls Salieri as "friendly, obliging, benevolent, full of joy of life, witty, inexhaustible in anecdote and quotation, a finely built little man with sparkling fiery eyes, a brown complexion, always tidy and clean, of lively temperament, easily aroused but just as easily pacified." His "benevolence" did not keep him from intriguing against Mozart to the latter's dying day, and Salieri poisoned Schubert's mind against anything German, including Mozart and Beethoven, Goethe and Schiller. His Italianate influence and insistence that only opera was the supreme form of composition did Schubert lasting harm. At that early stage composition was already a "must" with Schubert.

> To see him compose was interesting [wrote Spaun]. He seldom used the pianoforte, often declaring that this would interrupt the progress of his thoughts. He sat quietly at his small table, scarcely bothered by the conversation and noise of his fellow students . . . He stooped far over a sheet of paper and a textbook for he was extremely nearsighted. He gnawed on his pen, sometimes playing with his fingers upon the table as if trying a passage; and wrote fluently and easily with few corrections, as though it had to be just this way and not otherwise.

Not until he was fifteen did Franz hear professional performances such as Spontini's *Vestal Virgin*, Handel's *Messiah*, and Beethoven's Ninth Symphony. Mozart's music, especially the Requiem, *The Magic Flute*, and *Don Giovanni*, left him breathless. Zumsteeg's songs gave him his first glimpse of the Elysian fields in which he was to reign supreme.

Franz's voice changed. Although offered an imperial scholarship if he improved in mathematics, a subject that was to remain an enigma all his life, he declined. But before exchanging the school's harsh conformity for the longed-for freedom, he completed a symphony, the first of Schubert's blossoms in the Eden of Haydn and Mozart. He then followed his father into the teaching profession, but not, as usually claimed, to escape military service. Schubert's height, barely five feet, and his extremely poor eyesight would have ruled out conscription. He followed his father's métier, even became a licensed member of a profession which he despised, as a means of keeping himself in food and clothes.

Despite his father's continued hostility towards music and the long hours of drudgery, Schubert's musical surge could not be stifled. At age seventeen he wrote the B-flat Quartet in the unbelievable span of five hours. Further impetus was given by the musical atmosphere of the Grob family. As so often, a woman's smile inspired a genius. Sixteen-year-old Therese Grob who possessed a lovely voice, became the object of Franz's affections. For her he wrote his Mass in F major. Its first performance, during the centennial celebration of Schubert's church in the suburb of Liechtenthal, made him a local celebrity. The impressiveness of the occasion was heightened by the presence of old Salieri who was sufficiently impressed to claim Franz as his pupil. Even father Schubert was mollified and loosened his tight purse strings for a new, badly needed piano for Franz.

Inevitably 1814 became the decisive year for Schubert. Immediately after school closed, he sold all his school books and went to hear *Fidelio* at the Kärnthnerthor Theatre. He read Goethe's poems and under their overwhelming impression created his first masterpiece in song, "Gretchen am Spinnrade" (Gretchen at the Spinning Wheel). Without trial or transition the mature Lieder composer had emerged from an adolescent cocoon. Salieri was annoyed: "It is all very well to try your hand at Masses, but do not fritter away your time on such insignificant things as Lieder. The only thing for a real composer to concentrate on is opera."

In 1814 there was also born that closely knit circle of devoted friends, the Schubertiad, gaining a measure of fame for the one man around whom it revolved. In that circle Franz befriended gloomy poet Johann Mayrhofer, ardent champion of freedom in principle but Metternich's censor as a livelihood. Schubert, who later shared a room with Mayrhofer, set to music 47 poems by his friends, together with 57 by Schiller, 67 by Goethe, but only one by another Schubertiad member, Vienna's greatest poet, Franz Grillparzer. Remarked Mayrhofer on their relationship: "Our love for poetry and music made our association more intimate. I wrote poems and he set them to music. Many of them owed their very existence, development and dissemination to his melodies." Franz's path was freed of many obstacles by a later member of the group, Franz Ritter von Schober, witty, sensual, a dandy and ladies' man, second-rate actor and poet and, despite his cynical shell, the soul of goodness. He soon became an ardent admirer of Schubert and remained his loyal friend. Franz, in turn, set fifteen of Schober's lyrics to music.

The year 1815 saw an explosion of creative genius which produced the Second and Third symphonies, four operas, two Masses,
150 songs, plus numerous works for church and piano. Finally, 1815
saw the birth of "The Erlking." Related Spaun in his memoirs:

> We found him all aglow, reading [Goethe's] "Erlking" out of
> a book which he carried several times to and fro across the room.
> Suddenly he sat down and in the shortest possible time the
> magnificent ballad was hurled down upon paper. As Schubert
> had no piano, we hurried with it to the Konvikt; and there
> that evening "Erlking" was sung and received with enthusiasm.

Despite his opposition to his son's music-making, father Schubert
was strongly musically inclined, and enlarged his quartet group into
a small orchestra, one of numerous such ensembles which constantly
blossom in Vienna, by adding some amateur woodwind players.
They were fortunate to have a Schubert in their midst who wrote his
Fourth and Fifth Symphonies for them, creating them in a matter of
weeks.

Schubert's friends were now convinced that their little "mush-
room" was a genius and set out to garner fame for him and his creations. The first step was made by Spaun who sent a number of songs
on Goethe's poems to Goethe in Weimar. But the old court poet
had never been a connoisseur of the finer things in musical life unless
they were forced on him by a Beethoven. He was too steeped in the
provincial sounds of Zelter to be moved by Schubert's Lieder. Goethe
had the manuscripts returned unopened.

Upon the advice of Spaun and Schober, Schubert took a year's
leave of absence from teaching to devote himself to composition.
Life became austere but the mind was free to spread wings. The
result—105 songs, among them such gems as "Death and the Maiden,"
"To Music," "The Trout," and seven piano sonatas, written primarily
for private entertainments devoted entirely to his music. Undaunted
by the failure to get Goethe's ear, Franz's friends went a step further.
They submitted his songs to the foremost German publishing house,
Breitkopf & Härtel, hoping these professionals would immediately
recognize the greatness of their little friend and rush his songs into
print. But fate played a cruel hoax. The only Schubert Breitkopf &
Härtel knew was a Franz Schubert in Dresden, composer and director
of Italian opera there. Upon inquiry from the publishers, that honorable nonentity wrathfully replied: "To my immense astonishment I
reply that this cantata is not a composition of mine. I will keep it in
custody in order to ascertain ... who has so impolitely sent you such

a bungling piece of work, and also to unearth this fellow who has so mistreated my name."

In 1816 Johann Michael Vogl entered Schubert's life. At first meeting the giant baritone, who had sung the first Pizarro in Beethoven's *Fidelio*, seemed barely interested. But upon leaving, the towering singer turned to the diminutive composer and, with his hands on the little man's shoulders, remarked (echoes of Baron Grimm's words to Mozart): "There's 'something' in you but you are too little of an actor, not enough of a charlatan. You squander your beautiful thoughts without making enough of them." But Vogl soon caught fire: "To find such depth and maturity coming from such a small fellow is simply incredible . . . [these are] outpourings of musical clairvoyance."

> The impression Schubert's songs made on Vogl was almost overpowering [recalled Spaun]. Without invitation he again approached our circle, invited Schubert to his house . . . and when he realized the terrific overpowering effect his delivery had on us . . . he grew so enthusiastic over these songs that he now became Schubert's most ardent admirer.

Musical inspiration was fine but, hunger eventually forced Schubert back into the abhorrent task of teaching. Now it was the dull country estate of Count Johann Karl Esterhazy von Galatea, at Zselitz. The count was no exception when it came to taking advantage of Schubert. Franz was engaged at bargain rates and relapsed into the position of servant from which Beethoven had just raised the lot of the composer. Despite his menial position, Franz rather liked the place because its peace and quiet, interrupted only by noisy geese, gave him time to compose plus the rare feature of regular meals. Soon he was half resigned, half adjusted to life in the relaxed atmosphere of remote Zselitz, eased further by the presence of a pixieish chambermaid, remembered only as Pepi, who did her small part in broadening his worldly education.

Franz's eventual return to Vienna in the autumn had its compensations in the meeting of his dear friends but also drawbacks.

> In a half-dark, damp and unheated little room, shivering and composing . . . at six o'clock every morning Schubert sat down at his desk and composed without break until one o'clock in the afternoon, smoking a few pipes as he wrote. If I visited him, he immediately played me whatever was finished and wanted to know what I thought of it. If I especially praised a song he would say "Yes you see this is a good poem. When you read a bad poem nothing is right . . . I've refused many poems that have

been thrust upon me." [Composer Hüttenbrenner in his memoirs.]

Often Franz would be so immersed in creation that he would not bother to look up to see who a visitor was and, after a friendly absentminded nod, would continue without pause. Only in the afternoons would he and his friends meet in the intimate, smoke-filled atmosphere of coffeehouses which abounded in Vienna and sported such colorful names as "The Hungarian Crown," "The Black Cat," or "The Eye of God."

Contemporaries Beethoven and Schubert lived and created in similar surroundings: In Beethoven's quarters trunks and suitcases held, in total disarray, whatever wardrobe he possessed. A mattress filled with straw, night clothes and other wearing apparel strewn over furniture and floor, dirty dishes on the table, and several pianos, some on the floor without legs, all out of tune, heaped with ink- and coffee-stained manuscripts, completed the picture.

Schubert's lodgings matched Beethoven's: A piano heaped high with music, stringed instruments, music racks, a table and chair the only sign of comfort. From such dismal quarters the two men, both small in stature (Beethoven only five feet five) both creating in the atmosphere of Vienna, both giants of musical thought, proceeded in opposite directions, musically as well as philosophically: Beethoven: "Man, help thyself." Schubert: "Man is like a ball with which accidents and passions play."

Beethoven lived in the world of princes over whom he reigned in his own roughshod manner. In the same Vienna yet worlds apart, Schubert was acknowledged by a middle class of high artistic standards for whom he became a focal point. Theirs were not gatherings to which one came to be seen, nor were their musical evenings earth-shaking musical events—although the Schubertiad now included some of the foremost poets, musicians, and artists in Vienna. In that tightly knit world, far removed from the marble halls of Beethoven and the musty make-believe of Rossini (fickle Vienna's newest darling of the hour), Schubert was the sun around which his friends revolved within the orbit of their music sessions. Word went around that exquisite music was being made, and other devotees joined: Franz Grillparzer, Austria's greatest poet, Karoline Pichler, who brought with her the memory of similar music-making by Haydn and Mozart, and minor court officials.

By far the loveliest of the group were the Fröhlich sisters, gay, sparkling musical amateurs of whom Grillparzer said: "They intoxicated themselves with music." Their house was always open and music could be heard at all hours. When Leopold Sonnleithner, who made a hobby of collecting Schubert manuscripts, showed some of them to the Fröhlichs, they too caught the spark and welcomed the timid composer to their abode. The liking was immediate and mutual: "Schubert had a glorious disposition," wrote one of the sisters. "He was never envious or jealous like so many others. On the contrary, what pure joy he felt when lovely music was played. Then he would put his hands together, press them to his mouth and sit there wholly entranced."

Despite all efforts by Schubert's friends, the publishers in Leipzig and Vienna continued to turn a deaf ear. Diabelli openly declared that he would not pay a kreuzer for such rubbish nor even take it free. Thereupon the friends chipped in to raise the money and shamed Diabelli into putting some music in print. Surprisingly a hundred copies were sold at a private concert, sufficient to pay for printing another song. And, lo and behold, in that manner Schubert's debts were also paid for the first time.

But his luck did not hold. Mayrhofer, the morbid poet with the split personality, committed suicide. Spaun departed for Linz, Hüttenbrenner to his native Graz. Into the void stepped Moritz von Schwind, destined to be one of the great painters of the Vienna school. Seven years Schubert's junior, he was handsome, elegant and poor until he acquired sudden affluence by selling a painting of Faust for 2,500 florins. Loquacious and vivacious, sensitive and fiery, he became one of the brightest lights of the Schubertiad. Schwind's family home, the Mondscheinhaus (moonlight house), soon became the favorite meeting place of the group. The huge, massive house offered a magnificent view of the fortifications of the city and the alpine foothills beyond. In summer the group slept on the ground in the vine-shaded courtyard which in winter, became the scene of fierce snowball fights to the accompaniment of declamations from the *Iliad* or the *Nibelungenlied*. When they were not listening to Schubert's music, the members studied the new creations of poets and painters among them, rent the air with heated discussions, or filled their young souls with the thoughts of the new romantic era of Kleist, E. T. A. Hoffmann and Brentano. Later Schubert moved into the vicinity, close to Schwind and near the majestic baroque Karlskirche (memorial church to Charles VI).

Like Schubert, Schwind could not gain recognition in Vienna either. He had the good sense to leave, but not before he had immortalized his friends Schober, Schubert, Vogl, his almost-wife Anna Hönig, and himself in his drawing "Stroll Before the Town

Gate." In later years, he atoned for the world's neglect by immortalizing his timid friend and the entire gathering in his "Schubertiad" with the picture of Schubert's supposed great love, Countess Caroline Esterhazy, happily gazing from the wall on the inspired assembly.

Meanwhile another composer, Karl Maria von Weber, had set Vienna on its musical ear with his opera *Der Freischütz*. While Schubert's opera *Alfonso and Estrella* joined all his previous efforts in limbo, Vienna listened with baited breath to the rustle of German forests in Weber's music. Weber had met Schubert and had commented favorably on *Alfonso*, even promised to further a performance in Germany. When Weber's opera *Euryanthe* failed, however, Schubert rashly joined in the general criticism. He had acted in such a manner before, calling Beethoven an extremist only to imitate his style unabashedly later on. Weber, who never hesitated to criticize others, Beethoven included, was livid with rage at Schubert's criticism, and with the words "Let the fool learn something first before he begins to judge me," put a premature end to a budding friendship.

After the *Euryanthe* failure, fickle Vienna avidly looked for another style, and its seesawing enthusiasm reverted to Italian *rubati* and *crescendi*. Rossini became the man of the hour, and Rossini adulation reached new heights. He responded by personally leading a brilliant opera company to the "Capital of Music." "Rossini madness" grew apace with each performance until Italian music was again the rage of Vienna, drowning out Weber's German romantics, scuttling Schubert, and prompting even Beethoven to darkly ponder the state of "true" music in Vienna.

As inevitably as water from a spring, so music continued to stream from Schubert's pen. Totally unaware of their worth but compelled to write them, he created Masses, symphonies, fantasies. Yet when asked for an overture for orchestral performance, he retired into his timid shell and modestly declined: "As so many works by the great masters are available, for example Beethoven's overtures of Prometheus, Egmont and Coriolan etc. I must sincerely beg you to forgive me for not being able to serve you in this matter; for it would hurt me to appear with something mediocre." Haydn had reacted with similar modesty, recommending Mozart's work. But Haydn could afford to do so, Schubert could not.

Trouble had become Schubert's constant companion. He contracted a severe sickness, probably venereal disease stemming from furtive nocturnal excursions into the lowest strata of Viennese society. He lost his hair and was forced to wear a wig for some time. Contrary to popular belief, however, the disease did not cause his death. Similarities to Mozart increased: lack of regular meals, poorly heated, lighted and furnished lodgings, constant failure, discouragement and financial difficulties, coupled with an exhaustingly creative mind. All this, plus his nightly imbibing weakened Schubert's resistance against the final onslaught of typhus.

Another poison, which Salieri had administered to Schubert's youthful mind in 1823, was still strong enough for him to pursue the ever beckoning chimera of operatic success. Three more operas flowed from his inventive pen. Their fate? *The Conspirators* ran afoul of Metternich's censors because of the title and was returned unopened by the theatre after gathering dust there for a year. *Fierrabras* was rejected outright. *Rosamunde* was handicapped by a wretched libretto by the same Viennese authoress whose inferior book was largely responsible for the fiasco of Weber's *Euryanthe*. Unbelievably, the entire *Rosamunde* music was put on paper in five days but lasted only two performances at the Theatre an der Wien.

> A play by the disastrous Frau von Chezy was put on, "Rosamunde auf Cyprus" with music by Schubert [wrote Schwind to Schober] . . . [the overture] was unanimously applauded and, to my great joy, repeated . . . a ballet and the second and third entre-acte went unnoticed. The fact is, people are used to talking immediately after an act is over . . . In the last act there came a chorus of shepherds and huntsmen, so beautiful and natural that I don't recall hearing the like. It was encored and I believe it will give the chorus of Weber's "Euryanthe" the coup de grace. An aria, though horribly sung . . . and a short pastoral were applauded. A subterranean chorus was inaudible because the gesticulation of Herr Rott, who was brewing poison at the same time, did not permit it to come to life.

The Viennese who had come to see another "Zauberspiel" (magic play) drowned out Schubert's music in noisy laughter and then buried it under layers of dust in the backroom of publisher Spina, successor to Diabelli. Forty-five years later Sir George Grove, who went in search of the music with Sir Arthur Sullivan, reported:

> Spina produced a pile of music and says: Here is all I have that you wish to see. You shall go into my room with it and do what you like . . . First we spend an hour in incoherent raptures, then we get more reasonable and part it all into lots and begin to go

through it thoroughly . . . After settling about the instrumental things we open a bundle of about sixty songs, forty of which had never been printed. Some of them turn out charming, equal to anything of Schubert's or anyone else.

We made a final call on Dr. Schneider [of Spina's] . . . guided by a special instinct . . . He had again recourse to the cupboard and showed us some treasures that had escaped us before. I again turned the conversation to the Rosamunde music; he believed that he had at one time possessed a copy or a sketch of it all. Might I go into the cupboard and look for myself? Certainly, if I had no objection to being smothered with dust. In I went, and after some search . . . found, at the bottom of the cupboard and in its farthest corner, a bundle of music books two feet high, carefully tied . . . and black with the undisturbed dust of nearly half a century . . . the part books of the whole music of Rosamunde, tied up after the second performance in December 1823 and probably never disturbed since. Dr. Schneider must have been amused at our excitement . . . at any rate he kindly overlooked it and gave us permission to take away with us and copy what we wanted.

After copying music until the early morning hours, Grove and Sullivan, were still so exultant over their find that they vented their enthusiasm in playing leapfrog—Grove was almost fifty.

One day Schubert visited a boyhood companion of school days. The friend was briefly absent. While waiting Schubert discovered a little volume of poetry entitled *Die schöne Müllerin* (The Beautiful Maid of the Mill) by a poet with the apt name of Wilhelm Müller. Schubert immediately became so entranced that he could not resist the urge and slipped the lean volume into his coat pocket. When the friend looked for the book some time later, Schubert admitted his irrepressible attraction to the poems but excused his gentle larceny by showing the ones he had already set to music, ultimately the most beloved Lieder cycle in all music.

As his hair began to grow again, Franz threw himself with renewed strength into his work. There was a brief meeting of two worlds when Schuppanzigh, Beethoven's friend and first violinist of the famed Rasumovsky Quartet, played Schubert's A minor Quartet and Octet. Strange indeed are the fortunes of masterpieces. After the genuinely enthused Schuppanzigh publicly performed the Octet, it lay for about thirty years until discovered by the Viennese composer-conductor Hellmesberger; a similar fate befell Schubert's Ninth Symphony. Like every true genius, Schubert felt himself constantly growing and hoped the Octet would "pave the road to the great symphony." In typical self-deprecation he did not consider his Eighth "Unfinished" Symphony a great one. But perhaps the great C major Symphony was already taking shape within his mind.

During 1824 "Die Schöne Müllerin" cycle was published, but the Rossini floodtide swept past it and left it stranded. Schubert was briefly dismayed: "The dogs have no feeling or thought of their own, and succumb blindly to the noise and opinions of others." Happy-go-lucky Vienna, at the moment, could not be bothered with Beethoven's celestial struggles or Schubert's limpid thoughts. After war and privation, invasion and inflation, hunger and death, the people gorged themselves on the opulent Italian fare and their own naive Ländlers to lift their spirits, keep dancing, drown out rumbling stomachs, and blind themselves to the generally sad state of affairs.

Aside from the above angry outburst Schubert had unwavering faith in the good judgement of his countrymen and actually declared that he would leave ultimate judgement of his art to the Viennese whose innate artistic sense he trusted. It may have been difficult to hold such beliefs as his financial condition fluctuated from precarious to desperate. "If my publishers would only pay me a small fraction of what is due me! I've often gone to them for my honorarium but each time they declare that their expenses just happen to be enormous and that there is little demand for my compositions."

Necessity drove him back into employment with Count Esterhazy. He found country life less bearable this time and threw himself into composition as an escape from dreariness; particularly since his pupil and alleged great love, Countess Esterhazy, was actually mentally retarded and at the age thirty still played with dolls and hoops. Surrounded by spiritual aridity, Franz expressed loneliness and longing for the understanding companionship of his friends:

> Sometimes I endure miserable days . . . if we were only together . . . I would make light of every inconvenience . . . I would cry out with Goethe "Who will bring me back only for an hour of that lovely time!" . . . when we sat together . . . and showed the other his art's children, awaiting, not without some anxiety, the judgement that love and truth would deliver. That time when each filled the others with enthusiasm and thus all were inspired by the united striving toward beauty in its highest form. Now I sit here all alone in the depths of Hungary whither, alas, I have been lured, without a single person with whom I could exchange an intelligent word. [Letter to Schober, 1824.]

When his friends were available, however, he was not nearly as avid for their company and companionship:

Ten times he had promised to come and ten times he failed to show up [Schwind to Schober].

Schubert had promised to come. I waited for him all afternoon but he left me in the lurch . . . now I regale myself with the prospect of a ruined Easter Holiday [Schwind].

I went to visit Schubert who had invited us, but he was not there [von Hartmann].

Schubert made us happy by coming to our house. He was very amiable and talkative, but suddenly disappeared before anyone noticed it [Sophie von Kleyle].

Franz's attention to Vienna's favorite thirst quencher, that light clear wine of Roman vineyards, only too often proved his undoing. The secretly longed for strength and even brutality, self-confidence and assertion would then come to the fore and Franz would leave a trail of broken windows and smashed glasses. Only once did he rise to assert himself a la Beethoven. The scene was Bogner's Cafe at one o'clock in the morning. He had spent the night with friends, smoking, talking, drinking, when he was approached by a group of wind players from the opera orchestra who, after complimenting him, requested him to write music for their specific instruments. Schubert turned on them, suddenly all fire and fury:

> You are musical hacks! Nothing more . . . You set yourselves up to be artists? You're tootlers and fiddlers, the pack of you! It's I who am the artist. I am Schubert . . . whom the world knows and proclaims. Who has created great and beautiful things that you can't even understand, and who will create still more beautiful ones . . . the loveliest in the world! Cantatas and quartets, operas and symphonies. For I am not a mere Ländler composer as the stupid newspapers assert and the stupid people echo—I am Franz Schubert!—Get that into your thick skulls. And when the word "artist" is spoken, it means me, and not you worms and insects who demand solos which I shall never write for you . . . You creeping and gnawing worms whom my foot should crush, the foot of a man who reaches the stars . . . to the stars I say, while you wretched tootling worms wriggle in the dust and with the dust blow away and rot.

In Vino Veritas—the gnawing disillusionment of a frustrated genius vented on innocent bystanders. The next morning a friend found Franz asleep across the bed where he had fallen, in his disorderly room, with clothes strewn all over the floor and with his spectacles on as was his habit.

Schubert's growing maturity was not matched by growing popularity, but publishers became a shade more attentive. That did not keep them from depriving him of his just fees. He was actually treated more like an obnoxious mendicant than the genius who fattened their purses. Taking advantage of his timidity and constant financial distress, they seemed to be in a tacit conspiracy to get the most for the least. Probst in Leipzig, in refusing Schubert's songs, pleaded that he was too busy publishing the complete works of Kalkbrenner, and Hüther of Vienna, when inquiring about Schubert's new compositions, admonished him to hold his prices low because he was "only a beginner." Diabelli in Vienna grudgingly paid him a few florins per song, while he realized the equivalent of $15,000 on the "Wanderer" Lied alone!

Schubert, who had meanwhile fled the Esterhazy menage again, now was without income whatsoever. He still visited the Esterhazys but mostly in the company of Vogl. The singer by then had become so arrogant in his relationship with Franz that, according to a mutual friend, he "behaved like an elephant driver exhibiting a special rarity from the animal kingdom." Here and there the tender shoots of recognition broke through the ice of ignorance and neglect: the Leipzig *Allgemeine musikalische Zeitung* praised his Piano Sonata in A minor as "uncommonly attractive as well as a genuinely rich work"—Artaria in Vienna published his Sonata in D—the Gesellschaft der Musikfreunde commissioned his biography (which was never published)—publishers Cappi and Diabelli put on sale his engraved portrait. Despite their denials, the publishers could not conceal Schubert's growing popularity. But Franz had no illusions as to his state: "The artist shall eternally remain the slave of every contemptible shop keeper."

With the death of Salieri the post of second court conductor became vacant. Upon the urging of his friends, Schubert applied to Emperor Franz for the comfortable position which would yield twelve hundred florins. "Your Majesty! Most Gracious Emperor! In deepest reverence the undersigned permits himself to make the most submissive petition for the all-most-gracious award of the vacated position of Vice Conductor." In support of his petition he submitted a Mass and thereby encountered the pinnacle of Viennese official ignorance: Herr Eybler, imperial court conductor, had never heard of Franz Schubert! "A few weeks later," Franz wrote to a friend, "when I returned to learn the fate of my brainchild, Eybler told me that, though the Mass was good, it was not written in the style the emperor liked. On which I said goodbye and thought to myself: So, I'm not fortunate enough to be able to compose in the imperial style."

Dead Salieri's poisonous lure was still potent. Whenever the faintest possibility offered itself, Schubert would throw all caution, warnings, and past experience to the winds and throw himself whole-heartedly into opera. Thus in July 1826 he worked on the Bauernfeld libretto "The Count of Gleichen." Poet Bauernfeld's own terse epilogue, written posthumously on the manuscript tells the tale: "Set by Schubert. The instrumentation is lacking. He died before completing the work. Schubert had surely hoped for success. The censor and death decided otherwise."

Schubert seemed undaunted. In a letter whose very timidity nullified his chances, he again turned to Breitkopf and Härtel: "In the hope that my name is not wholly unknown to you, I herewith politely inquire whether you would not be unwilling to accept certain of my compositions for a cheap honorarium, as I greatly wish to become as well known as possible in Germany . . . It would be a special honor for me to form a connection with such a famous old house of art dealers." Of course B & H refused, offering him only free copies but no money.

Winter found the friends together in Vienna again and the Schubertiad resumed their music making. They celebrated the Viennese "Fasching," the dancing season before Lent, by giving their own "sausage" ball to which each one was obliged to bring a lovely girl. It remains a mystery who paid for the sausages and beer, abundantly consumed, but the dancing was spirited until the early morning hours. No wonder—what lovelier invitation to the dance than the music of Vienna played by Franz Schubert, in person.

There exists no authenticated record of a meeting between Schubert and Beethoven. Schubert may have visited the deaf recluse to show him several of his songs. It is certain that Beethoven was familiar with some of Schubert's music. With his nephew, he repeatedly played the four-handed "Variations on a French Song" dedicated to him. He discussed Schubert's songs in his conversation books, and when shown some more during his last illness, he studied them avidly and exclaimed: "Schubert has the divine spark in him . . . one song of his is worth ten of others."

Once more there was an attempt at steady employment on the part of Schubert, but, inevitably, his musical integrity collided head-on with the other players on the tragi-comical occasion. Friend and fellow composer Lachner had persuaded him to try for the post of conductor at the famed Kärnthnerthor Theatre. The rehearsal had barely started when the prima donna demanded changes. Schubert quietly but adamantly refused in the face of pleading friends, a hand-wringing director, and a raging prima donna. At the height of the altercation, the prima donna conveniently swooned but not before she had screamed, in true prima donna fashion, "I shall never sing another note of such a mess!" Whereupon Schubert calmly shut the score and walked out: "It's just as well. I'm not fitted for the job."

Beyond the musical realm, Schubert's relaxed habits could only be described as "Viennese." But he radiated such endearing charm as to outweigh any shortcomings, annoying as they might have been at times. Once Grillparzer had written a serenade for the Fröhlich sisters, and Schubert had set the poem to music on the spot. He also promised to accompany it should a performance take place. The occasion arrived, the people were assembled, the stage set—but Schubert had forgotten. The Fröhlichs arranged another public performance so that the composer might hear his masterpiece. Again the hour was at hand and the audience assembled, again no Schubert. A frantic search found him at an inn, leisurely smoking a pipe. He was rushed to the hall where he accompanied the song and brought down the house. Who could be angry with a man whose only comment was: "I had no idea it was so beautiful."

On March 29, 1827, carrying white lilies and a wax taper, Schubert marched in the funeral procession and extinguished his taper symbolically against the ground as Beethoven's remains were lowered into the grave. Returning from the sad occasion, the friends silently filed into their favorite tavern. Somberly they raised their glasses:

"To the memory of the great man whom we lost today." Schubert emptied his glass, refilled it, raised it again:

"To him who shall be next."

He drained his glass. Silence again oppressively fell upon the smoke-filled room. The macabre toast was to be for himself.

Flighty Vienna began to listen to Schubert's sounds. Schuppanzigh premiered the Octet. The *Wiener Tageszeitung* noticed it as "radiant, agreeable and interesting"; Leipzig chimed in. In Graz, the capital of Styria, a special concert was arranged in honor of "the composer from the capital." Schubert remained three weeks in Graz which had upon him the same exhilarating effect Prague had on Mozart. He ate and drank, played and improvised among admiring friends until he was dripping with perspiration. He also went to hear Giacomo Meyerbeer's opera *The Crusaders in Egypt*—"I can't stand it. Let's get out into fresh air." Schubert's reaction coincided with Schumann's and Hanslick's sarcastic comments in a later period.

Predictable winter hardships plagued him. He complained of sickness and headaches while composing the last twelve songs of the

"Winterreise" (Winter Journey) cycle. Depression haunted him: "I'll sing you a round of ghastly songs . . . they have unnerved me more than my songs have ever before." His friend Bauernfeld clearly diagnosed Schubert's plight:

> He found himself without courage and hope, staring into a gloomy future.

> In a voice filled with emotion, he sang us the whole "Winterreise." We were dumbfounded by the gloomy atmosphere of the Lieder. Those who knew him realized how deeply his creations bit into him and in what anguish they were born. Whoever has but once seen him composing—glowing and radiant eyes, yes even with a different manner of speech . . . will never forget the impression . . . I have no doubt that the excitement in which he wrote his most beautiful songs, especially the "Winterreise," was a contributory factor in his early demise.

The songs proved pearls before swine. While the Schubertiad was startled but enthused, Berlin, Leipzig, and Vienna declared the music "unworthy of the poems," and publishers continued their tacit fraud. Haslinger actually bought six Schubert songs for one florin per song!

Despite his deteriorating financial and physical condition, Schubert, somehow found the strength and inspiration for the "great" C-major Symphony: "No more songs for me," he told a friend. "I am fully occupied with opera and symphony." The Gesellschaft der Musikfreunde, to whom he dedicated the symphony, found it "unplayable." Ten years later Robert Schumann was to find the yellowed manuscript in brother Ferdinand Schubert's house. His glowing discussion of the "symphony of the heavenly length" brought it to Mendelssohn's attention who gave it its delayed premiere in Leipzig.

Pudgy in body and personality, without spokesman or patron, Schubert could not compete with the charlatans who launched their cheap wares on muddied waters. He had to be satisfied to hear his "Erlking" sandwiched between two guitar pieces by Hummel and Giuliani. Even when young Felix Mendelssohn accompanied it, the critics sneered that "the overrich and bizarre modulation did not compare with settings by Reichardt and Zelter." But one day Bauernfeld excitedly gave Schubert an idea.

> Your name is upon all lips and every new song is an event. You have composed the most glorious quartets and trios, not to mention the symphonies . . . master your inertia, give a concert . . . Vogl will assist you, others will deem it an honor to serve a

master like you with their artistic skill. The public will compete for tickets . . . a single evening will at least cover your
expenses for an entire year . . . a concert, take my advice, a
concert.

To everyone's surprise Franz roused himself into action. And equally
to everyone's surprise, the Gesellschaft der Musikfreunde opened
their famous hall for a concert on March 26, 1828, the anniversary
of Beethoven's death. It proved to be Schubert's greatest triumph
during his own lifetime. The hall was filled to capacity with an
audience brimming with enthusiasm. The box office receipts, eight
hundred florins, the largest sum ever held by Schubert, spoke for
themselves. Yet nobody but the people liked the concert. The critics
ignored the occasion while flooding the pages with paeans to Paganini's arrival. A Dresden critic called Schubert "a star of the second
magnitude as compared to the comet Paganini." Berlin mixed faint
praise with hints that the wild applause had been fanned by Schubert's
claque.

Ein Thaler und ein Groschen,	A dollar and a penny,
Die waren beide mein.	Both of them were mine.
Der Groschen wurde Wasser,	The penny turned to water,
Der Thaler wurde Wein.	The dollar turned to wine.

No proverb more aptly mirrored Schubert with money in his pocket,
and his small fortune soon melted away. After paying his debts and
treating himself to a new piano, he took his friends to hear Paganini
and found himself penniless as before.

But this new source of income buoyed his spirits and strengthened
his backbone. For the first time we notice firmness in his letter to
the publisher Probst: "I request that the edition be without mistakes
and I await it with longing. This work is dedicated to nobody but
those who like it. That is the most rewarding dedication." The newly
found impulse carried him along with renewed inspiration, culminating in his Mass in E flat, his main religious work, the C-major String
Quartet and the C-major Symphony. He was too busy to accept
invitations to his beloved Graz, too poor to accept Schindler's invitation to Budapest, too proud to ask him for the coach fare.

The excitement of creation plus neglect, sickness, privation, and
drink rapidly began to take their toll. All contributed to sudden
catastrophe although nobody, including Schubert, had realized the
steep decline. On October 31, 1828 he ate his last meal in the
tavern "To the Red Cross" but could not keep the food down. For
the next three days he kept up his routine although he was unable

to take food or drink. He even walked to town from the outskirts to arrange for lessons with Simon Sechter, the foremost teacher of counterpoint in Vienna. "For the first time I now see where I'm lacking and how much I have yet to learn." He was destined to take only one lesson. "Dear Schober: I am sick," he wrote his friend. "For eleven days now I have eaten nothing and drunk nothing, and wander, exhausted and tottering, from chair to bed and back . . . Be so good and help me out of this desperate dilemma with reading matter. Of Cooper I have read 'The Last of the Mohicans,' 'The Spy,' 'The Pilot' and 'The Pioneers.' If you have something else of his . . ."

Karl Holz, a friend of Beethoven, brought the latter's Quartet in C-sharp minor, Op. 131, and participated in its playing at Schubert's sickbed. While listening, Schubert worked himself into such a state of excitement that all were concerned about him. With his strength ebbing away his spirit remained restlessly active. He attempted to correct proofs, spoke of completing "The Count of Gleichen," even requested a new libretto from Bauernfeld. By nightfall he was delirious and had to be forcibly kept in bed. New doctors were called and diagnosed typhoid fever. During a brief period of rationality in two days of hallucinations, he called his brother to his bedside. Letting his eyes wander over the bare walls he finally rested them on his brother's face. "Here is my end," he said.

At the sudden loss, Vienna was stricken with belated remorse. Now a public concert could be arranged of Schubert's works only. Now a bust could be erected over his grave, next to that of his idol Beethoven. Schubert's friend Grillparzer wrote a moving inscription:

> The Art of Music entombed here rich Treasure
> But even fairer Hopes.
> Franz Schubert lies here

VIII

Imperial Interlude

"May Heaven and Hell destroy his happiness! May his family perish root and branch from the earth, and he himself be made to suffer through the persons he loves most! May his life be dedicated to destruction and his children go down in misery to their graves." Countess Károlyi pronounced the curse on the day her son was executed for his part in the abortive Hungarian revolt against the house of Habsburg. It was directed at a man who had been born two years after Schubert's death and was destined to ascend the throne of the Habsburg empire as the ruler of thirty million people at the age of eighteen.

The curse was to cast its evil spell over Franz Josef, Emperor of Austria and King of Hungary. Josef II had been dead three years when his sister Marie Antoinette went to the Paris guillotine, but Franz Josef sat helplessly as his brother Maximilian, "Emperor" of Mexico by the grace of France, died before a Mexican firing squad and Maximilian's wife went insane. Heard in stunned disbelief of the suicide of his only son and heir to the throne, Crown Prince Rudolf, of his wife, Empress Elizabeth, stabbed to death by a fanatic, his nephew Otto the victim of a mysterious disease. Finally stood by as Archduke Franz Ferdinand, successor to the throne, and his wife were assassinated at Sarajevo, triggering the holocaust of World War I which ultimately led to the dissolution of the Habsburg empire. "I have lost everything, my entire happiness, all my hopes . . . now nothing remains but my duty to which I hope to remain faithful as long as my old legs will carry me." "If the empire is destined to perish may it at least go down with honor."

It is an ironic twist that the man who was forced to say these words and who was destined to rule longer than any other monarch in history, was truly a man of peace. Amid the light-hearted frivolity of his beloved Vienna and the shaky foundations of his empire, Franz Josef was the rock of rectitude, the proud keeper of Habsburg traditions, devout observer of the time-tested verities of the Catholic Church and Spanish ceremonial.

Charles VI (1685–1750) had been the last emperor to insist on total observance of the Spanish ceremonial. Amid the dark, dank walls of the imperial court, the elaborate ritual was performed daily. "Spanish Reverence" forced nobles of the most exalted rank into obeisance, kneeling on one knee when greeting the emperor; citizens genuflected in Spanish Reverence at the mere mention of the emperor's name in proclamation. The court costume was Spanish, short black coat trimmed with lace, broad-brimmed hat turned up on one side, with long plumes, red stockings, and black shoes. During dinner the Papal Nuncio and foreign ambassadors attended, standing in the background, but were permitted to retire as soon as the emperor had taken his first swallow of wine. The meal began with the chamberlain on one knee presenting goblets of wine to the emperor and empress. They would pledge each other troth and health before attending to the meal. Such involved ceremonial required an enormous retinue. At state dinners each plate of food passed through the hands of no less than twenty officials before reaching the emperor. But, elaborate ceremonial and lavish entertainment could not mask Charles's indecision and weaknesses of character. Thoughtless cruelty was also a characteristic of that brilliantly artistic, contradictory ruler. When urged to look for an appointed heir since his marriage had been blessed with two daughters (one son having died in infancy) he declared that he would outlive the empress and hoped for a male heir by a later marriage, a hope which did not materialize. Charles VI, nonetheless, was sufficiently concerned about the dynasty to secure acceptance of the Pragmatic Sanction which insured succession to the throne by his daughter Maria Theresia.

Upon ascension, Empress Maria Theresia found her throne threatened from within and without. Yet the vivacious, attractive young queen upheld the empire while winning the hearts of her people. She "Viennized" court functions by giving the round dance equal footing with the minuet and modified the Spanish ceremonial. Such touches endeared her to the sentimental Viennese as did her passionate love for her handsome husband who was to become Emperor Franz I. Franz ardently reciprocated her love, with historic results: Maria Elizabeth was born in 1737, Maria Anna in 1738, Maria Karoline 1740, Josef 1741, Maria Christine 1742, Maria Elizabeth 1743, Karl Josef 1745, Maria Amalie 1746, Leopold 1747, Karoline 1748, Johanna 1750, Josefa 1751, another Maria Karoline 1752, Ferdinand 1754, Marie Antoinette 1755, and Maximilian in 1756.

When not so occupied, Maria Theresia defended her realm successfully against France, Bavaria, Spain and Sardinia, unsuccessfully against Prussia, resisted the Pope and suppressed the Jesuits, erected a new building for the Vienna University, created a military academy, the Maria Theresia Thaler (still the standard coin in Ethiopia) and the Maria Theresia Medal for exceptional valor, and, jointly with her consort and co-regent managed the affairs of state efficiently, ever mindful of imperial interests. This prompted her, despite her privately held views on the matter, to admonish her daughter Marie Antoinette to show proper respect to the mistresses of Louis XV lest royal privilege be blemished or the Franco-Austrian treaty shaken.

At no time did she lose touch with the people of her realm. Legend has it that she appeared before the Diet of rebellious Hungarian nobles with her infant son in her arms and so eloquently pleaded her cause that the session ended with the Hungarian aristocrats enthusiastically shouting their allegiance to the death on their drawn swords. Her innate warmth and love for her family (and she considered the Viennese her family) never deserted her. When her son Leopold, Grand Duke of Tuscany, became the father of a son, the message was brought to the empress while she was working in her chambers. Heedless of her informal attire, she rushed through the chambers and corridors into the Court Theatre. There, leaning over the red velvet railing of the imperial box, she shouted with motherly joy in Viennese dialect, "The Poldl has a boy, and on my wedding anniversary at that, isn't he gallant?" The theatre rose and shouted its congratulatory joy.

As the empress matured and viewed matters of state with an eye unclouded by youthful passion, she gently relieved her beloved husband and co-regent, gay, charming Franz, of many duties of state and took sole charge of her empire's fortunes. By then Franz was not averse to roving beyond the marital bed which had yielded sixteen children. It was no secret in Vienna that he viewed with great favor Eva Maria Violet, a lithe dancer; and Lady Montague, an English visitor, reported, "I saw the lovely Princess Auersperg. The Emperor makes no secret of his passion for her."

Maria Theresia viewed these escapades with a jaundiced eye. Yet public reaction was impossible lest she cause a scandal which would undermine the jealously guarded dignity of the *Herrscherhaus*. But if it was not advisable to interfere with extramarital joys of the imperial spouse, she was not going to permit them to her family at large, the Viennese. "She crushes every degree of libertinism beneath the weight of her displeasure," wrote an English visitor.

> A woman known to be [morally] frail, unless her frailty be confined to one lover and managed with the utmost attention to privacy and decorum, is certain to receive an order to leave

Vienna . . . It is not possible to conceive how minute and circumstantial a detail her inquiries embrace relative to the private conduct of her subjects of both sexes; their actions, amusements and pleasures, even the most concealed, are constantly reported to her. The presence of the Empress and the terror inspired by her vigilance, as well as her resentment operate as repressing all excesses . . . but the principle of frailty nevertheless exists.

In 1753 Maria Theresia created a special office, the Keuschheits Kommission (Chastity Commission) headed by her famous chancellor Prince von Kaunitz. Its agents had strict secret orders to investigate all rumors of licentiousness and spy upon all people suspected of being libertines as well as those who occasionally strayed from the marital path. The empress, now devoid of youthful joie de vivre, embittered and narrowly puritanical, pursued her anti-libertine aims relentlessly. "I have heard that a certain [highborn] person has persuaded a virtuous dancer of the Deutsches Theater to live with him," she wrote the Kommission. "Investigate this matter and verify the facts." When she heard that a count and young countess had become intimate friends, she ordered the deportation of the nobleman and the cloistering of the girl. Her anger flamed when she was informed that the young pair, forewarned, had foiled her efforts and escaped.

Josef II, Maria Theresia's oldest son, became sole ruler of the Habsburg domains at the age of thirty-nine. He immediately did completely away with Spanish reverence: "Only before God shall men kneel." Class distinction diminished further. Aristocrats became subject to the same penalties as ordinary citizens. Having been found guilty of larceny, Count Liechtenstein swept Vienna's streets in prisoner's garb and with shaven head side by side with other common criminals. But affairs of state were handled ineptly and Austria's importance among the powers diminished. The reign of Josef's brother and successor, Leopold II, lasted only two years. The plague took him despite tightly closed palace windows.

Leopold's son reluctantly ascended the suddenly vacated throne as Franz II. Many of the liberal innovations of Maria Theresia and Josef II were nullified, and Austria relapsed into darkness under this cynical, scheming despot. "The People? I know nothing of the people, I know only of subjects." At a time when the shout "Constitution" was heard throughout Europe, the word became so abhorrent to Franz that even physicians were forbidden the use of the word to describe the state of his health.

One of the men in exalted position who saw eye to eye with the emperor was his chancellor, Prince von Metternich, one of those enviable creatures of naturally noble bearing who move surely and easily in the highest social regions without climbing the steps, a perfect cavalier and embodiment of the Viennese aristocrat. Impeccably elegant in gold-embroidered sartorial splendour, he first came into prominence as Austrian Ambassador at Berlin and later in Paris. As Napoleon's star descended at Moscow, Leipzig, and Waterloo, that of Metternich rose. From 1815 to 1848, Vienna was the stage of this mightiest of chancellors. From there he directed the affairs of state in his inimitably high-handed and devious manner and managed for over thirty years to dominate the European political scene and outwit adversaries. Although he acknowledged the grand seigneur in Metternich, Napoleon hated him with a vengeance and openly called him "a constant liar." Metternich, in turn, hated the French for their revolution which destroyed the aristocratic and established order of which Metternich was a part. A special corner of his hate was reserved for Napoleon for having defeated, and humiliated, his, Metternich's, sovereign.

Metternich's music was played more or less harmoniously by the "Concert of Europe," and the main features of the map drawn at the Congress of Vienna lasted for ninety-nine years. The Europe reconstituted by democratic governments at Versailles in 1919 lasted only twenty. In domestic affairs, however, the chancellor and his associates were not nearly as successful. After the death of Emperor Franz, the crown went to his oldest son, "Ferdinand the Good"—but alas mentally retarded. Metternich temporized, terrorized, promised, suppressed, played party against party, conceded nothing. But it was impossible to keep the clock turned back forever. Danger signals in Vienna and the empire increased but were ignored. Unorganized protest gatherings, at first more annoying than threatening, were easily dispersed. The mood of the populace grew ugly. Shots were fired and the fire returned, first in the air, then point blank into the crowd. Vienna's hungry and oppressed sought refuge behind hastily erected barricades, regiments deserted, commanders refused to obey orders to shoot into the unarmed crowd. The 1848 revolution flared.

"Metternich must go!" The cry raced through Vienna's streets, rattled the windows of the imperial palace, was repeated from pale lips in imperial corridors. Metternich resigned, Ferdinand left the capital and later agreed to a constitution. But the court party thought differently, even though Hungary, Bohemia, and the Italian provinces had joined the revolt. Prince Windisch-Graetz, leader of the court party, declared martial law; loyal regiments were moved into Vienna to replace the mutineers. But the revolt had not yet run its course. The suppressed populace, seeing its recent gains evaporate, rose up once more. The court fled again. Only Count Baillet von Latour, the minister of war, remained at his post. Apprised of a threat to his life, the minister first tried to hide within the inner recesses of his office but finally agreed to meet a deputation of the revolutionaries. He was seized instead, dragged into the court yard, and there killed by a blacksmith's hammer blow. The enraged mob then stripped the body and hung it, naked and mangled, from the nearest lamp post.

But the Habsburgs were not to be denied. From exile Emperor Ferdinand approved of an attack on his own rebellious capital. Prince Windisch-Graetz again obliged, and Vienna's valiant but ill-armed citizenry, after five days' futile resistance, surrendered to the overwhelming strength of the professionals. The revolt was crushed, liberty stamped out; but the impossibility of further reign by Ferdinand was clear to all. On December 2, 1848 the entire court convened in exile in the city of Olmütz. There Emperor Ferdinand, before the court and the new ministry, was handed a parchment which he haltingly read: "Weighty considerations have led us to the irrevocable decision of renouncing the imperial crown. The renunciation is made in favor of our beloved nephew, his serene Highness, Archduke Franz Josef, whom we now declare to have attained majority." At age eighteen Franz Josef had become emperor.

The early reign of the inexperienced monarch was a nightmare. Reared in the century-old, stiff Spanish ceremonial of the Habsburg dynasty, or at least in its spirit, its upholding was uppermost in the mind of the cautious young man whose dash and elegance hid, at first, his limited vision and lack of spirit. Influenced by his scheming, ambitious mother, Archduchess Sophie, who had engineered his succession, he permitted the reactionary forces of the previous regime to go on a rampage. Parliament was dissolved, promises of a new constitution voided. Field Marshal Radetzky crushed the Italian insurgents and Prince Windisch-Graetz, ably assisted by Czar Nicholas and 75,000 Russian soldiers, snuffed out Hungary's short independence. All this, tragically, by a man who wished nothing better than to treat kindly his subjects of many diverse religions and nationalities.

His marriage, six years after his ascension to the throne, to Elizabeth of Bavaria, promised to bring fresh air into Vienna's musty imperial atmosphere. It had been love at first sight between the young emperor and the radiant young girl, a child of nature given to riding through the Bavarian woods with her hair flowing in the wind. But imperial ceremonial was immediately up in arms. Nobody in living memory had ever laughed out loud in the palace, or gone without gloves, or ridden unchaperoned, or demanded a bathtub in her chambers . . . . "Gott im Himmel!"—who had ever heard of immersing the entire body in water? Maria Theresia had gone far enough when she ordered the faces of her children to be washed once a day with a mixture of vinegar and water.

Although Elizabeth bore the emperor two daughters and the much desired successor to the throne, a gulf opened between freedom of spirit and bonds of ancient ceremonial. The total repression of the young empress at court, led by her husband's dour dowager mother, poisoned Vienna's pleasant air for her. Above all she felt lonely because she had not been allowed to bring with her one single person of her own entourage nor permitted to make friends at court, leaving her totally at the mercy of hostile courtiers. She began to travel in ever extending circles until her untimely end by an assassin's dagger in Geneva.

Her son, Crown Prince Rudolf, grew into a brilliant, morbid young man of many talents and great promise. Even Bismarck was impressed upon meeting him:

> Young Crown Prince Rudolf was pleasant as he indeed always is. But as to the development of his mental power and the maturity of his opinion and conceptions, these surpassed my expectations. His comprehension of political matters is no ordinary one and proves that, despite his youth, he has reflected independently and seriously on many subjects; he really surprised me. We were not always of the same opinion but he was able to argue his point excellently and what struck me most about this was the cautious manner in which he did so.

Within the small circle of eligible European royalty, selection was meager. Rudolf eventually married shy, retiring Princess Stephanie of Belgium, and Vienna enjoyed the glittering imperial pomp of the occasion with its innate exuberance. After the initial bloom faded, it became apparent that the pair were mismated. Estrangement became inevitable. The marriage would have lingered on (the words "separation," "divorce," or "annulment" did not exist in the Habsburg vocabulary) had not fate intervened in the person of vivacious young Baroness Marie Vetsera, wise beyond her years and madly in love with the crown prince who reciprocated ardently. Scandal loomed, and the emperor personally intervened and during a stormy audience sternly forbade further meetings. But passion had carried the young lovers beyond reason and restraint; double suicide at the hunting lodge of Mayerling ended one of the great romances of all times.

The crown prince's violent death deprived Austria of the leadership it was to need so sorely in the future. With clairvoyance he had foreseen the inevitable:

> The monarchy stands there, a mighty ruin which might last today and tomorrow but which will ultimately disappear altogether. It has endured for centuries; as long as people were willing to be led blindly all was well; but now the end has come. All men are free and the next conflict will bring down the ruin . . . graft, theft, rabble in high places, the crudest despotism, hand-to-mouth makeshifts. The state is sliding towards ruin . . . a great powerful upheaval must come, a social revolution from which, as after long illness, a new Europe will blossom.

Although the minorities responded loyally in 1914, Rudolf's prophecy was borne out in 1918. But the new blossoms were poisonous nightshades—communism and fascism—far more ruthless and oppressive than the old empire had ever been.

The death of the crown prince also cut the last link between Empress Elizabeth and Emperor Franz Josef. She resumed her travels and her absences from the hostile court, and its narrow-minded intra-court politicking which she detested, lengthened. Surprisingly fondness for her royal spouse never deserted her. Concern for his loneliness prompted her to devise a unique arrangement. After discreet investigation, she introduced to the emperor Katherina Schratt, a charming intelligent actress of the Court Theatre, who, in time, became the inseparable companion of the monarch and an unofficial member of the imperial family.

The friendship became so close that during Elizabeth's infrequent stays in Vienna, Katherina would have dinner with the royal couple in a triangle of mutual friendship, trust, and understanding. The empress' concern went even further. To comfort him during periods when she was travelling and the actress was on tour, she had a portrait of "the Friend" (the code word for Katherina in imperial correspondence) painted in one of her favorite roles and had it hung in the emperor's private chambers. The two women remained lifelong friends, were seen walking together, even took the same health cures together. After the death of the empress, the inconspicuously dressed emperor could be observed almost every morning leaving the summer palace of Schönbrunn by a discreet garden door leading to a narrow lane and Kathi's modest residence. There was actually no secrecy about it. By then Vienna had spun a sentimental halo about its much plagued emperor. Lovingly, smilingly Vienna understood, and the imperial walk to Kathi's home in Vienna and, in summer, in Ischl, was discreetly guarded by police.

Over the years Frau Schratt became the trusted companion of the aged monarch. Her growing circle of friends in the highest places, who often hoped to reach the emperor's ear through her, coupled with her discernment of the importance of newsworthy items, made her invaluable to the emperor as a major source of news and information. Since she had the rare faculty of coupling knowledge with discretion, she was often informed of important state secrets. "Please keep to yourself the information I sent you yesterday. Best Wishes. Franz Josef," reads one of the emperor's missives to her.

IX

Languid Lyre

Vienna seemed serene again. With the impossibility of discussing politics due to the ever-present informer, conversation of the short-memoried Viennese glibly reverted to the opera, the theatre, the latest scandal. Emperor Franz Josef loved Vienna, "the pearl of the empire," and lavished his attention on the city, although himself totally in-artistic. Despite his own personal frugality, he missed no occasion, be it in the field of art, music, religion, or entertainment, to display the splendor of the city and the court.

During the *Fasching* (pre-Lenten) season, when dancing occupied most of the Viennese most of the time, the court ball was *the* event. In the imperial ballrooms, hundreds of crystal chandeliers would reflect in hundreds of mirrors the splendor of the Habsburg Empire. Gala uniforms intermingled with white ties and tails, complete with decorations, ecclesiastic solemnity with the lavish gowns of the aristocratic distaff side. The entire empire seemed to converge on the court. Polish nobles in velvet berets edged with fur, Hungarians in rich scarlet embroidered in lavish gold, their gold-braided capes of pale green bordered with beaver fur, thrown across one shoulder and held across bemedalled chests with heavy gold cords. There the brilliant uniforms of Austrian officers would flash next to the em-peror's personal guard in lavish scarlet, the halberdiers in black, their patent leather boots reaching above the knee. In striking contrast, the hierarchy of the church added solemnity to the glittering array with their simple vestments of purple, brown, and black, often overlaid with precious lace.

What completed the gathering with gaiety and glamour were the charming women of the Viennese aristocracy in their exquisitely hued gowns, family heirlooms glittering on white necks, diadems on a profusion of hair artistically arranged. Intermingling with all, the bemedalled chests of diplomats, the mayor, high dignitaries. Scurry-ing among them with lighthearted laughter were pages in scarlet and white, either bearing the trains of highborn ladies or carrying scented messages removed from gaily heaving bosoms and accompanied by meaningful glances from behind gently waved fans. The cares of the world had fallen away, and life was gay and uncomplicated for the chatting, laughing, flirting young creatures, enjoying a high moment of their lives under the chandeliers and innumerable candles.

Laughter and conversation fell to a murmur with the appearance of the master of ceremonies at the main portal to the main ballroom. He rapped his staff, and silence fell over the vast expanse. Respectfully a walk opened in the center of the ballroom. All eyes were turned towards the entrance. The clock read exactly nine o'clock. Slowly, silently the portals were opened by invisible hands. The procession was led by the emperor, the empress on his arm, followed by arch-dukes and duchesses in time-honored precedence. Wearing the uni-form of a field marshal, including a tunic of pale blue, the emperor slowly walked the length of the ballroom, past the nobles of the realm, past respectful bows and deep curtsies, and took his place at the head of the hall. It was the signal for the ball to begin. The Hofkapellmeister tucked his violin under his chin, the Chief Dancer (an official title), a Lord of the Imperial Chambers, resplendent in the uniform of the Imperial Guards, bowed before the young arch-duchess highest in rank. The dance began, and soon hundreds of couples, arms entwined, eyes sparkling, danced the noblest of dances under innumerable chandeliers and before hundreds of mirrors.

If imperial trappings glistened at the court ball, they shone no less on high church occasions such as the *Fronleichnamsfest* (Corpus Christi). On that day the full panoply of church joined the pomp of empire to make an equally colorful spectacle. Each church in Vienna had its own Corpus Christi procession, but the one emerging from the court chapel was the one people by the thousands craned their necks for. An artillery salvo announced the start of the procession which slowly emerged from the flag-draped chapel in the inner court of the palace. A military escort in full regalia, officers with drawn sabers, preceded the procession, while soldiers held back the sea of the curious and the devout who knelt on the granite cobblestones while others filled every window, rooftop, tree, and balcony.

The first to be seen were lesser clergy, white-laced surplices over black habits, holding crosses high above their heads or carrying church banners. Next, the emperor's equerries in gold-embroidered red coats, pages in satin doublets, lackeys in scarlet jackets and knee breeches. In their wake the imperial *Kapelle* (band), complete with side arms, kettle drums sounding a muffled beat. Next the chamber-lains, their keys, symbol of office, worn on gilded chains, knights of Catholic orders in their somber ankle-length mantillas and plumed hats. Slowly out of the medieval recesses, the nobles of the realm followed, garbed in historic family attire, furred caps and capes, slashed boots, broad-brimmed hats looped back by gold aigrettes set with precious stones, diamond-studded swords at their sides.

The murmur of the vast, waiting crowd lining the Ring Boulevard subsided as the Archbishop of Vienna emerged from the deep shadows of the chapel under a baldachin carried by four acolytes, preceded by a priest in lavish soutane who, walking backwards, swung the censer toward the prince of the church. Through clouds of incense, the jewel-studded Holy Sacrament gleamed like the Holy Grail as the archbishop held it. Behind this solemn retinue, the emperor walked in majestic solitude in the full regalia of a field marshal. Several respectful steps behind came his staff of Marshals of the Realm, followed by the German Guard in red and gold, the Hungarian Guard with helmets gleaming and leopard skins proudly thrown back over their shoulders, the Imperial Guard on horseback, their lances and pennants swaying in the rhythm of the procession, the Swiss Castle Guard, carrying their traditional halberds, and the Police Corps of the Court, in black helmets with scarlet crests. Interspersed were members of the various ecclesiastic orders in scarlet, purple, black, or tan, and laymen from all corners of the empire wearing plumed headgear, glowing liveries, the most gossamer of lace.

Yet not all religious observances were public. The deeply devout foot-washing ceremony of *Gründonnerstag* (Maundy Thursday) was held in the *Rittersaal* (Knight's Hall) of the Imperial Court. Vienna's twelve oldest needy men of the people were selected for the great honor. They had been bought new clothes, and imperial carriages called for them at their humble homes to bring them to court. In observance of the occasion, all ladies and civilians present dressed in black with only officers in uniform. Upon a signal from the emperor, the twelve men were ushered into the vaulted hall. In order not to feel uncomfortable among titled strangers each had been allowed to bring a relative. Behind each chair, after the men were seated, stood an Imperial Guard in full dress uniform, complete with plumed helmet. First bread, then a complete meal was served the twelve honored guests by the emperor who received the plates from the hands of archdukes handed to them by imperial guards.

After the meal, the table was cleared by the archdukes and guards, and the sacred rite of foot-washing began while the court chaplain invoked the prayers for the occasion. As the emperor knelt before the first man whose feet had been bared, two archdukes advanced with golden basin and ewer. After the emperor had washed the feet of the first man, he moved on his knees to the second and so on until the complete ceremony was performed. Only then did he rise and was met by pages holding another golden basin and linens for washing his own hands. During the empress' lifetime, she performed the identical ceremony for twelve women. One foreign visitor privileged to witness the observance described it in her memoirs: "The Empress drew near the woman first in line, the oldest, and, kneeling down, dipped the corner of a napkin in water and touched the foot; having wiped it, she bent down her fine Imperial head and kissed it."

Having attended to the ceremony, the emperor turned to the imperial treasurer who presented, on a golden tray, twelve white silk purses tied with black and yellow ribbons, the Habsburg colors, each purse containing thirty florins. The emperor then gently hung a purse around the neck of each of the twelve old men and smiling waited while they murmured their thanks. The ceremony ended with the emperor and his entourage filing out while the old men remained seated until the immense hall had been completely emptied. Only then did members of the guard escort each man back to his abode in a separate carriage. Traditionally each carriage also carried a basket of food for the men's families with wine, of course, included.

Artistically Vienna languished after its first wave of classical genius. Having established its name throughout the world as *the* city of music, Vienna bided its time by playing host to the musical great. Paganini led the parade. Prince Metternich had personally invited the world's foremost violin virtuoso in 1817, but Paganini's sickly constitution had prevented the visit until 1828, in time to be heard by Schubert. The violinist marvel of the world was an ugly sight. Large head, pallid face, toothless mouth, skeletal black-clad figure, but all that did not matter: "When women hear my music, my melting tones, they begin to weep and I become their idol and they lie at my feet." Vienna continued to do so in twenty concerts.

Chopin arrived one year later. The Viennese, spoiled by pianistic acrobatics, listened absentmindedly, and only a small circle of connoisseurs rallied to his side. While a few remarked upon his "indescribable technical dexterity, the subtle coloring of his tone, the cleanness of his interpretation" as "the mark of genius," the large majority, Vienna critics included, thought him lacking: "He plays . . . with none of the dash and daring which generally distinguish the artist." Artistic success continued to elude him, and he left for Paris—and fame.

Liszt visited Vienna again. He had made a favorable impression years before when he had played there as a "Wunderkind." Now, in 1838, the city of music was at his feet. The handsome young man, his blond mane falling to his shoulders, with a lion's tempestuous piano temperament, dazzled the Vienna concertgoers, as well as the less musically inclined damsels, in and out of the concert hall.

After scoring pianistic triumphs in Vienna at the age of eighteen, Clara Wieck urged Robert Schumann, her future husband, to join her. But Vienna completely failed to grasp his musical and critical vision. Schumann, in turn, soon became annoyed with the petty intrigues which flourished in Vienna. Disenchanted he left. But in 1846 he and Clara, now man and wife and an artistic combination without peer, returned, determined to win the Viennese anew. But now even Clara's magic failed. Her mixture of the traditional—Beethoven, Schubert—with the new—Chopin, Schumann, and Bach*—fell on deaf ears. Only the guest appearance of Jenny Lind kept the Schumann's final recital from being a total fiasco.

Vienna adored the "Swedish Nightingale" just as America was going to do when she appeared under Barnum's sponsorship. Meyerbeer wrote an opera especially for her, the royal family honored her, and Vienna's enchanted young music lovers unhitched her horses and drew the carriage through the streets to her hotel in tribute. "I have never met such kind people as the Viennese. I cannot find words with which to describe my stay in Vienna," she declared. High praise contrasted with the disillusionment of the Schumanns: "We thought we had found our future heaven of refuge and now all desire for it has vanished."

A similar fate befell pianist-composer Anton Rubinstein. He too had been acclaimed as a child prodigy in Vienna. He returned five years later and found himself forgotten. Even Liszt's efforts on his behalf could not rekindle the spark. His concerts were ignored, his compositions rejected. Deeply hurt Rubinstein retreated to his native Russia. He returned fifteen years later, matured, famous, and had Vienna at his feet.

Vienna continued to languish in its torpor. Music had ceased to be an art. It had descended to the level of mere entertainment, was used to dazzle the senses and blot out or at least dim the unpleasant facts of beginning decay. Even the dignity of the Catholic Mass did not

* Bach had been neglected so long that he was "new."

escape the downward trend and was relegated to the same level of mediocrity and superficiality. Superstition was rife despite ingrained Catholicism. To meet a nun was a bad omen, but the sight of a chimney sweep portended good fortune. On New Year's eve chimney sweeps would mingle with the crowds of revelers, give away parts of their twig brooms as good luck charms, and be rewarded with handsome tips. When a child was born into a family its exact moment of birth, date, weight, and size would all be noted and the respective numbers played in the national lottery. Superstition reached into the highest circles:

> March 1, 1835 . . . My people told me that the cook yesterday played the lottery with the following numbers. No. 12 (the emperor having been born on the 12th of February). No. 43 (today being the forty-third anniversary of his ascension) and No. 67 (his age). The ticket cost her thirty kreutzer and this morning she had won 288 florin. We looked upon this as a good omen and Clement wrote it to the Empress who showed the note to our good Emperor. [Princess Melanie Metternich in her diary.]

The Viennese Sunday was divided between piety, gaiety, and dissipation. The Day of Rest was eagerly awaited. By the burgher to sit in slippers, robe, and mustache-bind and read the Sunday papers; by the student to hike into the Vienna Woods with his girl, knapsack, and mandolin; by the pious and the music lover to attend church. The church in Vienna became the Sunday concert hall, Mass a matinee with programs and singers announced in the newspapers in advance. On Sunday, the question "Which concert are you attending" became "Where are you going to Mass?" and the papers in the coffee houses and homes were eagerly scanned to decide whether one should hear Miss X from the imperial opera sing a Sanctus in one church or Countess Y sing a Benedictus in another. The society opera-lover would attend the Augustin Church. There long kid gloves, silk, and lace abounded as society gathered to hear their favorite singer and, incidentally, attend Mass. As soon as the solo swelled from the organ loft, all congregants would impiously turn their backs to the altar to behold the soloist. And when the "musicale" ended, the congregation would unceremoniously file out amidst animated chatter, leaving only a devout handful to partake in the balance of the service. Promptly the door to the choir loft would be besieged by dandies of all ages, resembling more a stage door than a church portal.

From church, society would repair to the Corso, a portion of the

Ring Boulevard, to see and be seen, greet friends, discreetly or flamboyantly display the latest fashion or latest liaison, or flirt with dashing cavalry officers sporting monocles and riding crops. Thence to a fashionable restaurant or a drive in an open carriage to the restaurants, cafes, and beer gardens in the Prater where one could also listen to Vienna's famous salon orchestras or military bands. The Prater, a wooded park extending four miles along the bank of the Danube, was one of the few points of contact between aristocrat and burgher. The latter, with family or girl friend in Sunday best, would attack Schnitzel and beer as the aristocrat drove by on his way to the races.

At night, one and all, aristocrat and laborer, wandered out to the nearby villages there to drink the young wine from nearby hills, a tradition immortalized by Benatzky's "Grinzing Song." Thus the most welcome Sunday sounds were the pealing of bells and the tinkling of glasses, the chanting of hymns under vaulted medieval arches and the braying of street songs under a vintner's bough.

If the world was changing in quest of new values, Vienna took no note. Still basking in past glory, it lay mostly dormant or viewed political, artistic, and musical innovations with hostility born of lethargy. But despite all delaying tactics, the superficial, reactionary era known as Biedermeier was coming to an end. Regression, barrenness, indecision, and lack of critical and directional sense came under attack from within and without its walls. While Lortzing, Meyerbeer, Herold, and Flotow continued to fill Vienna's flabby operatic paunch with mediocrities, Mendelssohn, on a visit to Vienna, openly criticized its lack of a first-rate orchestra comparable to those of Leipzig, Mannheim, and Paris. Within, the Viennese playwrights Ferdinand Raimund and Johann Nestroy held a satirical mirror to Vienna's slack image. The decline of aristocratic patronage, the tremendous growth of Vienna's populace, the rise of middle class and proletariat, the emergence of a new type of monied "aristocracy" —all created new standards, new patronage, and a clamor for artistic and political rejuvenation.

Suddenly also, the Machine Age dawned. Emperor Franz Josef inaugurated the first Alpine railroad over the Semmering Pass, finally linking the southern part of the empire with the capital. The opening of the Suez Canal was celebrated in 1869 with Verdi's *Aida*, and 1879 saw the light of Edison's first incandescent electric light bulb. The phonograph, invented by him two years earlier, was destined to revolutionize music and carry it to the multitudes.

Two decades before Edison's invention, the city had been released from medieval bondage. By the imperial "Christmas Decree" of 1857, the towering fortifications fell. The Viennese, who had long spilled beyond their confines into the suburbs, watched with tearful melancholia as the walls came down and a new Vienna arose. Ancient, lethargic Vienna had shed its strait jacket. If there was a new dawn on the horizon, the city was ready for it.

X

Jew Street

Against the background of artistic stagnation and spiritual paucity, the development of Conservative Synagogue chant in Vienna stands in sharp contrast in its spiritual and artistic vigor. The history of the Jew in Catholic Vienna had not been happy. The annals reveal confiscation of all Jewish possessions in 1370, pogroms in 1406, public burning in 1421, ghetto in 1626, expulsion in 1670, destruction of synagogues and desecration of cemeteries. Even when such active persecution had ceased, Jews were not allowed to own land, practice any crafts or professions, medicine, arts or sciences, could not be represented in court. They were forced to report at set intervals to the "Jews Office," were required to pay "Jews Taxes"; even their private lives, at times, were regulated by the state as few Jewish marriages were permitted and only by special permit. A "foreign Israelite" could not reside in Vienna without a "Toleration Permit," each one considered individually. Foreign Jewish travellers were allowed to remain in Vienna overnight only by special police permit. For Jews wishing to visit longer, a special permit was issued with a validity of no more than two weeks, to be renewed or refused at the whim of the Jews Office.

Even after the chains of the Vienna ghetto, locked and unlocked at appointed hours, had been abolished, the Jews still remained in their dark quarters on the Judengasse (Jew street) and Judenplatz (Jew square). From there they emerged each morning in their long black silken caftans and high silk hats, with old clothing, cheap jewelry, and trinkets overflowing from their trays and pockets. With their side locks and beards flowing, they would hawk their wares in their peculiar sing-song, returning each night to the bosoms of their tightly knit families, to teach their children, to study, plan, dream, pray.

Anti-Semitism in Vienna reached something of a highpoint in modern times during the reign of devout, narrow-minded Empress Maria Theresia whose distaste for everything Jewish became proverbial. At the end of the eighteenth century a ray of liberalism began to enlighten Vienna under Emperor Josef II. The obligation of wearing beards and staying off the streets on Sundays and Christian holidays was lifted. Jews were permitted to engage in crafts and professions. They were not full citizens, however, could not own real estate, and were loosely restricted within the city. In 1867 a new constitution lifted all restrictions. But anti-Semitism, fostered through centuries, abetted by Maria Theresia and later by Dr. Karl Lueger, mayor of Vienna, was too deeply ingrained to be abolished by decree.

Eased conditions under Josef II enabled the Jews to officially re-establish their community in 1790. Eventually the building of a synagogue was permitted in 1826, and Rabbi Noah Mannheimer, a leader in the synagogue reform movement designed to update Jewish liturgy, was elected spiritual head of the community. He found Koppel Markbreiter, cantor since 1792, unequal to the task of modernizing the service. In a drastic move he strove to eliminate the office of cantor altogether in his synagogue. Rooted in the melodic orthodoxy of Eastern Europe, however, the Jewish community in Vienna strongly resisted Rabbi Mannheimer's desire for drastic innovations. Finding himself stymied, the rabbi hit upon a brilliant idea: Why not combine the finest features of orthodoxy and reform, of East and West, thus bringing a new image—conservatism—to Judaism. He succeeded brilliantly in his task and conservative Judaism started its course from Vienna across the Old and New Worlds.

The composer Ignatz Moscheles, friend of Beethoven and teacher of Mendelssohn, had written music for the Vienna synagogue as early as 1814. On the occasion of the opening of the temple, Beethoven and Schubert had been approached to write a cantata but, unfortunately, nothing came of it. In carrying out his self-appointed task, Rabbi Mannheimer soon realized that a new cantor had to be engaged. It was a fateful day for Judaism when Salomon Sulzer was engaged for that office.

Sulzer arrived from Hohenems in Austria at the age of eighteen. He too was imbued with the controversial spirit of Judaic reform. Again Vienna wrought its spell of sublimation in creation. Soon Sulzer espoused the theory that

> it behooves us to fight an entire break with the past, by abolishing all traditional and inherited liturgy. It appears to me that the confusion of the synagogue service results from the need of only a reformation which should remain on historical ground . . . Jewish liturgy must satisfy the music demand while remaining Jewish; and it should not be necessary to sacrifice Jewish characteristics to artistic forms.

Such an opinion happily coincided with the wishes of the Jewish community and Rabbi Mannheimer's intentions. Sulzer warmed to his task: "The old melodies and singing modes which became national should be improved, selected and adjusted according to the rules of art."

Sulzer's innovations soon proved to be much more than mere improvement. Aside from being a tenor and performing artist in his own right, he proceeded to create an entire new Jewish musical literature and liturgy. Frances Trollope, British author and traveller who heard Sulzer's service in 1837, went into raptures:

> There is so wild and strange a harmony in the songs of the children of Israel as performed in the synagogue [of Vienna] that it would be difficult to render full justice to the splendid excellence of the performance without falling into the language of enthusiasm . . . The volume of sound exceeds anything of the kind I have ever heard; and, being accompanied by no instrument . . . while a dozen voices make up a glorious chorus, it produces an effect equally singular and delightful . . . Some passages of these majestic chants are so full of pathos, that the whole history of the nation's captivity rushes upon the memory as we listen.

Franz Liszt was also deeply moved:

> In Vienna we knew the famous tenor Sulzer, who served in the capacity of precentor in the Synagogue, and whose reputation was so outstanding . . . We went to the Synagogue in order to hear him . . . For moments we could penetrate into the real soul and recognize the secret doctrines of the fathers. Seldom were we so deeply stirred by emotion as on that evening, so shaken that our soul was entirely given to meditation and to participation in the service.

Thus the unique art of Sulzer created in Vienna a synagogue chant which, though innately Jewish, remained inscrutably oriental to the gentile while carrying distinctly modern overtones to the Jew. Aided by his innate artistry and feeling for Jewish tradition and somewhat influenced by the Vienna Catholic Mass, Sulzer created masterpieces for the Jewish service which exhibited a unique blend of antiquity, piety, and modernity. They coincided with the new, liberal spirit of Vienna which lasted until Hitler's march into Austria. Sulzer became one of Vienna's prominent citizens. He was honored by the emperor, the Czar of Russia, and the Sultan of Turkey. He became professor at the famed Vienna Conservatory and an honorary member of the Academy of Arts in Rome. Finally, on his seventieth birthday, he was made an honorary citizen, a signal honor for a Jew in Vienna.

Jews had always been attracted to Vienna. Legend has it that a
Jewish community existed in the Vindobona of Roman times. As
enlightenment gained, the Jewish influx into the capital of the empire
increased. The liberal spirit of Vienna stood in marked contrast to
the medieval feudalism which still prevailed in other parts of the
realm. Furthermore, Vienna, a city of world renown, offered the
best opportunities for the inspired, the talented, the ambitious. Finally
there was a certain assumption of safety in numbers. Most Jews in
Vienna lived in the northern districts of the city, close to the railroad
stations at which they had arrived from eastern provinces. The trend
increased after the collapse of the empire. In the countries newly
carved out of the former empire, the Jew fled in fear of becoming the
scapegoat for past Habsburg sins and sought safety in the largest
concentration of Jews in that part of the world—in Vienna.

That influx, in due time, gave Vienna great men and women in
many walks of life. Perhaps the earliest Jewish name of prominence in
the city's annals is that of suave, diplomatic Salomon Rothschild,
scion of the famous banking house, whose financial shrewdness
served even the mighty chancellor Metternich. But regardless of his
exalted financial position, Rothschild encountered in Vienna the
identical restrictions his co-religionists had to endure. His petition to
establish residence in Vienna was not handled by the Jews Office,
however, but became a matter of confidential correspondence on the
ministerial level.

> [Although] foreign Israelites may reside here only by obtaining
> the special toleration permit . . . special exceptions can be made
> only with the personal approval of the Emperor. Meanwhile,
> your Excellency may rest assured that we are only too well
> aware of the advantage that would in many respects accrue to
> the Imperial State of Austria through the settlement of such an
> eminent firm within its borders not to advise his Majesty most
> emphatically to give his consent as soon as a formal application
> in this matter is received. [Minister of the Interior to Minister of
> Finance, 1819.]

Even with such high recommendation, Salomon still had to con-
tend with existing anti-Jewish measures. All the Rothschild money
could not acquire a house in Vienna, and he countered by renting an
entire hotel. Eventually open-handed diplomacy carried the day with
the chancellor. Rothschild built hospitals, railroads, supported the
sagging fiscal system, financed Austria's steamship company, became
Austria's banker. His efforts finally bore fruit and he was made the
equal of a Viennese street cleaner, an Austrian citizen. This was

followed by another dispensation in 1843: He was granted the privilege of acquiring real estate. So useful did diplomat-banker Salomon Rothschild prove to the imperial house and its administrative right arm, Prince Metternich, that there ripened an enduring friendship between the house of Rothschild and Metternich. Inevitably the day arrived when the roles were reversed. While the Vienna mob of 1848 burned him in effigy, the seventy-six year old chancellor fled into exile with a cash loan and a letter of credit from Rothschild in his travelling bag.

The enlightened period of liberalism under Emperor Franz Josef brought about a flowering of Jewish intellect unthinkable in the near-medieval repression of only half a century before. Vienna not only provided ground for slow, fruitful development as in the days of Beethoven and Brahms, it became the fertile bed from which sprang original, uncompromising theories, experiments, and achievements.

Theodor Herzl, the prominent Vienna journalist, was shocked into realizing the evil of anti-Semitism when covering the Dreyfuss trial in Paris. Upon his return to Vienna, that rude awakening resulted in his book, *Der Judenstaat* (The Jewish State), and the beginning of Zionism. It culminated, long after the death of its spiritual father, in the State of Israel.

Sigmund Freud laid bare the never-before explored jungle of the human mind, the "inner self," the motives behind our dreams, thoughts, and actions. The unparalleled achievements of the "Father of Psychoanalysis" still reverberate in the world.

Gustav Mahler was to reach the zenith of his career at the Vienna Opera. Although Mahler and Freud lived for ten years in the same city, they did not meet, due to Mahler's surprising hesitation, until very late in the composer's life. Their eventual meeting in 1910 resulted in a four-hour talkathon. Afterwards Freud commented that he had never met anyone who had grasped his theories and revelations as readily as the intellectually sensitive Mahler.

Peter Altenberg wedded Viennese charm with poetic genius in gently erotic poetry, and Arthur Schnitzler and Hugo von Hofmannsthal, two masters of the spoken word carried Austria's literary fame far beyond its borders. Schnitzler, who abandoned a medical career for poetry, created subtle word paintings of a degenerating society, pleasure loving and pleasure seeking aristocracy, willowy maidens seduced and abandoned in a cloud of morbid sadness, a middle class caught adrift, seeking, gropingly, its place in the sun. A pleasant lethargy pervades Schnitzler's world, a self-destructive virus of laissez-faire sleeping sickness made more deadly by slow injections of melancholy despair. The privileged are self-centered, the under-privileged darkly discontented, filled with nebulous desires but with no plan or will for improvement. Vienna—a society ready to be led to the slaughter.

Hofmannsthal, on the other hand, depicted all that was eternal in Vienna. Blue blood mixed with Jewish blood brought about an unusually rapid maturing of poetic gifts. The Viennese writer Hermann Bahr, having read Hugo's writings, visualized him as a man in his forties, trained by Jesuits, who may have spent two decades in Paris. To his surprise he met a youth of seventeen whose mental and poetic capacities had ripened into brilliant bloom. Hugo served with a famous mounted regiment then plunged into Romance languages. Respected, aristocratic, the future librettist and collaborator with Richard Strauss in his most famous operas, soon exhibited an irrepressible penchant for the bohemian life—and poetry.

His poetry became a paean to the mighty voice that was Vienna: the romantic whisper of the Vienna Woods, the medieval organ voice of St. Stefans, the cherubic voices of the Vienna Choir Boys. The sights, the perfumes of lilac parks, the splendor of the Ring Boulevard, the Heurigen inns, the opera, the dance halls of the suburbs, all found expression in his poetry, immortalizing the everlasting spirit, the ageless soul of Vienna. Where Schnitzler saw only the painless poison of decay, Hofmannsthal painted Vienna in its highest intellectual colors, far brighter than when Grillparzer reigned as Vienna's great poet.

MARIA THERESIA

HVNGARIÆ   BOHEMIÆ REGINÆ
  AVGVSTÆ   CONIVGI
   ORBIS   DELICIIS
NOSTRI TEMPORIS   PALLADI

MARTIN DE MEITENS PINXIT.   D D D
PHIL. ANDR. KILIAN SVMPTIBVS SOCIETATIS SCVLPSIT.   OMNIVM HVMILLIMA
                                                          DEVOTISSIMA.

1   Maria Theresia, Queen of Hungary and Bohemia

2 Kärntnertortheater and Kärntnertor (Carinthia Gate) in the city
wall on the right

3 Theater an der Wien before restoration—*Fidelio* opened here

4 The Burgtheater in the nineteenth century

5 Stage design for opera *Il Pomo d'Oro*

6 Gluck at the spinet

7 Lipizzaners of the Spanish Riding School

8   The young Mozart

9　Joseph Haydn about 1791

10　Ludwig van Beethoven

11 Franz Schubert

12 A court ball about 1898

13 Johann Strauss, son, with first wife,
Henrietta Treffz

14 Johann Strauss, father 15 Josef Lanner

16 Johann Strauss, son, with brothers Josef and Eduard

17　Gustav Mahler as a young man

18　Anton Bruckner

19　Johannes Brahms

20 Franz Lehar

21 Richard Strauss

22 Stage design for the *Rosenkavalier*

23   Schrammel musicians and guests "beim Heurigen"

24   A Mozart matinee during the Vienna Festival Week

Empress Elizabeth

26 Emperor Franz Josef

Archduke Franz Ferdinand and wife in 1901

28 Emperor Franz Josef in 1910

29 Arnold Schönberg (by Egon Schiele)

30   Clemens Krauss

31   Bruno Walter

32   Anton von Webern   33   Alban Berg

34　The bombed-out State Opera in 1945

35　The rebuilt State Opera

THE DANCING CITY

XI

The Good Taverns

Brahms was at a crossroads. "I believe I am growing." But there seemed to be no room in which to grow artistically. He was sick of the life of the roving virtuoso, wanted to fasten himself, sink his creative roots. The quiet little Duchy of Detmold had, for a while, given him peace for creation but little more. In Leipzig the premiere of his First Piano Concerto in D minor, with himself as soloist and Joachim conducting, had been a nightmare. "A production—now given decent burial—of unrelieved dreariness and aridity," wrote one critic, "three quarters of an hour of ranting and raving, pulling and tugging, patching together and ripping apart of phrases and embellishments—screaming dissonances and discordant noises in general."

His native Hamburg had been no less cruel. When Brahms applied for the post he coveted, conductor of the Hamburg Philharmonic, he was passed over. What made the rejection doubly stinging was that he lost out to a singer. But his friend Julius Grosser had written a glowing letter after a stay in Vienna:

> How lovely it was—the people are much more easygoing and friendly than here; life is easier; nature and surroundings help us to overcome a great deal of worries which are hard to shake off under these grey northern skies . . . One thing is certain, whatever joy I possess in life, in its goodness and beauty, I acquired in Vienna, and I therefore cherish the most grateful feelings for this most charming of all cities.

And another friend, Louise Dustmann, a singer of renown, completely "Viennized" after five years with the Vienna Opera, had also praised the city, as had Clara Schumann, who was still enamored with Vienna despite her and Robert's failure to succeed there. Brahms arrived in "The Holy City of Musicians" in 1862.

Vienna was then regaining the crown of "music capital of the world" which it had temporarily lost to Paris. In background, musical history, prestige, and creative climate it had more to offer than any other city, and the chances of success were infinitely greater there than anywhere else in Europe. Its opera ranked among the foremost in the world, its philharmonic orchestra was nearing its peak; together with the older Gesellschaft der Musikfreunde (Society of Friends of Music), which carried the names of Beethoven and Schubert on its roster, and the famed seat of musical learning, the Vienna Conservatory, they attracted artists from every corner of the globe.

Brahms did not know what to expect but realized that he might have an uphill fight on his hands in the face of such fame, glamor, and a wealth of home-grown talent. His worries were dispelled after the first concert with the Hellmesberger Quartet. There was immediate rapport; Brahms and Vienna had discovered each other. "My concert went off splendidly, far better than I had hoped . . . the quartet was favorably received, I had an extra-ordinary success as a pianist . . . I played as freely as if I had been sitting at home among friends and certainly this public is far more stimulating than our own. You should have seen how attentive they were and heard the applause."

Vienna had regained its intuition and took Brahms to heart. Contemporary pianists Tausig and Epstein and composer-pianist Cornelius were eager to play his compositions, and Vienna publishers clamored for them. This success was doubly surprising because at no time did Brahms intend to blind the public with any display of virtuosity which was anathema to him. Yet the Viennese sensed the outflow of genius and intuitively reached out for it. It was the second time that a native of Hamburg, stifled in his own habitat, triumphed in Vienna. Sixteen years earlier the poet Friedrich Hebbel had arrived in the Austrian capital. Then also the city had sensed greatness and had embraced his creations.

On his thirtieth birthday in 1863, Brahms was offered the post of conductor of the Singakademie, one of Vienna's finest choruses. He accepted, and with the first concert realized his high ideals. Never before had Vienna been treated to so severe a musical menu—Bach, Beethoven, Brahms, and Schumann. The Viennese reveled in it which only tended to show Hamburg's snub in a doubly glaring light.

With pianist Tausig and composer Cornelius friends and admirers of both Brahms and Richard Wagner, at that time also living in Vienna, a link seemed established between the two composers. Through a mutual acquaintance, Brahms and Wagner eventually met in Wagner's lodging. The meeting opened with stiff formality because four years earlier Brahms had openly joined the anti-Wagner-Liszt camp by co-signing an ill-timed "Manifesto." But when Brahms played his "Handel Variations" Wagner could not help but remark:

"One sees what can still be done with the old forms in the hands of one who knows how to deal with them."

But this was to remain the only meeting. Third parties fanned dislike between the two masters. Nevertheless a friendship of brief duration did blossom between Brahms and Mathilde Wesendonck, an unbridled admirer of Wagner (who had dedicated the "Wesendonck Lieder" to her). This did not prevent Mathilde from seeking Brahms' closest friendship and from issuing repeated invitations to him whom she described as "one of the least prejudiced men of our time."

His mother's death in 1865 severed one more tie with Hamburg, but his father then visited Vienna and later described his stay as "living between heaven and earth." It was in the shadow of the deaths of his understanding mother and his great friend Schumann that Brahms' greatest masterwork germinated; it was to raise the young composer, overnight, to artistic maturity and fame. The "German Requiem," the spiritual testament of a deeply devout soul and one of the few monumental masterpieces of Protestantism, was immediately ranged with Bach's B-minor Mass, Handel's *Messiah*, Beethoven's *Missa Solemnis* and Mendelssohn's *Elijah*. The conductor Herbeck performed the first three movements in Vienna, but despite critic Hanslick's praise, the reception was cool. It took the solemn setting of the Bremen cathedral to add emotional impact to a magnificent performance and spell success. Suddenly the name of the thirty-five year old Brahms loomed large in London, Paris, and St. Petersburg.

But despite successes all over Europe, Brahms constantly retraced his steps to Vienna. His growing dislike for the unsettled life of the virtuoso decided him to refuse tempting offers from Cologne and Berlin. His decision was greatly strengthened when, after the successive retirement of Hellmesberger and Rubinstein, he was offered one of the most prominent posts in Vienna, that of conductor and director of the famed Gesellschaft der Musikfreunde. With their orchestra and their Singverein, a magnificent choral ensemble of three hundred voices, Brahms gave Vienna three glorious years of music. Vienna gave its rousing approval, and the composer came to realize that Vienna was the best soil for sowing and reaping his musical seeds. His delightful "Liebeslieder" (love songs) waltzes attest to his growing love for Vienna just as his "Triumphlied" (song of triumph) proved his patriotic joy at the German victory in the Franco-Prussian War in which his political idol, Chancellor Otto von Bismarck, was the leading force.

Despite the obvious artistic triumphs which Brahms scored in Vienna, he was eventually eased out of his position. Conductor

Johann Herbeck had incurred imperial displeasure by an indiscreet remark and had been removed from the position as director of the opera. His clique, looking for another prominent position for its ambitious darling, asked for Brahms' post. Weary after three strenuous years as conductor and chary of an open fight, Brahms resigned before tempers could flare. Unfortunately Herbeck had barely lifted a baton when pneumonia cut him down. After Brahms' resignation became known, offers from Düsseldorf, Leipzig, and Cologne were not long in coming, but he decided as he said in favor of "the good taverns of Vienna." At age forty Brahms made two decisions: one—never again to accept a permanent position, two—to grow a beard. He now devoted about three months to guest concerts, usually in autumn, and spent his summers with friends in the Austrian provinces, Germany, and Switzerland and winters and springs in Vienna and his beloved Prater: "It isn't really spring without a few evenings in the Prater . . . . . . nowhere does one enjoy the amiable and gay character of the Viennese so much as in one's stroll through the Prater" (Brahms to Billroth).

The success of his two "Serenades for Orchestra" and of his "Haydn Variations" had given Brahms the courage to try for the high plateau of symphonic writing. Brahms' fear of symphonic writing at times almost amounted to a mental block. "I shall never compose a symphony. You have no idea how the likes of us feel when we hear the tramp of a giant like him [Beethoven] behind us." When the ardent labor of many years—his First Symphony—was finally born, Brahms heard it in the quiet atmosphere of Karlsruhe under Dessoff before he dared to bring it to Viennese ears. A month later, in December 1876, it was premiered in Vienna. Hanslick the critic rhapsodized: "fervent emotional expression—noble song—a proud national possession." It was on the same occasion that Hans von Bülow, following Schumann's earlier prophecy, made his famous pronouncement on the "three B's, Bach—Beethoven—Brahms" and soon thereafter labelled the work the "Tenth Symphony," the worthy successor of Beethoven's nine, thus conferring Beethoven's mantle on Brahms.

But the severity, exacting execution, and demanding intellectual concentration of the work caught Vienna unprepared. Despite Hanslick's glowing review, the Viennese listened with reservations. Quite the reverse was the case with Brahms' Second Symphony conceived among the enchanting Carinthian lakes. "It is all rippling streams, blue skies, sunshine and cool green shades. How beautiful it must be in Pörtschach" (Billroth to Brahms). The Viennese completely agreed.

The premiere under Hans Richter on December 30, 1877 demonstrated that Beethoven's motto, "from the heart, may it speak to the heart," still applied. The Viennese loved it and in ovation forced a repetition of the third movement. Carinthia can also claim to have inspired the First Violin Sonata and the Violin Concerto. But before this happened Brahms received satisfaction from his native city. Hamburg invited him for the fiftieth anniversary of its philharmonic orchestra and the occasion turned into a rousing ovation for its native son.

Life, at that time, took Brahms for as giddy a rollercoaster ride as his frugal nature would permit. He lost the friendship of violinist Joachim, who resented his taking sides in his marital dispute, and conductor Levi, whose ardent admiration for Wagner Brahms resented. He was compensated by a closer friendship with Bülow, the famous conductor-pianist. The disillusioned Bülow, still smarting from his wife Cosima's (Liszt) desertion and marriage to Wagner, changed from an ardent Wagner champion into an enthusiastic proponent of Brahms. Bülow headed the superb court orchestra of Meiningen whose musicians played their parts from memory and standing up! There Brahms' works received excellent performances. The music-loving Duke of Saxe-Meiningen graciously put the orchestra at Brahms' disposal, and the composer reciprocated by dedicating his "Gesang der Parzen" to the ducal pair and a violin sonata to "My Friend Hans von Bülow."

A summer at the German spa of Wiesbaden proved equally if differently inspirational: There Brahms met Hermine Spiess, a brilliant, vivacious Lieder singer. He was completely swept off his feet, and many a song with the ink barely dry went to the young scintillating creature. "You must be in the grip of a strong, wholesome mid-summer passion," wrote his friend Billroth. "I believe there is something behind this . . . one does not choose such words and write such songs merely out of the habit of composing." Hermine reciprocated Brahms' rare ardor: "What a splendid fellow Brahms is! I was again completely overwhelmed, enraptured, enchanted, carried away . . . He is eternally young." A rare portrait of Brahms, so different from the caustic and gruff man of later years. Passion bore splendid artistic fruit. Brahms' Third Symphony was born in Wiesbaden, and in its joyful air the rift between him and his friend Joachim was healed.

In Vienna, Brahms' name had become a household word. Every day through winter and spring the squat, bearded master could be seen walking, silent and absorbed, or sitting in his favorite inn or cafe with the inevitable cigar and a glass of beer. Only in the company of his friends was he, like Beethoven, "aufgeknöpft," did he open up. Those convivial friends also accompanied him at a rapid pace through the Vienna Woods. Only they could make the bourgeois Brahms discuss everything from art to politics, everything but music. In their company he would sit down at a time-worn, tavern upright piano, its top weirdly ornamented with the rings of many beer glasses, its ivories stained by innumerable cigar butts. Enveloped in the blue haze of cigar smoke, he would play dance music for hours, an occupation which had provided a meager livelihood in his youth. Nor would he hesitate to sing folk songs in a beer garden to the blaring of a third-rate band, accompanying himself by beating time with his walking stick on the table top (one of his favorites—the American "Ta ra ra boom dee a"). Similar scenes were repeated during the summers in Ischl when half of Vienna was there.

As he grew older and was beset by frequent ills, Brahms grew fond of Italy. The sunlit landscape, the carefree atmosphere, the masterpieces of the Renaissance cast their spell. But not Italian music which he openly called "ghastly." The native music of Hungary and Vienna, however, had a lifelong attraction for him; we have only to think of his "Hungarian Dances," "Zigeunerlieder" (Gypsy Songs), and the "Love Song Waltzes."

Six years elapsed between his Second and Third Symphonies, the latter being premiered by Hans Richter in December 1883 with the Vienna Philharmonic. It depends on whose reviews one reads as to whether the work was a tremendous success, surpassing that of the Second Symphony, or whether it registered only a *succès d'estime* with the connoisseurs. What actually happened was all-out hissing and catcalling by the Wagner and Bruckner factions, led by Hugo Wolf. But the Brahms tide could not be stemmed, and faithful Bülow conducted the entire symphony twice in one concert.

In 1889 Hamburg finally made Brahms an honorary citizen. The University of Cambridge had already conferred a Doctor of Music on him as had the University of Breslau, and the London Philharmonic had a gold medal struck in his honor. Franz Josef conferred the Order of Leopold on him and in 1896 the decoration *Letteris et Artibus*, the highest Austrian decoration for intellectual and artistic achievement. Bavaria awarded Brahms the Order of Maximilian, the Royal Academy in Berlin made him a member and the French Academy followed. All these honors were welcome but could not change the man: "When a nice melody comes to my mind, it pleases me more than an order of Leopold, and if it enables me to make a success of a symphony, I had rather that than the freedom of any city."

Yet the paradox that was Brahms deepened with age. There was the conflict between the romantic who wished to roam and the classicist who wished to stay, the cleft between genius and bourgeois, the chasm between cruel sarcasm and kind understanding, the gulf between outward rudeness and innate warmth. There was longing for home and children, yet all his youthful loves took their one-sided course into nowhere. Clara Schumann, Brahms' life-long ideal of womanhood, illustrates the point. There was at first the friendship of young Johannes, putting himself devotedly at the service of the wife of his desperately ill friend. After Schumann's death that friendship inevitably blossomed into a deep passionate longing, acknowledged by both. Yet when the question of marital union arose, Brahms shrank from a binding decision. Any one of those sensitive, artistic, charming women who fell in love with him might have consented to marry him, yet when in later years he was asked why he had never married, he concealed his enigmatic reasons gruffly: "None of them would have me; if there had been one who would, I would not have endured her because of her bad taste." Only on rare occasions did he vent his frustrations to Clara: "One would like to be in bonds and win what makes life worth living and one dreads loneliness." "How I hate the people who prevented me from getting married." Yet it was primarily Brahms who recoiled from binding decisions because he felt more than realized that to bind himself to another soul was to lose his own. Fortunately for him the wonderful women who fell in love with him recognized the artist's need of freedom and none ever pressed her advantage.

Unfortunately, with each disappointment in love Brahms grew more bitter and sarcastic. The examples of his rudeness are legion. After Max Bruch had played his "Odysseus" for him, he addressed the young composer: "Tell me, where do you get your beautiful manuscript paper?" Or he would pointedly inquire in the presence of one of his dear friends, the Jewish composer Karl Goldmark, "Do you find it unusual that a Jew should compose a setting to Luther's text?" Even in unimportant matters he would bring his caustic wit into play. When a cellist complained that Brahms' powerful piano accompaniment had drowned out his own instrument, Brahms retorted: "Lucky man." Brahms was ruefully aware of this uncontrollable, acrid humor which alienated many and thus added to his solitude: "I have no friends! If anyone says he is my friend, don't believe it."

Whatever gentle, warmhearted acts he "committed" were done furtively, such as his contribution to the education of Schumann's children or his endowment to the Hamburg Philharmonic. Or when he hid money in a copy of Handel's "Saul": "Dear Father! If at any time things should go badly with you music is always the best consolation. Only study my old 'Saul' attentively, you will find something there that will be of use to you."

Another occasion for his lasting benevolence was when Franz Jauner, the director of the Vienna Opera, recommended the budding Anton Dvořák to Brahms. How Brahms assisted the young composer has been described by Dvořák's own pen:

> I read your [Brahms'] last most cherished letter with the most joyful excitement; your warm encouragement and the pleasure you seem to find in my work, have moved me deeply and made me happy beyond expression. I can hardly tell you, dear master, all that is in my heart. I can only say that I shall all my life owe you the deepest gratitude for your good and noble intentions towards me, which are worthy of a truly great artist and man.

Brahms himself was deeply grateful for the appreciation of his own friends: "You can't imagine how important and valuable your approval is to me," he wrote his friend Billroth. "One knows what one wanted and how seriously one wanted it. Then one should also know what really has been achieved, only one prefers to hear it from another person and is glad to believe the kind words. My heartiest thanks for praising my song and thus—giving it to me." Brahms could appreciate the praise of Billroth because the world-famous surgeon was also a music connoisseur par excellence in whose spacious home the musical elite gathered to hear premieres of Brahms' chamber music. The critic Hanslick dubbed those sessions Billroth's "jus primae noctis."

By then Brahms had become a tremendous force for balance and one of the few composers of his time who had sought and found his own destiny outside the Wagnerian pale. He had always been opposed to the tendencies of the Wagner-Liszt school ("I have a perfect horror of all that smacks of Liszt"), but he was fully aware of Wagner's greatness: "I once told Wagner that I'm the best Wagnerite alive. Do you think me so narrow-minded that I cannot be charmed by the gaiety and greatness of 'Die Meistersinger'? Or so dishonorable as to keep it a secret that I think a few measures of his work are worth more than all the operas written since." Wagner, on the other hand, had only derision for Brahms which in later years prompted him to call Brahms a "street singer" and a "Jewish czardas player." It is therefore not surprising that Brahms remained passive while being made anti-pope to Wagner by Vienna's Wagner-hating clique led by Hanslick, whose once justified conservatism had degenerated into fanaticism against Wagner and Anton Bruckner.

Despite the floodtide of success, Brahms' inborn sense of thrift, which bordered on frugality, never changed. The little restaurant "Zum Roten Igel" (At the Red Hedgehog), at the time Vienna's oldest, had become the informal meeting place of the city's musically illustrious. At mealtime Brahms avoided the main dining room frequented by officers and officials in preference to the "Stube," the intimate backroom with its checkered tablecloths and discreet service. There he dined and debated with Nottebohm, the Beethoven biographer, Max Kalbeck, his own future biographer, Hanslick, and composer Ignaz Brüll. He had become a Viennese composer and enjoyed the role. The group was often joined by Goldmark, "the Makart of Music," and composers Heuberger and Gänsbacher, or Pohl, the Haydn biographer. Soon another young face joined: Eusebius Mandiczewsky, Brahms' factotum and friend, librarian of the "Gesellschaft." When death took some of Brahms' closest friends, Nottebohm, Pohl, the painter Feuerbach, "Mandy's" affectionate nature made him the ideal companion for the aging Brahms and filled many voids. The voids grew larger with advancing years. Brahms' sister Elise died and so did charming Hermine Spiess at the untimely age of thirty-six. The year 1894 removed Spitta, friend Billroth, and Hans von Bülow.

There were some compensations. Brahms discovered a new singer of songs in Alice Barbi. So captivated was he by her classic Italian beauty, her womanly charms and vocal accomplishments, that he once, on the spur of the moment, told her accompanist to buy himself a beer, and treated Vienna to the rare spectacle of himself accompanying her publicly on the piano. Despite the December-May relationship, Alice reciprocated Brahms' strong feelings, and for months they were inseparable.

Except for such rare whims, Brahms had all but retired from the concert stage. He spent his sixtieth birthday in Italy nursing a friend with a broken left leg and was much gratified by the many congratulatory telegrams. Only one of them did he resent. When the staff of the Vienna Conservatory mistakenly congratulated him on his seventieth birthday, he returned the telegram: "Not accepted, I protest."

He suffered another severe blow in a disagreement with the most important woman in his life, Clara Schumann. The break came about because Brahms took it upon himself to have the first version of Schumann's "Spring Symphony" published without consulting Clara who preferred the second version. Clara was understandably indignant. Actually their disagreement was only a stage in a gradual cooling of their friendship caused by Clara's irritation with Brahms' new friends and also his often coarse joking which offended Clara, now at a ripe old age of seventy-two. Brahms, who could not bear the breakup of this life-long friendship took the, for him, unusual step of seeking reconciliation on Clara's birthday. Their friendship restored, it regained a warmth that had been absent since their youthful meetings.

His more and more deeply felt sense of loss and futility was compounded by the belated offer of the position he had sought so avidly in his youth. At sixty-one he was offered the conductorship of the Hamburg Philharmonic. Brahms' reply could not conceal, after all the years, his initial disappointment:

> There are not many things which I had desired so long and so ardently at the time, that is the right time. Many years had to pass before I could reconcile myself to the thought of being forced to tread other paths. Had things gone according to my wish, I might today be celebrating my jubilee with you, while you would be, as you are today, looking for a capable younger man. May you find him soon, and may he work in your interest with the same goodwill, the same modest degree of ability and the same wholehearted zeal, as would have done yours very sincerely
>
> J. BRAHMS

But the bitter cup had not been drained. After a stroke, Clara died in May 1896. In his anguish and sorrow Brahms again turned to creation as he had done at his mother's, Robert Schumann's and Feuerbach's deaths. "Vier ernste Gesänge" (Four Serious Songs) were dedicated to the memory of "the most beautiful experience of my life, its greatest wealth and its noblest content."

What added to the misery was his mistake in taking the wrong train to the funeral site. He thus arrived too late for Clara's funeral ceremony and had to rush directly to the cemetery. The physical effort, superimposed on the emotional strain, caused an overflow of bile and brought on yellow jaundice. Examination upon return to Vienna revealed a serious liver condition and sent him to the spa of Karlsbad. The diagnosis of the Karlsbad doctors was alarming: "serious swelling of the liver combined with complete blockage of the gall ducts" leading into the final stage, cancer of the liver.

Meanwhile his fame grew. Leipzig capitulated and started its season with three Brahms concerts in which composer-pianist Eugene d'Albert played both piano concertos in one evening. D'Albert called the occasion "a wonderful and unforgettable hour." Meiningen, true to Bülow, followed with a Bach-Beethoven-Brahms concert; Zürich, one of the earliest "Brahms cities," topped its season with the "Triumphlied" and Beethoven's Ninth Symphony presented in one concert. In Karlsbad Brahms was surrounded by his friends, and despite alarming loss of weight seemed unaware of the gravity of his condition. Subconsciously, however, his plight must have impressed itself upon his mind and contributed to the ethereal, other-worldly beauty of the "Eleven Choral Preludes," the last one a clairvoyant fantasy on "O World I Must Depart from Thee."

Upon returning to Vienna, Brahms suffered a mild stroke. Being rapidly sapped of strength but not of willpower, he continued his walks but stopped composing. His skin a suspicious yellow, his walk unsteady, his body stooped, he was still seen at concerts. On January 2, 1897 he attended the concert of the Joachim Quartet to hear his G-major String Quintet and was deeply moved by the tumultuous applause. That accolade was surpassed when on March 7 Hans Richter conducted his Fourth Symphony with the Vienna Philharmonic:

> Immediately after the first movement a storm of applause arose, so continuous that Brahms at last had to come forward from the back of the director's box and bow in acknowledgement. That ovation was repeated at the end of all four movements and after the finale it simply would not stop. A thrill of awe and pain ran through the entire audience, a clear presentiment that they were greeting the suffering and beloved master for the last time in this hall [Hanslick].

Brahms forced himself to attend yet another performance, the premiere of his friend Johann Strauss' operetta "Die Göttin der Vernunft," and refused to acknowledge the seriousness of his situation: "I have been laid up a little, for a change, so writing is uncomfortable for me. But otherwise do not be alarmed, my condition is unchanged and, as usual, all I need is patience" (letter to his stepmother). But soon even to Brahms the signs became unmistakable: "I am going downhill, every word, spoken or written, is a strain." Two days later he was unable to leave the bed. Life began to leave his emaciated body. His face averted from friends and life, wordless, soundless, he lingered on unconscious until April 3.

XII

The Waltz

Paris, 1789. On the rubble strewn area once occupied by the Bastille stood a lone pole. To it was nailed a board with crudely lettered words: "Ici l'on danse." No more fitting expression could depict the joy of a people after liberation from oppression. "Here we dance"— the joy of freedom expressed in the most genuine, the most elemental way, to jump for joy, to dance. The dance—the carmagnole—was the incarnation of a people's feeling, a repudiation of a cynical, tyrannical era trampled into the dust of history. The artificial, aristocratic minuet was swept away by the bacchantic round-dance of the people, the oldest of all dances. It was the natural motion of rejoicing, of jumping, stamping, and whirling, in a hand-entwined circle or in pairs, in contrast to the confined, refined, measured turning, bowing and scraping of the minuet.

Society at large had been well aware of this always joyous, often ecstatic expression of the people and did not always approve. The rotating motion of waltzing (from the German, to turn, to roll) had been forbidden for nearly five hundred years. Hopping and whirling had been banned as early as the reign of Charlemagne who wished to create a more dignified dance atmosphere. Medieval Nuremberg decreed that "nobody may swing or turn a woman while dancing." Frankfurt and Magdeburg fined rotating couples, while Saxony described their motions as "improper and horrible," and from Vienna's pulpits was ranted in vain: "God preserve pious young men from such maidens as delight in evening dances and in letting themselves be swung around and round and allowing themselves to be kissed and mauled about; indeed they cannot be honest while each entices the other to harlotry and offers a sop to the devil."

Such harsh edicts and opinions stemmed from ecclesiastic piety which saw in the round dance, particularly when danced by pairs, a shameless and pagan love pantomime. Coupled with such real or imagined impropriety were reasons of health. The dances were often physically too strenuous and emotionally too rousing for the official tastes of the time. But after the triumph of the revolution, the people prevailed. The fast skipping-dance as well as the slower round-dance became again their own, ringing the death knell to past mores of the highborn.

In Vienna, where classes were not quite as harshly defined and animosity seldom as strong as in France, the picture was somewhat different. Austria's gentler sense of humor, from the court down to the man in the street, created a more relaxed air and attitude. Because the poor were not quite as hopelessly wretched as their Paris counterparts and not without their own shred of dignity, the spark of revolution did not ignite until half a century later. Nor were the nobles as brazenly ruthless and avaricious as those of France. An innate urbanity ameliorated even such unsolvable social rifts and class chasms as did exist. And many adjustments came about through thoughtful deed and gradual change or in the wake of France's thunder. Empress Maria Theresia included the Ländler, a slow round-dance, side by side with the minuet in the court dances. Such an act was well understood by the populace and strengthened the bond between court and people.

In such a typically relaxed atmosphere, the winds blew well for the seed of the waltz. The poet Bauernfeld expressed it succinctly when he could find no other birthplace for the waltz but "the Falstaff among German cities, Vienna, old and stout." Amid medieval fortifications, Gothic churches, and Spanish ceremonial, the lusty spirit of the waltz matched a lust for life further demonstrated by statistics. Vienna, a city of a quarter million inhabitants, in 1786 consumed 454,063 barrels of Austrian wine, 19,276 barrels of Hungarian and Italian wine, and 382,578 barrels of beer. This washed down equally huge amounts of *Schnitzel* (breaded veal) and *Backhändel* (fried chicken) and mountains of rich baked goods, and was finished off with impressive quantities of coffee topped with whipped cream. Good food and drink were cheap enough to be afforded by all but the very poor, and the dance fitted well into the Vienna version of the good life. As Bauernfeld put it:

Muntere Feste, Schmäuse, Tänze	Gayest feasting, banquets, dances
Volle Becher, weisse Nacken	Brimfull tankards, snowy necklines
Süsse Ruhe, tiefer Frieden	Sweetest rest and deepest peace
In dem Lande der Phäaken	In the land of the Phaeacians
Von dem Finger an der Wand	Of the writing on the wall
Von der Mene Tekel Mahnung	Of the mene tekel warning
Von dem Popanz Politic	Of that ogre politics
Hatte Wien doch keine Ahnung	Happy Vienna had no inkling

Full stomachs and dancing feet tended to make people forget political restrictions, military defeats, national frictions, floods, and epidemics.

Mozart's friend, the tenor Kelly, described Vienna's growing dance mania: "The passion for dancing and masquerades was so strong among the Viennese ladies that nothing could make them curtail their favorite amusement . . . the women are particularly famous for their grace and movement in rotating, an exercise of which they never tire. I for my part considered waltzing from ten o'clock at night till seven o'clock in the morning a form of continued frenzy."

Music in Vienna, in one form or another, never stopped. When the Viennese aristocrat or burgher, delightfully exhausted, finally sought rest and slumber, the folk singers, who had plied their trade since the middle ages, were still or again awake, accompanying their songs with fiddle, harp, or bagpipe. They usually sang the music of the Austrian countryside, and the tempo was that of the Ländler. They bore such colorful names as "Baron Jean," "Tanz Leni" (Dance Leni) or "Juden Lisl" (Jew Lisl). Some formed small groups with fiddle, guitar, and bass or clarinet. They played and sang in coffeehouses, beer gardens and wine cellars. Morning would find them in the inns along the Danube where the boats brought news to be transmitted in song, new melodies and new customers to inns whose medieval trade-signs identified them as at "The Golden Bear," "White Lamb," "Golden Rooster," or "Blue Star." In many of those smoky, low-ceilinged inns, music could be heard until the early morning hours, some never closed, never stopped serving and playing. There was music, day and night, summer and winter, year in year out. The folk quartet, with accordion added, became the favorite of Emperor Franz Josef. Schrammel's quartet stood out among them, and today all folk music quartets are "Schrammel Quartets" in Vienna.

Some folk singers became favorites. Schubert and his friends would take rides into the countryside to hear Johann Baptist Moser sing his songs in the 1820's. Prince Metternich so enjoyed the singing of Johann Fürst that he had him sing at his palace. Antonia Mansfeld, a willowy, saucy beauty, had aristocratic carriages drawn up for many blocks wherever she sang and was called upon to sing before Emperor Napoleon III when he visited Vienna. Milly Turrececk, "Fiaker Milli," was immortalized by Richard Strauss in his opera *Arabella*.

Certain songs and their creators became enshrined in Vienna folk-lore: "Du guter Himmelvater" (Thou Good Father in Heaven) by Krakauer, "Der alte Drahrer" (The Old Philanderer) by Sioli, or

"Wien, Wien, nur du allein" (Vienna, City of My Dreams) by Siczinsky. No song, however, surpassed the popularity of the "Fiaker Lied" by Gustav Pick, which extolled the virtues of that Vienna specialty, the carriage drawn by two fast frisky horses, which is seen in Vienna to this day. They came open or, if privacy was desired, closed, comfortable, and intimate, complete with curtains and mirrors. It was a matter of professional honor for the driver to go at top speed. Jovial and fast with repartee, he would doff his bowler or high hat and invite "His Grace" to engage his conveyance. The most celebrated of the fiakers, "Bratfisch," Archduke Rudolf's personal driver, was often hired when discretion was advisable. Austrian nobility in general took pride in being excellent horsemen. If an aristocrat drove his coach-and-four at top speed down the Prater boulevard, the highest compliment would be "he drives like a fiaker." The inimitable Alexander Girardi sang the "Fiaker Song" for the first time in 1885 and immediately made it his own. It swept Vienna and remained green for nearly a century. The only other song ever to rival it was the "Grinzing Song," composed by Ralph Benatzky in 1918.

Sioli, Siczinski, Krakauer, Turrececk, Girardi—their forefathers had come from Italy, Poland, or Bohemia, but Vienna wrought its spell and in the end their names became enshrined in the annals of the city. Everybody—the washermaid with the huge polka-dot bow, her trademark, in her hair, the fiaker with his bowler, spats and striped pants and indispensable slender "Virginia" cigar, the aristocrat with resplendent uniform and nasal dialect, all sang the songs, considered them their own, and thought pridefully of their city. And they all danced. The Viennese writer Adolf Bäuerle tells us how

> the Mondscheinsaal [Moonlight Hall, one of Vienna's famous dance halls] made an immortal name for itself by the mortality rate of the young who danced there . . . It was the fashion to be a dashing dancer and the man had to whirl his partner from one end of the hall to the other with the greatest possible speed. If one round of the immense hall had been considered sufficient one might have allowed this bacchantic dance to pass. But the circuit had to be made six or eight times at top speed and without pause. Each couple endeavored to top the performance of the other and it was no rare occurrence for apoplexy of the lungs to put an end to such madness.

In time the exhausting jumping step gave way to the sliding motion which proved more graceful, particularly in rapid rotation. The waltz thus proved to be all things to all people: narcotic to the poor, energizer to the young, rejuvenator to the young in heart, mad joy to all. "As soon as the first measure starts faces light up, eyes sparkle, bodies sway in anticipatory motion," wrote Count de la Garde, a French visitor. "The graceful spinning tops form, start moving, cross each other's path, pass each other by. It was a spectacle worth seeing. Those marvellously beautiful women . . . carried along by the irresistible music, reclining in the arms of their partners . . . finally the ecstatic delight breathed from charming faces when fatigue forced their owners to leave the heavenly regions."

Nobody wished to remain outside the dance's magic circle. Women who had passed their bloom would engage dancing partners for the evening. The price would vary according to the dancing skill, dress, and general appearance of the partner of the evening. Handsome, tall, elegant men who could swing their partner lustily all night long commanded as high as two gulden per evening with supper always included.

The dance halls of Vienna were legion, ranging from the vast, glittering ballrooms of the imperial palace to the intimate, low-ceilinged halls in the suburbs beyond the walls. The best known were the "Mondscheinsaal" and later the "Sperl" whose name Johann Strauss father immortalized. But their fame was eclipsed by the glamour and splendor of the "Apollosaal" opened by Sigmund Wolfsohn. London-born Wolfsohn, who emigrated to Vienna at the age of thirty, was a man of startling ideas, decades ahead of his time. Originally a doctor and surgeon, he left his profession to manufacture surgical instruments. He so excelled in that field that in 1801 he was awarded a gold medal by the Berlin College of Medicine and was given a diamond ring and one thousand ducats by the Czar of Russia. He reaped even greater fame when his agile mind turned to the manufacture of artificial limbs. His mechanical marvels put an end to those hideous wooden stumps on which victims of imperial ambition had hobbled and earned him the gratitude of untold thousands. His restless mind also devised wheel chairs and rupture belts, all manufactured cheaply to be available to many. Nor were the high-born and the wealthy slighted. For them a "health couch" and beauty creams were produced and marketed. Once a field had realized its potential it became uninteresting to its creator who looked for new fields to conquer, new gold mines to discover. Eventually he began to eye Vienna's richest vein whose potential had never been fully realized—amusement.

In January 1808 he opened the "Apollosaal." The date just happened to coincide with the wedding of Emperor Franz and his third wife Ludovica d'Este. Over four thousand people jammed into the immense establishment on opening night at twenty-five florins per person. Wolfsohn had gauged and gouged correctly. The elaborate luxury of the Apollo was the right, final touch that had been missing for the pleasure-starved Viennese. The many halls had been ingeniously decorated in Turkish, Greek, and Moorish styles; crystal chandeliers and glittering candles abounded in that concoction of rich splendor and garish variety.

> Five enormous ball rooms, four large drawing rooms. Marvellous greenery and flowers abounded everywhere amid waterfalls and grottos and a lake with real swans in it. Garlands, flowering shrubs turned the place even in winter into a veritable garden, the whole being reminiscent of the luxury of ancient Rome . . . Triumphal arches on marble pillars led from floor to floor, the names of the emperor and the empress were emblazoned everywhere together with the heraldic emblems of the city. Said a Viennese wit: "There the bones of our ancestors did not rest—they danced." [Ernest Decsey, a contemporary Viennese writer]

Nor was the musical side neglected. Johann Nepomuk Hummel, a fashionable pianist-composer of the day, had been engaged and with him a new word appeared in the musical vocabulary—concert waltzes —half-hour suites of waltzes especially written for the occasion. They had little in common with the future music of Strauss but rather harked back to the minuet and were all but impossible to dance. But there was no paucity of dance music at the Apollo. The German conductor Reichardt visited the pleasure dome in 1809: "The love of dancing here is now intensified to the point of becoming a mania." Dancing was the sole subject of conversation by young and old, highborn and low, he added, and by his estimate one fourth of the city's population danced every night.

The dancing mania was but a prelude to the nightmarish dance of death which Napoleon led in his invasion of Austria. Heaps of dead soldiers, swollen corpses floating down the Danube, legions of maimed men became a common sight. Was this to be the end of Austria, of Napoleon? The campaign seesawed as the French invader was defeated at Aspern but won at Wagram. Finally, on October 20, 1809, a new peace treaty was signed and Austria saved from annihilation.

If anything, Vienna's thirst for amusement, its hunger for forgetfulness became more frantic with the coming of peace. The Apollo became the symbol of the near-hysterical joy to be alive. The unreality of the situation was deepened when Napoleon, the victor, asked for and received in marriage the hand of Marie Louise, the daughter of defeated Emperor Franz of Austria. Now there was reason to dance as never before. When Alexandre Berthier, Duke of Neuchâtel, arrived in Vienna on behalf of his master, a party for the French guest and his retinue was arranged, at the Apollo of course, attended also by the Austrian Emperor and his daughter. After a brief introduction at which the emperor marvelled at his invention of artificial limbs, Wolfsohn led the imperial party through the multitudes of ballrooms, even the thirteen kitchens drew attention.

After Leipzig Napoleon's erstwhile victims assembled in the conference known as the "Congress of Vienna" which lasted five weeks and dispersed in frenzy. The atmosphere of the Congress fitted Vienna's inclinations. Festivals, parades, banquets, fireworks, balls, operas followed each other in breathless succession regardless of the cost to the bankrupt participants and their retinues of aristocrats, statesmen, adventurers, and charlatans and their lavishly attired ladies, courtesans, aides, and servants. All were caught up in that Vienna madness which relegated politics and statesmanship to a position of decidedly secondary importance. The great, near-great, would-be-great, mingled and danced. The minuet is dead, long live the waltz! The Congress danced, night and day.

The only personage of royal blood in Vienna who reluctantly stayed aloof from all the glitter was Marie Louise, Emperor Franz' daughter, who had been married to Napoleon. She had subsequently returned to Vienna with her entourage in carriages sent by her father. With her was her young son, the King of Rome and later Duke of Reichstadt, half Napoleon, half Habsburg. Although she would have dearly loved to partake in the feasting, her delicate position as the wife of the man whose downfall the Congress celebrated, made it unwise to appear in public. Also, the presence of her son, heir to Napoleon, complicated matters. "Little Napoleon is an object of alarm and terror to most European cabinets because many chimerical hopes of millions of Frenchmen float on his head," wrote the historian Friedrich von Gentz at the time.

Such reluctantly self-imposed seclusion did not keep her from later bearing two children while her husband languished at St. Helena. This came about not by extra-sensory conception but through close contact with General Albert von Neipperg, her dashing one-eyed equerry, thoughtfully supplied by Chancellor Metternich. Fearful of an inevitable international scandal, Marie Louise hid the bastards for years from the world and her own father until a secret wedding could be arranged after Napoleon's death. Only then did the children, appropriately named Albertina and William Albert, officially begin to exist. Emperor Franz had no choice but to acknowledge his bastard grandchildren. Italianizing their father's name Neipperg (originally Neuberg, New Mountain), he made them Count and Countess of Montenuovo.

"Le congrès danse mais ne marche pas"—the Congress dances but doesn't get anywhere—remarked a participant. Nevertheless kingdoms were dismembered or created at breakfast, treaties concluded or broken at a hunt, boundaries redrawn at a ball, spoils casually divided during supper, nationalities parceled out as a grocer measures out flour or sugar—all watched over by ever-present, alert Metternich. And surprisingly the main features of the map drawn at Vienna lasted until 1914. But the political picnic was interrupted by a thunderstorm. Metternich described it in his memoirs:

> Having met till three o'clock in the morning . . . I had given orders not to be awakened should a courier arrive. In spite of the order a servant brought me at six o'clock in the morning a dispatch marked "Urgent." When I saw on the envelope the words "from the Consul General in Genoa," having been in bed only for two hours, I laid the dispatch, unopened, on the nearest table and went to sleep again . . . sleep, however, would not return . . . at half past seven I decided to open the dispatch. It contained information in six lines. "The English Commissary Campbell has just appeared in the harbour to inquire whether Napoleon had been seen in Genoa as he has disappeared from the island of Elba. This question being answered in the negative the English ship has put out to sea." I was dressed in a few minutes and before eight o'clock I was with the emperor.

> 7 March 1815 . . . The announcement of Napoleon's escape from Elba and his return struck the party like lightning from a clear sky. Thousands of wax-lights seemed to go out at once . . . Although politicians are accustomed to control themselves, these terrible tidings were written on their faces. Talleyrand showed the deepest, Stewart the most conspicuous marks, and the Czar's pallor shouted what his lips would not have breathed.

The music played on but the party was over. The exit was swift. The illustrious vanished overnight from the Vienna scene, so serenely gay only yesterday, in frightened haste. The historic one hundred days blazed briefly and furiously before Napoleon's candle was snuffed forever at Waterloo. An era had ended. An era began.

XIII

The Craze

The news had gotten around—"the music at Jüngling's Cafe is a dilly."
If Beethoven had heard about it he, busy with his Ninth Symphony
and deaf anyway, did not care. But Schubert, Schwind, and Schober
frequented Jüngling's and were charmed by the music of a trio led
by a gangling eighteen-year old lad who answered to the name of
Josef Lanner. Another boy, barely fifteen, also heard about it while
helping his father run a tavern. Johann Strauss played a fair self-
taught fiddle. The boys met and made it a quartet. As news of their
lively music-making spread farther and the demand for it increased,
they moved to larger quarters. First to the inn "Zum grünen Jäger"
(The Green Hunter), thence to "Roter Hahn" (The Red Rooster),
and finally to one of the most famous Vienna coffeehouses, "Reb-
huhn" (The Partridge), the hangout of artists, musicians, and minor
officials who lingered to enjoy the superior light-music Lanner and
Strauss provided.

A close friendship soon developed between the flaxen-haired, gentle
Lanner and raven-haired, lusty Strauss. They shared lodgings, ate,
drank, and pranked together and, most of all, made music together.
As Lanner's reputation grew, so grew their group to twelve members.
Soon the boys became bored with the musical trash offered as light
music. They who had started as *Wirtshausmusikanten* (inn musicians)
pooled their talents and began the historic move of the waltz from
the low-ceilinged taverns of the suburbs to the high-ceilinged palaces
of aristocratic Vienna. While Johann made love to the cafe-owner's
daughter Anna, Lanner began to write his own music to mirror the
warmth and love he felt for his native city. The first true Viennese
waltz was born, and credit goes to Josef Lanner for alone lifting the
waltz to historic preeminence. Johann Strauss son tells of the music-
making of his father's and Lanner's time:

> Musical composition at that time was manifestly a simpler affair
> than at present. In order to produce a Polka ... it was only neces-
> sary for an idea to strike one ... and, oddly enough, something
> always did strike one. One had so much confidence in its doing

so, that we older ones would often announce a waltz for such and such an evening, while on the morning of the appointed day not a single note would have been put to paper. In such a case the orchestra generally betook itself en bloc to the composer's lodgings and as soon as he had produced a theme and a few pages of the piece everyone started practicing and copying. Meanwhile the miracle of inspiration repeated itself and the other half was composed. Thereupon there would be a rehearsal of the whole on the spot. The entire procedure only took a few hours and as a rule it met with enthusiastic reception upon presentation that night . . . Lanner hardly ever composed anything except in that fashion . . . When on occasion he fell ill and was unable to write but was committed to a piece for which not a single bar had as yet been written, he would simply send my father a message reading—"Strauss, how about an idea?" That same evening the piece would be given—naturally as Lanner's, to be received with a fresh ovation.

History somewhat thwarted Lanner, because a genius of another musical world, Carl Maria von Weber, had also taken a passing interest in the waltz. In his "Aufforderung zum Tanz" (Invitation to the Dance), the man who had created German opera had also given first full recognition to the new dance form. More than that, he had breathed life, emotion, into it. Beyond sheer melody, repeated and promptly abandoned to make way for another eight-bar tune, he had elevated the entire structure by adding an introduction and coda. Vienna understood and so did Lanner, and his "violet-scented" melodies flowed out in his first great Vienna waltz, "Die Schönbrunner," at the famed Dommayer's Casino.

Now Lanner's fame exploded like a powder charge. Publishers vied for his waltzes with the ink still wet, and demands for personal appearances multiplied. Two orchestras were made out of the one and Strauss put in charge of the new "Lanner" orchestra. But ambitious Johann was champing at the bit. Temperamental and moody, less stable but equally as talented as Lanner, he hated his position in the shadows. Finally it was Strauss who broke the partnership of many years. It was not a pleasant farewell. After an ugly scene in public in which the two friends and part of the orchestra came to blows, there was a parting of the ways. It was typically Viennese of Lanner that he mourned the loss of his partner in his "Trennungswalzer" (Separation Waltz). Fourteen musicians decided to throw their lot in with Johann and a new group was ready. Now to find engagements and income, because the girl he had courted was with child and Johann had to marry her. After the bloom of courtship had withered in the frost of marriage, the union soon became inharmonious but three sons, Johann, Josef and Eduard were to do them proud.

Despite fierce competition, at age twenty-four, Johann landed a six-year contract at the "Sperl," Vienna's most popular dance hall for the gay smart set. That too proved only a stepping stone when he emerged into the full glory of gay Vienna society with an engagement at the most fashionable of Vienna ballrooms, the Apollo. Strauss' waltzes, more commanding than Lanner's, caught on immediately. To critic Hanslick, steeped in the elaborate framework of classical composition, the waltzes of Lanner and Strauss were incomprehensible in their voracious waste of melody: "The narrow compact of the waltz does not permit the slightest development of melody; as soon as it has come to a close it disappears without a trace, making way for the second, the third, the fourth, until all five themes have been played . . . that means at least five new themes [for every waltz] . . . this is inartistic wastefulness which must exhaust even the most talented."

Hanslick had not counted on Strauss' inexhaustible font of musical fertility. Not only was there a seemingly endless melodic flow but Strauss also asserted his own personality by changing the deadening monotony which even Lanner had not escaped. Lanner, for his part, had started to give his waltzes titles which greatly aided their popularity—and sales. Strauss went further. If three-quarter time had to persist, each waltz was to have a personality of its own. And if inspiration did falter on rare occasions, Strauss had no qualms about reaching into Beethoven's or Weber's pockets.

Both men grew. Lanner reached his pinnacle in 1829 when he became Hofballmusikdirector (Director of Court Ball Music). By 1830 the Strauss orchestra had grown into a finely-honed instrument of nearly two hundred musicians which he divided into as many as six ensembles to enable him to fulfill all his obligations. During the pre-Lenten season of 1832 alone, Vienna recorded 772 balls, attended by over 200,000 people. Strauss' main tie remained with the "Sperl" and at the ripe age of twenty-six he was foremost in his field. The German playwright Heinrich Laube described him as "The Austrian Napoleon":

> The waltzes are to the Viennese what the Napoleonic victories are to the French. Napoleon cost his Frenchmen many sons, the Austrians have only to pay a few gulden and a few wakeful nights and their reward is a Strauss with colored plumes for the ladies . . . [a play on words—"Strauss" in German meaning ostrich] All eyes were turned to him, it was a moment of wor-

ship . . . the power wielded by this black-haired musician is potentially dangerous; it is his special fortune that no censorship can be applied to his waltz music and the thoughts and emotions it arouses . . . Very characteristic is the beginning of each dance. While Strauss intones trembling preludes . . . the Viennese tucks his girl in his arm and in the strangest way they sway themselves into the measure . . . then suddenly the resounding trill rings out, the actual dance begins with whirling rapidity and the couple hurls itself into the maelstrom.

Whoever saw the dancing Viennese felt compelled to comment in various shades of approval. Chopin noted that "the Viennese have time for nothing but their waltzes," unconsciously expressing disenchantment at his own lack of success in Vienna. Even Wagner could not extricate himself from its charm. "The Waltz is a more powerful narcotic than alcohol. The very first bars set the audience aflame. The thing surpasses belief."

Strauss' enterprise grew. Some nights he conducted three orchestras, rushing from one to the other because the announcements had promised a "personal appearance of Herrn Strauss." Most of his time, however, was reserved for his main orchestra of one hundred players. From them he was able to extract a degree of perfection in light music never before attained. With each ball, concert, and season demanding fresh material, Strauss soon seemed driven by demons. As the work load grew, interest in his family diminished, and he left the rearing of the boys entirely to Anna. The family meanwhile had moved to the Hirschenhaus (House of the Stag) where they were to remain for over fifty years. Its spacious quarters, nevertheless, seemed in constant turmoil with three to five children, innumerable guests, plus constant rehearsals.

Inevitably the crowded, quarrelsome household became unbearable to the father. The mercurial composer, irritable and temperamental, soon developed a split personality: the public idol of Vienna and the irascible tyrant of his family. Strauss, courted by society, had outgrown the earlier attraction he had felt for the innkeeper's daughter whom he now regarded as a social liability. The situation was relieved as well as intensified when Strauss, commensurate with his spreading fame, accepted engagements in Germany and Hungary. While his trips removed the irritable tyrant from the midst of his family, it also further loosened whatever family ties remained.

The constant presence of instruments, music, and musicians in the house soon influenced the boys. Johann heard his father rehearse almost daily, commanding with voice and violin until the shaky rhythms shaped into razor-sharp precision and the waltz flowed with "Schmiss und Schmaltz" (verve and sweetness). Inevitably a further point of conflict developed. While father Strauss was justly proud of his position and accomplishments, he was unalterably opposed to the music-making of his oldest boy, Johann, whom he wanted to enter the banking business, removed from the vagaries of a musical livelihood: "That boy now wants to write waltzes himself, although he doesn't know the first thing about it and even I am at pains to present something new in eight or twelve bars." But the shrewd quiet mother, sensing Johann's musical urge, fostered, often secretly, his love for music. Somehow Johann got hold of a fiddle. You simply had to have a fiddle in Vienna. The father, upon discovering his son playing, conducting, and bowing before a mirror, broke the instrument across his knee and peremptorily sent the boy back to book-keeping school. But the mother smuggled one of father's violins to the boy and the practicing continued in secret.

Things grew worse in the Strauss household. Adulation had become indispensable, especially by the female of the species, singly and en masse, to the world-famed musician. This, in addition to increased travel, further deepened the rift between Johann and Anna. Berlin beckoned. The constant rivalry between Berlin and Vienna, between north and south, Hohenzollern and Habsburg, Protestantism and Catholicism, their different intellectual and artistic means of expression was a heady challenge to any artist, Strauss not excluded. No Beethoven, Mozart, or Schubert had ever been more famous beyond Vienna's borders. All-Saints Day 1834 saw Strauss and his orchestra in Berlin. It became one of the rare occasions when Vienna scored an undisputed triumph on German soil. The notably cold Berliners went headlong "Viennese." Vienna's world popularity began with Strauss' dance fiddle; the legend grew. He was capable of the utmost refinement as well as of crude circus stunts if the occasion demanded it, but Strauss could do no wrong.

It was inevitable that the vain, emotionally mercurial man should succumb to the ever present lure of female adulation. But it does not speak highly of his discernment or moral fibre that an insignificant little modiste, a hatmaker, garnered the prize. Emilie Trampusch had little to offer save her undisguised admiration, her young body and, in the beginning, tranquility. The smoldering rift between Johann and Anna erupted into open scandal. Meanwhile he triumphed in Dresden and Prague, was overwhelmed with offers to stay in Berlin or come to Russia, but when the pre-Lenten season came around and its innumerable balls clamored for Strauss, he was back in Vienna.

The Bohemians might have their polka, Paris its cancan and quadrille, the Poles their mazurka, but the waltz was king.

October 1837 found Strauss in Paris. Intellectually Paris reigned supreme through the luster of Diderot, Balzac, Meyerbeer, Madame de Staël, Gautier. After only four days in the French capital, Strauss gave the first concert. It was a *succès éclatant*. Berlioz, Auber, Cherubini were in the audience as Strauss electrified the jaded crowd. His success was doubly surprising because it was achieved with a small orchestra of only twenty-six instruments. It had been rightly assumed that the famed Vienna composer would be cordially received at court, but not even Strauss had dreamt of giving thirty concerts in Paris alone. Meyerbeer praised him, Halévy complimented him as did Cherubini. Ancient Talleyrand offered an age-wrinkled hand in admiration. Even morose Paganini was moved to congratulations. Berlioz, however, did him the supreme honor. In his famous *Journal de Debats* he praised Strauss, comparing him to Gluck, Beethoven and Weber: "We have had no conception of the supreme art, the fire, the intelligence, the superb feeling for rhythm in this orchestra . . . the swift interchange of light and shadow in the violins . . . bring forth such exquisite modulations that they become witness to the training of these artists."

On April 11, 1838 the S.S. *Princess Victoria* discharged Strauss and his orchestra on English soil. But despite past triumphs all was not well. The musicians were unhappy. They had not been consulted concerning the extension of the tour to England. Difficulties in staid Britain arose almost immediately. England was ill-disposed towards the waltz, due to lame Byron's expostulations upon it. Strauss was robbed, his men poorly housed, he was haled into court. When all tiresome, irritating, and costly obstacles had been overcome, Strauss was ready for England. But was England ready for Strauss? Music, at that time, was not nearly as treasured or popular in London as it was in Vienna or Paris. Strauss changed British opinion overnight. He was aided by a nineteen-year-old girl who had just ascended the throne of England—Victoria. In the social whirl preceding and following Queen Victoria's coronation, he swept England off its feet and had to give as many as three concerts a day. In 120 days he gave 72 concerts in addition to countless private balls and parties, a gargantuan task sapping the strength of the strongest. Again there was a sputter of mutiny among his men, but Strauss would not hear of return. He seemed as possessed, driven by will power and acclaim, but finally relented and the troupe returned to France. With continental soil under their feet, the men rebelled. They had not seen their families for an entire year and clamored noisily for return to Vienna. But Strauss' will prevailed, and back to England they went where only strong claret could banish the cold from their bones. Strauss suffered an attack of influenza. Coughing, sneezing, and wheezing he feverishly, in every sense of the word, continued the tour. Only threats of lawsuits could now keep the orchestra together, and only doses of opium prescribed by an English doctor could keep Strauss on his meandering course across England.

Finally he succumbed to the strain. He collapsed in Leicester and arrived in Dover with high fever. Now even he realized the impossibility of going on and reluctantly released his men. Recovery was further impeded by a relapse en route to Strasbourg due to inclement weather and poor coach facilities. He arrived in Strasbourg delirious, watched over by one musician who had loyally stayed with him. Seemingly on the threshold of death, Strauss reached Vienna and his distraught family and was nursed back to health by his loyal wife while the mistress waited across the Danube. Anna Strauss saw little of the fabulous sums Johann had earned on tour. She had barely enough to keep the children in shoes. Much of the money had been used to keep his rebellious musicians in comfort and much went to "that woman."

His slow recovery was not hastened by the knowledge that by his long absence he had forfeited the favor of the court. The new emperor, Ferdinand, looked askance on Strauss' coronation music for the British queen. Philip Fahrbach, a popular journeyman musician and composer, had been appointed conductor of the imperial balls, and Lanner conducted the coronation music. Upon full recovery, however, Strauss' popularity soared again. When, at a special soiree at the Sperl he introduced that new Parisian novelty, the quadrille, Vienna's enthusiasm broke all records. More than ever before Vienna danced to the fiddle of Strauss night after lusty night. Soon all Europe danced as Strauss played. Women and critics strewed his path with such rhetorical flowers as "exhilarating," "voluptuous," and "unequalled."

With health and popularity restored, Strauss quickly lost the little interest in his family that remained. His adoring audiences beckoned as did Emilie Trampusch. She would attend all his concerts, applaud enthusiastically, and afterwards go on long moonlit rides with the famous man whose attentions she had so fully captured. She began to dress lavishly, flaunted French perfume and diamond brooches, while Anna Strauss scrimped and worried. Soon Vienna whispered that Emilie was with child, Strauss' child.

Anna, who at first had passed off the affair as just another one in a long line of passing fancies, became worried as funds were diverted and the home neglected, yet she worried in silence. But when the illegitimate child was christened Johann, she could not contain her anger. She issued an ultimatum—and lost. Strauss moved out of the Hirschenhaus and in with Emilie. Soon his second family grew until he was the father of one son and four daughters by her. Thus the private life of Johann Strauss became as shabby as his new abode. He was to spend the rest of his life in a dingy, disorderly apartment, more crowded than the home he had left. He shared it with Emilie, five children, assorted bird cages, a dog, and two monkeys. It is impossible to grasp how a man of Strauss' stature and temperament could bear the contrast between the nightly lavish glamour and the dank crowded hole which he now called "home" and to which he returned with every greying dawn.

Anna Strauss, descendant of a long line of shrewd shop- and inn-keepers was a woman of tough fiber, practical and provident. Johann the father was gone, but Johann her first-born showed every inclination of being born to music. Ignoring the absentee father's advice and orders, she tenaciously saw to her son's education. Johann studied the violin, composition, and conducting. But although he studied the writing of Kyrie, Agnus Dei, and Benedictus, his mind was filled with waltzes, Ländlers, and polkas. Only one of his sacred compositions, a "Graduale" for four voices and brass, survived, and Johann used it to good advantage when applying for an orchestra license.

More than anything else, Anna wished her son to succeed in the field in which his father excelled. The final divorce decree and subsequent near-poverty could not dampen either Anna's resolve or Johann's ambitions. Although trembling at his father's ire, he applied, at age nineteen, for a license "to play music for entertainment in public places with an orchestra of twelve to fifteen persons." He was still a minor to whom licenses were usually not granted, but his musical background and education convinced the authorities of his musical maturity.

Johann was fully aware of the debt he owed the name of Strauss and selected and trained his fifteen musicians with great care. Finally, on October 15, 1844, the day was at hand. It was an important occasion in Vienna's annals. This was not the debut of just another dance orchestra, this was "Johann Strauss, Jr." and the place, the Café Dommayer, famous since Lanner's day, was in an elegant suburb of Vienna near the emperor's summer palace. And Johann seemed well-prepared—with four waltzes, two quadrilles and three polkas. The news of another Strauss orchestra had spread like wildfire, and on the set date musical Vienna streamed out to Dommayer's. Long before the announced hour of six, the huge hall was packed with standees crowding every nook and niche, while outside thousands milled, causing all traffic to stop. "It was more difficult to secure a table than to obtain a seat in the House of Lords," recalled an English visitor. The announcement of the debut had caused a sensation. Many accused Johann of a cheap trick, of exploiting his father's name and fame. A clique of Johann senior's partisans set out to break up the evening. The news pitted partisans of both sides against each other before the first note had been sounded. Outside the casino additional police had to be called to open a precarious route for the carriages arriving for the concert. Inside the waiters had given up the pretense of serving anybody in the packed hall where circulation had become impossible. And nobody had really come to eat, or drink, or dance, but only to see and hear a new Strauss.

Johann had inherited his father's black mane and paleness of face. Today he seemed paler than usual as he stepped before the sea of curious, intense, even hostile faces. But the moment had arrived, and resplendent in new blue waistcoat with silver buttons and silken vest with hand-painted flowers, Johann looked out over the vast, blurred mass of tightly pressed humanity. He did not hear their polite applause or subsiding murmur—the pounding of his heart drowned out all other noises. He raised his fiddle to his chin, a hushed silence fell. The overture to the opera *The Deaf-Mute of Portici* was mildly applauded and promptly dismissed. They were waiting for his own music, and the opening waltz "Gunstwerber" (Favor Seekers) was exactly what they had come for. A waltz in the best Viennese tradition but with a new flair, new verve, new charm. It seemed as though the pent-up excitement and emotion would literally raise the roof of the vast ballroom. People cheered and shouted, clapped, waved their handkerchiefs. Yet what seemed at first the limit of enthusiasm was only its beginning. The next waltz had to be repeated five times, the waltz "Sinngedichte" (Thought Poems) nineteen times! Never had elegant Dommayer's seen anything like it. Bedlam! There seemed to be no end to it from that sea of enraptured faces, flushed with the excitement of the hour. And the climax was yet to come.

At one o'clock in the morning, after seven hours of playing, Johann, now ensconced as Vienna's newest idol, his black eyes flashing with the triumph of the hour, imperiously bade the crowd silence. The sound which next wafted through the thronged hall was not one more child of his young and fertile imagination, but the most famous waltz of his father. "Loreleyklänge" (Sounds of the Loreley) demonstrated his filial loyalty, remembered in his hour of triumph. Vienna understood. When the waltz ended Vienna was his; there was a thousand-throated shout, a wave of love mingled with tears. The audience, with hearts full, understood the gesture of homage from son to father and was grateful. Newly won friends, former foes, they all surged forward and carried him off on their shoulders.

When the last bravos had subsided, Vienna had more than a new waltz king, it had a Strauss dynasty. But only Johann knew that the day had been as much a triumph for his mother as for him. After witnessing Johann's triumph, the music critic Wiest leisurely returned in an open fiaker during the greying hours of morning. Slowly the carriage rumbled past Lanner's house, the true father of the Vienna waltz who had died a year before: "I looked up at the windows, all dark and quiet as the grave. In that house there once lived a Viennese who also composed good waltzes. Good night, Lanner. Good evening, Strauss father. Good morning, Strauss son."

XIV

The King

The rush was on. Everybody wanted Johann to play at his ballroom as Vienna clamored for its newest idol. But what most fascinated the gossips was the question of the future relationship between father and son. Would the youngster's unheard-of success make them rivals or would it cement their relationship? The father watched with mixed emotions, proud yet sad; his own name and reputation enhanced and threatened at the same time. Overnight a famous son, a new threat, had arisen. Before it had been Lanner, now it was another Strauss.

Johann showed his respect by constantly placing his father's music on his programs. But while he admired his father as an artist, his loyalties always remained with his mother. When father and son finally met, their reconciliation solved all questions except the matter of the mistress and abandoned wife. It was even rumored that Strauss senior had invited the son to join forces but in deference to his mother Johann declined. Other matters of musical standing resolved themselves, but with increasing difficulty. With Lanner dead, Johann took over the position of director of his military band, while the father continued to lead his own regimental band. Both would conduct their respective bands attired in high shakos and crossed white-leather belts over brightly colored uniforms, one red, one blue. On changing of the guard, they would conduct their bands opposite each other, then would salute each other smartly and march off in opposite directions. If the father included Beethoven, Cherubini, and Mendelssohn in his programs, the son played Liszt and Wagner. Strauss senior reached the zenith of his public life when he was appointed Imperial Director of Ball Music, in which position he presided over many a brilliant festivity at the famed Redoutensaal. The visiting Count de la Garde described it as "An enormously long hall in which six hundred people could be seated. The walls were covered with the finest Gobelin tapestries. Above these were long mirrors reflecting and counterreflecting all the formal elegance made dazzling by the brilliance of the crystal chandeliers."

But despite outward splendor, the chinks in the empire's armour became apparent even in its capital. Outwardly the picture seen by de la Garde was dazzling:

> Numberless carriages traversed the city in all directions. Most of them were preceded by agile forerunners, in their brilliant liveries, who, swinging their large silver-knobbed canes, seemed to fly in front of the horses. The promenades and squares teemed with soldiers of all ranks dressed in the varied uniforms of all European armies. Added to these were the swarms of servants of aristocracy in their gorgeous liveries and the people crowding all vantage points to catch a glimpse of military and diplomatic celebrities . . . Then, when night fell, the theatres, the cafes, the public resorts were filled with animated crowds, apparently bent only on pleasure, while sumptuous carriages rolled by, lighted up by torches borne by footmen . . . In almost every big thoroughfare there was the sound of musical instruments and of joyful tunes.

Yet the cynically observant eye noticed the other side of the coin, a country dominated by a standing army of soldiers, a kneeling army of priests, a crawling army of spies. The contrasts deepened in 1848. While Vienna danced to the entrancing strains of Strauss, butcher shops and bakeries were plundered by the desperate populace. If the people, sucked by taxation and beset by spies and hunger, found forgetfulness in dancing, the spirit of rebellion, despite despotic measures, found fertile ground also. The Habsburg dynasty trembled as waltzing Vienna exploded in riot, as Metternich the all-powerful and Ferdinand the weakling fled, together with cabinet and aristocracy.

In the ensuing blaze the march displaced the waltz. Marches were not new to Vienna. Beethoven had written them as had Mozart and Schubert. But the new marches were dedicated to a different purpose, to stir and make feet march more willingly to battle and death. Vienna's gaiety screeched to a halt on an ugly note. The subsequent period of repression and reprisal was eerily accompanied by Straussian fiddles. Revolution seemed crushed, but the quiet was deceiving. Like a dormant volcano it was to erupt again seventy years later. Then the rampaging stream of social unrest would finish in 1918 the work begun in 1848 and topple the crumbling edifice of a worn-out order.

To nobody's surprise, Strauss father and son also found themselves on opposite sides in the matter of politics; the father siding with the *Herrscherhaus* (the ruling dynasty) while junior was mildly imbued with the spirit of revolution. It was before a gathering of officers that

Strauss senior first played the composition dedicated to and named after Austria's distinguished Field Marshal Radetzky. The Radetzky March was not only Strauss' most notable success but it was also to prove his most lasting. Together with Haydn's National Anthem and Strauss junior's Blue Danube Waltz, it was to comprise the triumvirate of popular musical treasures identified with Austria throughout the world. Yet its immediate reception by peoples struggling for freedom was hostile. Wherever Strauss went, Prague, Heidelberg, Brussels, or Paris, there arose protests against the man who dedicated music to those who had trampled freedom. Only Tory England received him without incident. Upon his return to Vienna he announced his first concert with trepidation. But the short-memoried Viennese forgave quickly. Even the bad omen of two broken violin bows in one concert could not diminish the joy and satisfaction of his continued popularity. But the symbol preceded reality by only six days.

After a chance messenger had informed the family, they found the man Vienna idolized, alone, naked, dead. One of the daughters Strauss had sired by Emilie had infected him with scarlet fever. The house was stripped bare of furniture, piano, rugs, food, linen, living spirit. Emilie Trampusch, the woman whom Strauss had showered with gifts and love, had fled with her children, leaving behind nothing but the bare mattress on which the body rested. While placards announced that Hofkapellmeister Strauss would personally conduct a gala affair in honor of Field Marshal Radetzky, an immense sea of Vienna's music-loving humanity, and three bands, followed him to his grave. Forever thereafter Strauss son was to be haunted by the horrible specter of death he had witnessed. It was to grip him with unrelenting dread to the end of his days.

Although the men from his father's orchestra had approached Johann and urged him to take over, the questionable taste was not overlooked when Johann appeared at the helm of his father's ensemble only eight days after the latter's death. The severe criticism could not be mollified by a memorial concert featuring only the father's music. At the age of twenty-four, however, with an aged mother, two brothers, and two sisters to support, Johann could not be burdened with sentiment. Thus, during the early reign of a young, inexperienced emperor, advised by reactionary, hated advisers, it was a young musician who continued to make life bearable: "A young man of eighteen had ascended the throne of Austria," wrote the contemporary music historian, Ernest Decsey, "and Johann Strauss, Jr. became, uncalled and unconsciously, his co-regent, one of the most winning powers in the dark house of Austria." During one night Johann might appear with six of his orchestras which had announced his personal appearance. While he obligingly fed the voracious appetite of Vienna's balls, he consistently attended to serious music as well, even included Wagner excerpts in his programs at a time when the doors of the Vienna opera were closed to Wagner.

If the father had rushed through life with a premonition of its short span, Johann, in every gesture expansively prepared for a long, rich life. Vienna, as usual, quickly forgave his lack of sentiment, but it was more difficult to appease the emperor who did not easily forget the young composer's revolutionary compositions and the playing of the Marseillaise in 1848. But when in later years Johann's march "Viribus Unitis" was dedicated to the emperor, there was instilled the regard which was to last to the end of their days. "The Emperor lived on Strauss music," wrote a member of the court. "To be exact Franz Josef reigned till the death of Strauss."

Johann and Vienna grew. The young emperor was determined to make Vienna the model of a world city. He built railroads, encouraged trade and industry, remodeled "his" city from medieval fortress to world metropolis. When Vienna's forbidding but ineffectual bastions were razed, Johann wrote his "Demolition Polka" to fit the occasion. On the ground where the walls had stood, work began on what was to be the world's most grandiose boulevard. Vienna grew, and a new middle class grew with it—and demanded more entertainment. Johann had long been its idol. His flashing eyes, black curly hair, and flowing moustache, combined with elegant tailoring and dashing conducting, made him the most famous man in Vienna, second only to the emperor. No important occasion took place without Strauss music. One woman even stipulated in her will that Strauss play at her funeral. He and his full orchestra thus played waltzes in her funeral procession, the gayest danse macabre ever, possible only in dancing Vienna.

But Johann's physical endurance could not match his musical power. One day he simply fainted from exhaustion. Wiser than his father, he did not ignore the danger signal. But the orchestra had to go on, for two reasons. A tyrannically benevolent Vienna public demanded it, and music was the sole support of the entire family. A family council, chaired by the mother, was held at Johann's bedside and decided that brother Josef should take over. Josef, with his long hair resembling Franz Liszt, was far removed from music. After having resisted his father's efforts to make him an officer in the Austrian army, he had become a successful inventor. Under family pressure he relented and, once decided, went about his new task with an inventor's inquiring tenacity. He was stiff, solemn and sparing in his motions, and the Viennese, surprisingly, loved him for the very contrast to Johann. Although he shouldered the responsibility of conducting, he was at first not at all interested in composition. He wrote one waltz entitled resolutely "The First and the Last," then another, "The First after the Last," and then 222 more. The fertility of the Strausses welled up in his inventor's mind and asserted itself. The most lasting composition of a man who had spent his early life over a drawing board was "Dorfschwalben aus Österreich" (Village Swallows of Austria), an idyll of outdoor village life which earned him the title "Schubert of the Waltz."

Johann's rest was of brief duration. When the promoters of a Russian railroad project approached him to conduct in the resort town of Pavlovsk near St. Petersburg, he accepted. The undertaking was as profitable as it was strenuous, with two concerts to be given each week, each lasting three to five hours. History repeated itself as the Russians thronged the concerts, heaped him with adulation; women vying for his attention filled his room daily with fresh flowers, while men carried him on their shoulders after the concerts. One nobleman challenged him to a duel because his wife had sent flowers. Johann invited the Russian to his suite, overflowing with flowers, and asked him to point out those the wife had sent. The noble apologized. But the musical taste of the aristocratic Russian audiences was not too high: The most applauded number was the "Bauernpolka" (Peasant Polka). "The Czar and the entire audience applauded it as no Beethoven symphony was ever received," wrote Strauss. "This polka is a miserable piece of trash. I doubt whether it would create such a to-do in Vienna."

During Johann's absences from the capital, brothers Josef and Eduard carried on the Strauss tradition. The brothers were of three totally different types, even in outward appearances. If Johann patterned himself after Emperor Franz Josef, right down to sideburns and moustache, Josef emulated Franz Liszt's long mane, while Eduard, the youngest of the three, fashioned his pointed moustache and goatee after Napoleon III. Eduard made his first appearance on February 5, 1859 at a monster ball at the wintergarden of the Diana Bath. His brothers made it an unforgettable occasion, each bringing his own orchestra! Fifty dances, waltzes, quadrilles, polkas, mazurkas, were played that evening and there was dancing without end. At the monster quadrille which ended the ball, each brother took a turn with his orchestra. Then, upon a signal given by Johann, Vienna viewed the never-to-be-repeated spectacle of the crashing finale, conducted by all three brothers before their bands—in unison! Eventually it became a fashionable game in Vienna to guess which of the three brothers had collaborated on what composition. It was known that they did so on occasion, but they kept their secret by simply signing the compositions "Strauss."

Eduard had also had other ambitions. He had wished to follow a diplomatic career before he was inexorably drawn into the magic Strauss circle. After his debut with the orchestra he became a stabilizing influence in that world of musicians, prima donnas and impresarios. Once he had become an integral part of the Strauss dynasty, Eduard began to study with Sechter, the teacher of Bruckner, and, inevitably began to compose. His combination of handsome appearance and brilliant conducting soon made him the best known of the three. In Vienna all women's heads turned when "der schöne Edi," handsome Eddy, passed. When he conducted in London, Queen Victoria addressed him: "You remind me very much of your father . . . It seems like yesterday when he played at my coronation ball. I remember the pieces. Could you play some of them?" But Eduard's outward dash was oddly balanced by a morbid interest in catacombs, funerals, and pestholes which, in later years, brought about a disastrous decision concerning Strauss manuscripts.

Vienna bloomed and blossomed. On May 1, 1865 the emperor officiated at the opening of his pride and joy, the fabulous Ringstrasse. The boulevard was sixty yards wide and six miles long. It had a four-lane center for carriages, flanked on each side by tracks for horse-drawn street cars, tree-lined riding paths, and wide side walks. Franz Josef had overridden all opposition to his ambitious plan. Part of the Mölkerbastei (bastion) with the Beethoven house, the rococo Schubert house, and the Burgtor (the gate leading to the court) were all that was allowed to remain of the ancient walls. Stately old palaces and gleaming new edifices now shouldered each other and were interspersed with forsythia, lilacs, and roses in public gardens and parks. But not all was perfect in the young emperor's design for his Vienna show piece. An over-abundance of styles placed the neo-gothic city hall next to a neo-Grecian parliament and opposite the baroque Burgtheater, while the two massive museums, and a monument to Maria Theresia between them, were conceived in lavish Renaissance. Too much space was allotted to some building and not enough for the lovely new opera house which seems crammed in near a busy intersection.

As Franz Josef's Vienna became worldly and elegant, its social structure also underwent a decisive change. Nobility still received in their marble palaces, but a new aristocracy of industrialists and financiers had assumed a leading role patronizing the arts and freely mingled their newly acquired titles with some of the oldest in the realm. Art was to gain from the newly "arrived" who vied in their support of art and artists. But, since they had little background or acquired taste to distinguish between the mediocre and the inspired, the noble and the commonplace facile, Vienna often wallowed in mediocrity.

The social change in Vienna was most vividly illustrated in the household of Baron Moritz Tedesco, a member of Vienna's new financial aristocracy. Jewish by birth, Bohemian by nature, his palatial home was frequented by the literati and the musical intelligentsia although (or perhaps because) it was presided over by his mistress, Henrietta ("Jetti") Treffz. The sparkling woman in her forties, to whom Mendelssohn had dedicated songs, about whom Berlioz had spoken in glowing terms, whose brilliant voice had been compared to that of Jenny Lind, was acceptable in the Vienna of 1860. Life in the sumptuous household of millionaire Tedesco, offered all that seemed worthwhile in life to Jetti's middle-class background—until she met Johann Strauss.

Johann had reached thirty-seven, handsome, famous, wealthy, unattached. He could have chosen among the highest and wealthiest of society. Yet he seemed oblivious of all the adoring females who vied for his favors, whose scented, ardent love letters he often discarded unopened. His choice was received in Vienna with open-mouthed disbelief—Henrietta Treffz. As the tacitly acknowledged lady of the house, she had invited Strauss to conduct at a ball at the baron's palatial home. The very night of the ball they fell in love. Fate had intervened and nothing else mattered, not her liaison, not that Jetti was ten years older than Johann, not that it meant leaving a baronial home. With understanding and tact, Tedesco not only acceded graciously to the demands of such tempestuous love but sped Jetti into Johann's arms with a considerable monetary gift.

The two were married in St. Stefan's Cathedral in a simple ceremony attended only by a few close friends. If mother Strauss objected to the choice, she kept silent because Johann was obviously happy. Johann and Jetti had both emerged from middle-class backgrounds, and were brilliantly musical. He was in many ways inferior to his worldly bride, but her theatrical experience, her social prominence, her beauty and shrewd mind, all now completely devoted to her husband's fame and fortune, were to have historic consequences. "She is irreplaceable," wrote Eduard to his wife. "She writes all bills, copies all music for the orchestra, looks after kitchen chores, and supervises everything with a care and kindness that evokes admiration." The happy pair moved into a villa in Hietzing, Vienna's most fashionable suburb, which provided the outward symbols of luxury and financial security as well as privacy and seclusion.

After the initial shock had abated, Johann was more in demand than ever. So uncontested was his fame that even a fine conductor and composer like Émile Waldteufel was relegated to the background. Paradoxically, Johann's waltzes were not played at court; the emperor had a long memory. But Jetti knew people and pulled strings, and finally Johann was appointed to the coveted position of Hofkapellmeister which his father and Lanner before him had held. Johann's music uniquely appealed to all; it permeated the court, the ballroom, the inn, and united the city in a "chord of harmony" which made the young washerwoman swing her skirts saucily and made the emperor smile.

Soon Jetti prevailed upon her husband to leave the task of conducting at nightly appearances to his gifted brothers and conserve his strength for composition and foreign appearances. At about this time Johann's eye fastened on the poem of an insignificant poet, Karl Beck. One line immediately struck a responsive chord: "An der schönen blauen Donau" (By the beautiful Danube). And conductor Herbeck had just requested a choral composition. Choral singing, long suppressed by Metternich for fear of large assemblies, had seen a revival since 1848. Johann was eager to oblige. The result was an immortal gem, Austria's unofficial anthem and his greatest waltz— "The Blue Danube." It could not have come at a more appropriate time. Austria had suffered the disastrous defeat at Königgrätz at the hands of Wilhelm I and Bismarck. Every troop train had brought thousands of wounded soldiers back from the front, and morale in Vienna was at an all-time low. By modern standards it was a comic-opera war of seven weeks duration, but the humiliation of the defeat, because of the inferior equipment and firing power of the Austrian troops, made it far from comical. It also brought to the fore the ostrich-like attitude of the Viennese. Responsible people were outraged when, on the very day of Austria's worst defeat, two thousand Viennese crammed into a Venetian Summer Festival in the Prater. "Freut Euch des Lebens" (enjoy life); Vienna danced while the monarchy was sinking into quicksand.

Strauss saved the day by giving Austria—and the world—The Danube. Flowing past woods and meadows, mirroring vineyards descending hills to the water's edge, steep precipices crowned with

monasteries or the stark ruins of once proud castles. The Danube—
river boats and peasant songs, the Nibelungenlied, quiet sunlit landscapes, the bustle of Vienna. The Danube is hardly ever blue except
when it reflects a clear sky; it is steel gray, silvery. Johann Strauss
made it forever blue and the world believed him. But at the premiere
the insipid text of the choral version gave it the kiss of sleep. Johann
shrugged his shoulders and wrote "Künstlerleben" (Artist's Life).
The "Blue Danube" was forgotten. Paris was to waken it from
slumber.

In 1867 Napoleon III opened the Paris International Exhibition;
Europe stood in awe, and nations vied to contribute to its splendor.
Despite political dilemmas and military defeats, the Austrian Embassy
was one of the hubs in that gay whirl, and Countess Pauline Metternich Sandor, wife of the ambassador, was one of the most influential
personages in her role as adviser to Empress Eugénie. Johann was
at first completely submerged in the city where Jacques Offenbach
reigned supreme. Countess Metternich saved the day for Strauss by
deciding that his orchestra should play at the glittering gala-ball of
the Austrian Embassy. "No-one thought of dancing," wrote one of
those present, "everyone wanted to listen to his waltz. And how
Strauss played . . . with what fire . . . We had thought Waldteufel
perfect but when we heard Strauss we said to ourselves, you had never
heard a waltz before." It was on that occasion that the world heard
"The Blue Danube" for the first time without words, for orchestra
only. "Mr. Strauss dances his own waltzes—with violin, arm, neck,
shoulders, head. It is impossible to sit still . . . he makes the very
pillars of the hall twirl and dance," wrote the journalist Villemessant,
influential owner of Le Figaro, who also gave a special soiree for
Strauss which the great of the world attended—Ambroise Thomas,
Turgenev, Flaubert, Gautier, Dumas father and son. Strauss graciously reciprocated with a dinner for Le Figaro's entire editorial staff,
replete with a brand-new "Figaro Polka" and of course "Le Danube
Bleu."

The spellbound Prince of Wales heard Johann and would not take
"no" for an answer. In England, where Wagner fought and argued
with one and all, where Anton Bruckner's organ magic was all but
ignored, Strauss triumphed. Johann also honored his father's memory
by playing his coronation music for Queen Victoria, arranged variations on English folk songs, and as the highlight of the season, played
"The Blue Danube" in Covent Garden with full symphony orchestra.
The world now clamored for the "waltz of waltzes." Publisher
Spina in Vienna had to use over one hundred plates (as compared to

three for the average successful piece) to comply with the demand for that one waltz coming from all of Europe, America, Australia, Russia, the Orient.

Johann returned to Vienna a conquering hero. If he was exhausted his inventive spirit showed no signs of it as he composed in rapid succession such gems as "G'schichten aus dem Wienderwald" (Tales from the Vienna Woods), "Wein Weib, Gesang" (Wine, Woman and Song), the hymn to the spirit of Vienna, ranging from the sprightly to the dreamy and sensuous, and also arranged for another European tour which was crowned by a command performance at the Royal Opera House in Berlin. Behind it all the fine hand of Jetti could be seen by all except Johann's mother who refused to acknowledge the ex-mistress of a *nouveau-riche* Jew.

Meanwhile brother Josef and Eduard had carried on the Strauss tradition with aplomb and soaring popularity. Some considered Josef even the finer musician in the light of such waltzes as "Dorfschwalben" and "Mein Lebenslauf ist Lieb und Lust" (My Life's Course Is Love and Joy). Only a Viennese could have dreamt up a title so typically Viennese. Unfortunately the "Schubert of the Waltz" passed away before his artistry could fully assert itself. Shortly before a fateful last journey to Warsaw in 1870, Josef made an odd request of his erratic brother Eduard. Whoever outlived the other should burn the other's compositions, manuscripts, and arrangements so that no stranger would have access to them. Unfortunately, Eduard did carry out his brother's stipulation. Thirty-seven years later, he made arrangements with a Vienna furnace maker and on October 22, 1907 commanded a van, loaded Josef's entire library in it and perhaps also the manuscripts of Johann, and watched for five hours while flames devoured much of the musical history of the Strauss family.

Death was a specter Johann had been unable to face since the death of his father. He stayed away from his mother's funeral as well as from his brother's. Josef had collapsed of a heart attack while conducting in Warsaw and, in falling, had injured his head severely. Fahrbach was called from Vienna to finish the tour and Josef was treated in a Warsaw hospital. When no improvement was noted he was belatedly transferred to Vienna but a brain tumor had developed and rendered even the famed Vienna medical specialists helpless. The responsibility of the orchestra now rested entirely on Eduard's shoulders.

A chance remark, more courteous than encouraging, led Johann onto the path of the operetta. Paris still reigned supreme in that field and its symbol signed his name Jacques Offenbach. He was

a lean, little, nervous man with a large jumping adam's apple, thick
side-whiskers, and piercing blue eyes behind black rimmed pince-nez
on a black silk string. The son of a German cantor, Offenbach came
to Paris at fourteen to study music where two other German Jews
were reaching fame, Heine and Meyerbeer. Unable to break into
grand opera, he ventured into "little opera" or operetta with tremendous success. Having conquered Paris he invaded the Vienna
which loved the honest sentimentality of poet Ferdinand Raimund
but also relished Johann Nestroy's sarcastic parodies; thus the Viennese were fertile ground for Offenbach's sly insinuations, sensuous
intimations, and broad parodies of weakly erotic gods and pompous
generals. To the swish of can cans with gibes at everyone worthy
of his cynical humor, including the reigning houses of Europe, he
quickly conquered Vienna where three theatres performed his
operettas simultaneously.

"You should try your hand at operetta." Offenbach could afford
such advice to Strauss. Vienna, at that time, had no such genre. The
crude form of the "Singspiel" which had culminated in Mozart's
operas had found no echo in the lower echelons of the Vienna stage
and had all but died after the 1848 revolution. Although the Viennese flocked to Offenbach's performances, there also rankled in their
hearts the fact that Paris should rival or even surpass Vienna in anything musical. Offenbach's chance remark had fallen on eager ears.

Jetti, being a woman of the stage, was all afire with the possibilities
of a stage work by Johann, and her opinion and experience should
have carried weight. But Johann would have none of it. Having
been eminently successful in his particular sphere, he was reluctant
to leave the solid ground of the waltz and attempt a flight into the
unknown of the operetta. The leap from the compact small form to
the involved large form seemed too risky in the face of Offenbach's
supreme position. He pleaded ignorance of the stage; some of the
world's greatest composers, he argued, had failed before the challenge of the stage—look at Schubert, Schumann, even Beethoven.

But what of Suppé? Franz von Suppé, the nephew of Donizetti, had
been born in Dalmatia and educated in Italy. To the end of his days
he spoke only broken German, but had become Viennese by sub-
limating the Italian style into the Vienna theatre. Offenbach had been
the final impetus Suppé had needed. His first operetta success, *Die
schöne Galathé* (The Beautiful Galatea), was quickly followed by
Leichte Kavallerie (Light Cavalry), *Boccacio*, and *Dichter und Bauer*
(Poet and Peasant). Despite obvious inferiority to Offenbach, his
popularity grew because his work was created in Vienna and because

of the anti-French sentiment of the 1870–71 Franco-German conflict.

Johann still remained unmoved until, through a ruse, some of his melodies were sung to him with prepared texts and sounded delightful. Suddenly he knew that he had to try his hand at operetta. His eye fastened on a libretto by Josef Braun entitled *The Merry Wives of Vienna*. He started with gusto and Maximilian Steiner, impressario of the historic Theater an der Wien, delightedly offered his popular soubrette, Marie Geistinger, for the main role. Strauss had intended it for Josephine Gallmeyer, star of the rival Carltheater, who was not available. Upon hearing the news Johann's enthusiasm dissipated and he withdrew the score.

If Strauss was obstinate, Steiner was determined. With the instinct of the man of the theatre he felt that Strauss could drive Offenbach off the Vienna stage with a distinctly Viennese creation. He set to work with an army of librettists to "fabricate" a libretto. It became Strauss' lot to be constantly hampered by such concoctions which survived only by virtue of his music. The result of Steiner's collaborators was "Indigo and the Forty Thieves" (promptly dubbed by the Viennese "Indigo and the Forty librettists"). February 19, 1871 was set for the premiere and all Vienna was there. The house was sold out days in advance and even opera director Herbeck was forced to watch the performance from a camp stool in the orchestra. Vienna loved it despite Hanslick's scathing criticism of the libretto. Johann's conducting alone was a rare treat, and when he swung into the main theme, "Ja so singt man in der Stadt wo ich geboren bin" (Yes, thus We Sing in the City where I Was Born), the house began to sway with the music and rose with shouts of jubilation. What if the text was asinine and the plot fabricated. It was four hours of Johann Strauss and it loosened the greatest tumult since the premiere of Wagner's *Die Meistersinger* the previous year. The ice was broken and a deluge of unsolicited librettos started.

What interfered with further operetta composition was the venture Strauss father had dreamt of but never achieved—a tour in America. Strauss son was to add it to his conquests. Boston had had the foresight to invite Johann to its musical festival which lasted from June 17, to July 4, 1872. Johann's dread of traveling (he traveled in railroad cars sitting in the aisle and drinking champagne) was overcome by the fee of $100,000, enormous today, fabulous in 1872, plus free transportation and lodging for himself, Mrs. Strauss, and two servants, the money to be deposited in a Vienna bank in advance. It was too flattering, too exciting, too lucrative to be refused. They sailed on June 1 from Bremen on a crossing which took fourteen days to New York. Boston went all out to welcome the "Waltz King," and huge placards showing Johann's crowned head adorned all main thoroughfares. He was to play fourteen concerts in an enormous hall, built especially for the occasion, seating 100,000 people. Johann was horrified at these "continental" dimensions which almost prohibited music-making, particularly with only one (!) rehearsal scheduled before the actual performance. That fellow guests Verdi and Bülow had to face the same problem was of little comfort to him.

Six husky policemen were needed to protect him and the servant who carried his violin. Men cheered him, women kissed the hem of his coat and fought for a lock of his hair. The music space alone, at which he looked down from a wooden tower of dizzying height, was filled to overflowing with 20,000 singers plus a sizable orchestra. His heart sank as he looked down over that sea of faces hanging on his every move. A cannon shot rang out. It was the signal for Johann to relay his opening beat to one hundred sub-conductors for a semblance of an opening in unison.

> I could only hear the people immediately around me; there was no question of giving a performance in any artistic sense. How on earth was this row to be brought to an end? I shall never forget what I went through, to the end of my days. My chief concern was to wind up in some sort of style if it were humanly possible . . . Thank God I brought that off somehow and they began to applaud and cheer.

Besides his full repertoire, Strauss presented Boston with his "New Jubilee Waltz" and the "Star Spangled Banner"—in waltz tempo. Strauss "the irresistible," "the electrifying" drove Boston to the brink of happy madness and the American press was unanimous in their opinion that "Johann Strauss was the first king America was willing to crown."

Laden with treasures and indelible memories, Strauss and his entourage landed in Europe in a state of happy exhaustion. An epidemic of cholera prevented them from rushing back to Vienna and Johann wiled away his time by giving concerts for royalty at play in Baden-Baden. But he was also seriously thinking of another operetta. The libretto was an adaption of Sardou's *Carnival in Rome*. Again it was a success only because of Strauss whose lilting tunes packed the house. Despite its foreign title, it was Johann's first truly Viennese operetta and one of the great attractions of the Vienna International Exhibition of 1873. Even the great Gounod was curious enough to hear the newest Strauss opus.

One week after the exhibition opened the financial roof of Vienna caved in due to a giant bank failure. The repercussions were disastrous. The stock market was forced to close, huge enterprises collapsed, and wealthy men were beggared overnight. Suicides multiplied. Vienna had invited the world to a feast but it turned into a funeral. Police and the army had to be called out to restrain the furious masses clamoring for their vanished life-savings. But even such a catastrophe could not depress Vienna for long. The pawn shops might be crowded and the grave diggers busy, but the chestnut trees were blooming in the Prater, and Strauss had written a new waltz.

Earlier, however, Max Steiner had acquired another French farce; it was by Offenbach's own librettists, had been published as *The Supper at Midnight*, and had all the ingredients of Parisian farce—satire, comedy, conflict. But its very French flavor made it unsuitable for Vienna. Adapt it, somebody suggested. Steiner turned the play over to two clever Vienna writers, Haffner and Genee. The result was the libretto for *Die Fledermaus* (The Bat). It was one of the few books Johann was ever to enjoy and was worthy of his music. The story sparkled, and the great ball, the highlight of the operetta, solved all problems of arias, waltzes, and the like which Vienna demanded. Johann was captivated by its evident possibilities and went to work with youthful zest. Jetti turned all visitors away except Steiner, Haffner, and Genee. The inspiration of composer and librettists proved mutually intoxicating. Within forty-three days and nights, Johann Strauss created his first masterpiece for the stage, a true comic opera only one step below Mozart's *Marriage of Figaro* and Richard Strauss' *Der Rosenkavalier*, only to see it doomed by Vienna's financial collapse. The incredible happened: *Die Fledermaus* lasted for only sixteen performances. Johann's masterpiece was a Sleeping Beauty destined to be awakened by the least likely of Prince Charmings—Berlin. There it glittered in one hundred consecutive performances. Only then did Vienna awaken to its glories.

The least dismayed had been Johann who, at fifty-one had written his most youthful masterpiece. He shrugged and went on a tour of Italy replete with gala concerts and receptions. Great was his surprise when he heard of the record-breaking run in Berlin. Steiner, incredulous but encouraged, rescheduled the work and the flood gates opened. People fought for tickets, Hamburg followed with two hundred performances, and Paris delighted in the operetta of the Vienna master who, overnight, had become the prince of the musical stage. Offenbach could not stem the Strauss tide. Old and in poor health he could spare time only for his last masterpiece, *Tales of Hoffmann*, while Paris danced to Strauss' *Fledermaus*.

As Italy enthusiastically whistled and sang Strauss tunes, Johann briefly became an Italian composer with *Cagliostro in Wien*, *Das Spitzentuch der Königin* (The Queen's Lace Handkerchief), *Der Lustige Krieg* (The Merry War), and *Eine Nacht in Venedig* (One Night in Venice). But all of them were mired in a libretto morass of mistaken identities and idiotic plot which escaped failure only through Strauss' music.

Yet, when the Ringtheater burned in December 1881, only Johann's *Merry War* could raise the Viennese from the gloom of the disaster. The fire, one of the worst disasters in the history of the theatre, broke out on stage before a performance of Offenbach's *Tales of Hoffmann*, and the billowing curtain fanned it into the audience. People tried to escape in panic only to find that the doors opened to the inside. Hundreds of corpses piled up inside the exits, and it took weeks to identify the dead. The fire is credited with having inaugurated the asbestos curtain and doors opening towards the outside in theatres all over the world. Offenbach's opera was kept off the Vienna boards for years.

What, by its very title, should have been one of Johann's greatest successes, *One Night in Venice*, became one of his worst failures:

> The nature of the book is such that with the best intentions in the world I could not find inspiration in it. Its coloring is neither poetic nor humorous. It is a scatterbrained, bombastic affair without out a trace of action . . . I never saw the libretto dialogue, only the words of the songs. There I put too much nobility into some parts of it which were unfit for the whole. There is nothing in this book to which a noble interpretation could be applied. At the last rehearsal I discovered the entire story! I was simply horrified. No genuine feeling, no truth, nothing but nonsense. The music has nothing in common with such crazy, inartistic material . . . Only one thing gives me satisfaction—that it was found impossible to prevent failure in Berlin. I should rejoice still more if the whole thing was soon to be shelved. Anybody can steal it who wants to; I shall shed no tears.

This exasperated disclosure shows Johann's inept, haphazard approach as the main reason for his many failures. *Cagliostro in Wien* would have been another, a local, seasonal success doomed to oblivion, had it not been for two names—Johann Strauss and Alexander Girardi. Although of Italian ancestry, Girardi embodied every lovable Viennese trait, a sensuous flexible voice, lively mimicry, a sense of humor, and a ready wit. He had never had musical training, but an unfailing ear and memory bridged the gap. The combined artistry of Strauss and Girardi carried the day. They had much in common. Each was a genius in his own right. Both were spoiled, moody, and both longed for the gaiety of their make-believe world; they were friends, they respected each other. This did not preclude occasional rifts. In *The Merry War*, for instance, Girardi, in true prima-donna fashion, insisted that Strauss insert a special solo number for him. Strauss reluctantly acceded, and its success proved Girardi's theatrical instinct correct. The *Nature Waltz* was not only the high point of the operetta but, together with the "Fiakerlied," the greatest triumph of Girardi's career. It made him the undisputed idol of Vienna: "On your shoulders rests not only every play, but the very existence of the Theater an der Wien," wrote Strauss. "You can imagine how every author who writes for that theatre clings to you as closely as possible . . . for it is you alone who decides whether he is to be or not to be . . . Tell me how you want this. I shall not go on with my orchestration until I know your views."

No prima donna, not even the great soubrettes, Geistinger or Gallmeyer, could approach Girardi's pre-eminence in Vienna's theatrical life. As the Viennese writer Herman Bahr put it:

> For the last twenty years every actor down to the last provincial town, when he tries to be irresistible, copies the vulgar yet mysterious, quiveringly agitated voice in which Girardi speaks. That they all assume his innocently cynical glances would not mean much. But there is not a young man among us, who, when approaching a girl does not involuntarily mimic him.

Strauss' brilliant music continued to support fumbling librettos. Pressure and intrigue plus his own laxity and ineptness gave some of the best texts to Millöcker and Suppé. But Johann could afford to take his misfortunes with equanimity. He had reached the pinnacle of his career. The grandson of the inn keeper bought a chateau in Ischl, where the emperor spent his summers, a town house in Vienna, and another sylvan retreat in Lower Austria. And the musical miracle did not cease. After nearly forty years, creative invention continued at a swift pace.

At long last, however, the gods became jealous of the cup which never stopped brimming over. While life outwardly continued its mad whirl, foundations began to crack. Jetti, for one, was forced to admit that a woman ten years her husband's senior was becoming a trouble factor in the glamorous life of a man like Johann. The idol of two continents was constantly enticed by women of all walks of life, their approaches ranging from a request for a lock of his hair to an invitation to an assignation or open liaison. Johann felt himself the equal of these challenges, but Jetti at sixty-two was beyond middle age. To compound the problems, an illegitimate, blackmailing son suddenly appeared out of Jetti's past, a past unknown to Johann or rather willingly left unexplored in the rush of early passion. Death made short shrift of the deteriorating situation. After a particularly depressing letter, probably from her son, Jetti suffered a stroke. Broken in health and spirit, it was only a matter of days before she passed on.

As in the past, death was an apparition which Johann could not face. He had never been able to forget his father's naked body on the bare bed in the bare room. Now again he fled, from the house, from Vienna. He was lost. For many years his irresolute streak had been counteracted by Jetti's firm management. If re-marriage is to be the highest tribute to a previous one, then Johann paid Jetti the supreme compliment by remarrying—within six weeks! It was not one of his old flames or recent flirtations who bedazzled Johann's senses, but a stranger from Cologne, Fräulein Angelika Diettrich. Practically at first sight the celebrated, middle-aged composer lost his head to the beauty in her early twenties. While Vienna openly mocked, scoffed and shook its collective head, they were married and moved to Strauss' estate for a secluded honeymoon.

Married bliss which Johann had enjoyed for so long and to which he again eagerly looked forward soon evaporated. "Men are as young as the woman they wish to conquer," but "to conquer may lend youth, to possess demands it." There was an age difference of thirty years but, more important, the difference between a productive and an idle mind. "Lili" soon became bored at the country estate, her shallow nature craving lights, male adulation. They moved back to Vienna, to the house Jetti had planned, the house the *Fledermaus* had bought. Inevitably things began to go awry.

In such an atmosphere, the work of dispirited Johann was doomed to failure while Suppé triumphed. Determinedly Johann started again; *The Queen's Lace Handkerchief* proved a financial success but his marriage reached the brink of bankruptcy. While Johann busied himself with *The Merry War*, Lili began an insidious campaign. She renewed old "friendships" and began to spread gossip about the "old man" she had married. Ugly scenes ensued in which she openly scorned and berated the "old man." *Old*—with one word she had hurt him more than a thousand bad newspaper critiques. He had felt rejuvenated when he had married that delectable creature after months of dissension, death and mourning. He, the spoiled darling of his people, the celebrity of two continents, the creator of imperishably young music—*old?* More and more he retired from ridicule and malice to the solitude of his study, continuing his own world of illusion, attempting to escape from his strife-torn life.

The knot was cut abruptly. One day Lili simply vanished from the Strauss home while Vienna knowingly nodded its head. To add to the injury, the man she had found more attractive than her husband was Max Steiner, Johann's friend who, as director of the Theatre an der Wien, had championed Strauss' music and given it innumerable splendid performances.

Sick at heart, confused, Johann kept on working. *Simplizius Simplizissimus*, a sordid tale of the Thirty Years' War, completely unsuited for Johann's music, was such a failure that he withdrew the work from Munich and St. Petersburg where it had already been scheduled. He even asked the publisher to withdraw all sheet music. On an appropriate theme, however, he could still write effective music. Like most Viennese, Johann felt deeply for the emperor who, in 1888, at fifty-eight, had already reigned for forty years, and was lonely by virtue of his high office. The Viennese had long forgiven his early mistakes and now a nimbus of adulation began to surround him although military, political, and family misfortunes dogged his every step. Among the many wreaths of devotion laid at Franz Josef's feet, none was more heartfelt than the "Kaiserwalzer" (Emperor's Waltz) dedicated to the "Emperor of Vienna."

Strauss now found himself with two popular rivals in Vienna, Millöcker and Suppé, both of whom were successful while Johann's works failed. Satisfaction of another sort came to him. Poetic justice had finally dealt with Angelika. Steiner, who had never intended to marry the flighty creature, had deserted her. Johann, for his part, began to notice another Strauss. There had lived in the Hirschenhaus of his youth, Albert Strauss, a banker (no relative) whose experienced financial advice had often been sought by Johann. The banker's son had married a charming girl, Adele Deutsch, but died only three years after the wedding. Johann and Adele met by chance, and soon the lonely man was attracted. They began to see more of each other and mutual attraction grew. But grave obstacles loomed. Johann was Catholic, Adele Jewish, an impossible combination in Vienna. Besides, Lili still masqueraded in the role of the forsaken, misunderstood spouse.

Johann was determined. Again he visualized love and tranquility after the hectic Lili interlude and decided not to let the chance slip from his grasp. To attain his goal he took steps for which the emperor never forgave him. He temporarily took up residence in the German Duchy of Saxe-Coburg-Gotha, turned Protestant, and started divorce proceedings against Lili. After the law had disposed of Lili, the marriage of Johann and Adele was performed in Germany. As a Protestant, Johann would never again conduct at the emperor's ball, but, apparently more important, at fifty-eight, he had recaptured his "third youth."

The well which had bubbled so richly began to flow again. While in later years the proverbial blackness of Johann's hair had to be maintained by artificial means, the laughter of his music, the sparkle of his eye needed no stimulant but the elixir of musical invention and Adele's love. And Cagliostro's words, "Könnt ich mit dir durchs Leben fliegen" (could I but fly through life with you), ended his love letters to the woman who had made his third marriage "the best of all." The house in Vienna became home again. There he was surrounded by Adele's loving care and the mementos of Strauss fame, portraits, busts, the violin of his father, innumerable laurel wreaths, and music, music everywhere. There he again received, with Adele by his side, Vienna society which flocked to his soirees.

His mood infected all who came in contact with him. Bülow, bitter and morose, relaxed in Johann's presence, placed Beethoven symphonies and Strauss waltzes on the same program. Liszt, who liked Strauss melodies best, next to Schubert's, frequently improvised on them. Wagner played Strauss pieces four-handed with his daughter and even conducted them on occasion. When Johann went to Bayreuth he may have nodded with satisfaction on hearing the Waltz of the Flower Maidens in Wagner's *Parsifal*. Mahler produced the *Fledermaus* in Hamburg and Vienna, Rubinstein played the waltzes with his robust enthusiasm, but Alfred Grünfeld, the Viennese pianist, was Johann's favorite interpreter on the piano. To him he dedicated his waltz "Voices of Spring" and, after hearing him play it, exclaimed: "That waltz isn't really as beautiful as it seems when you play it." There was perhaps no greater Strauss admirer than Brahms whose friendship bordered on adulation. It was he who asked for one of Johann's manuscripts for his collection. When Adele's daughter asked him for an autograph on her fan he inscribed it with the opening bars of the "Blue Danube" and the words "Leider nicht von Brahms" (Unfortunately not by Brahms).

It was at that happy time in his life that Johann's eye fastened on Maurus Jókai's novel *Saffi*. He had always been an enthusiastic admirer of Hungary's devil-may-care men and its dazzling women. The playing of the Hungarian gypsy, the unrestrained sobbing of his violin touched his heart. For once he realized the immense possibilities of the combination of Maria Theresia's baroque era and the gypsy milieu. Unhesitatingly he approached the Viennese writer and journalist Ignatz Schnitzer for libretto adaptation. Schnitzer suggested the perfect title *Der Zigeunerbaron* (The Gypsy Baron).

For once Johann approached composition with forethought and care. To insure perfection and harmony between spoken word and musical invention, Schnitzer, a master in his own right, insisted that Strauss compose first while he in turn would fit the words to the music. Completion took two years, and the workmanship surpassed even *Die Fledermaus*. The *Gypsy Baron* had every ingredient one might wish for. There was a touch of opera, the tears of love and joy and sorrow so dear to Viennese hearts, the universality of the waltz, and, above all, the dashing czardas of Hungary. The premiere on October 24, 1885 was a triumph. The audience laughed and wept, raved, shouted, sobbed, screamed, stamped and applauded the glorious occasion. With Strauss conducting and Girardi in the main comic role, Vienna went wild. Not since the "Blue Danube" and the *Fledermaus* had Vienna seen such enthusiasm, after so many near-misses.

But now success disturbed Johann as much as setbacks. "Strauss Jubilees" began to crop up all over Europe. While he was willing to accept the honors, he was less keen on being reminded that he had already fiddled and composed for forty years, a time span not in agreement with his youthful image. But he knew of no escape and "suffered" gracefully. Vienna led all others in joyfully proclaiming his first appearance at Dommayer's. Congratulations rained from all of Europe. A jubilee performance at which he conducted turned into happy bedlam. The world was truly at his feet. It was still at his feet ten years later at the fiftieth anniversary. Johann, his beloved Adele by his side, acknowledged the accolades, the outpouring of love and veneration with a mixture of joy, melancholy, and discomfort.

There remained only one regret in this picture of bliss. Strauss had always harbored the secret desire to write a "serious" work. He had reached a point where he could afford to pursue artistic aims without regard for monetary considerations or popular whims. And that aim was nothing less than an opera. He briefly considered a Shakespearean text but was suddenly dazzled by the play *The Kiss* by the Hungarian writer Doczi which enjoyed a brief success at the Burgtheater. The result was *Ritter Pazman* (The Knight Pazman).

Vienna did him the honor of a production at the Imperial Opera. No expense was spared, a star cast assembled, a gala production mounted. Although the mountains moved, only a mouse was born. Hanslick, by now an ardent Strauss fan, put it succinctly: "What we miss in this higher sphere is not the accomplished man of taste and first-class musician—but simply our old beloved Johann Strauss." The opera folded after nine performances. No man ever took defeat in better spirit: "One thing I am glad of and that is that no one accused me of triviality . . . In any case I set more store by the smallest of opera successes of mine than by anything else." Shades of Schubert who died thinking of himself as an opera composer while throwing away immortal songs.

But music Strauss had to write, and back he went to the things he knew best. *Princess Ninetta* was light fare again, and Vienna loved it. Emperor Franz Josef attended and personally received Vienna's aging darling: "I have enjoyed myself immensely . . . It is very curious, but your music ages as little as you do. You have not changed at all although it is a long time since I saw you last. I congratulate you on your new opera."

If the experor had remarked that Strauss had remained unchanged, Vienna had not. After the razing of the walls and outer fortifications, the suburbs had been incorporated into the city and Gross-Wien, Greater Vienna, emerged. Perhaps the greatest change was the emergence of the middle and working classes as social, political, and artistic forces. "People's concerts" started; a second opera house opened and was destined to create great singers and memorable performances.

Johann watched it all from his studio window. He too had entered into a new field. Hanslick had pronounced the ballet from *Ritter Pazman* the "crowning jewel of the opera" and had suggested that Strauss join the ranks of famous ballet composers. Johann was enthused about the idea and started work on "Aschenbrödel" (Cinderella) when he heard that Mahler would consider it for the Vienna Opera. His studio began to hum again. A celebrity of such renown, however, could not entirely shut himself away from an admiring public. During a matinee he conducted the overture to the *Fledermaus*, caught a cold in the drafty house, and left the theatre feeling chilled. Despite heavy perspiration and lightheadedness he continued work on "Cinderella" until three o'clock in the morning. The next morning he awoke with high fever which developed into double pneumonia. The truth was kept from him, but he soon became delirious. On June 3, 1899 he awoke and found Adele, as always, by his side. He kissed her hands and sank to eternal rest.

Vienna, Europe's gay city, wept. Its citizens, from street cleaner to emperor, mourned. The streets were silent, only Vienna's churches tolled their message of grief and loss; 100,000 people paid homage, the greatest outpouring since the death of Austria's greatest poet, Grillparzer, and the floral tributes appeared "as if the gardens of Vienna were being carried to the grave." The world and Vienna had reason to mourn. An era, a way of life had been laid to rest. Brahms and Bruckner had died three years earlier. Johann rested close to Brahms and Schubert as the Singverein intoned Brahms' "Fahr wohl."

An era had ended but the waltz lived on. Only five years later a young Hungarian stood at the lectern of the Theater an der Wien anxiously peering across the footlights as he conducted an operetta of his own. It was not his first, but *Die lustige Witwe* (The Merry Widow) was to be Franz Lehar's most famous. Vienna caught fire again. *The Merry Widow* was one of the few worthy successors of *Die Fledermaus* and *Gypsy Baron*. It was universal operetta whose waltzes the Austrians as well as the Hungarians or Prussians and the rest of the world could understand. Others tried their hand and succeeded to a lesser degree. There was Oscar Straus (with the one *s*) who, after failing to become a German Offenbach in Berlin, returned to Vienna and success with his *Walzertraum* (Waltz Dream). Leo Fall and Edmund Eysler registered seasonal successes in a form which was becoming increasingly commercialized. Emmerich Kálmán, a compatriot of Lehar, was a notch above the rest and proved it with his *Countess Maritza*. But only collectively did they approach the musical phenomenon that had been Johann Strauss.

Since Josef's death in 1870, Eduard Strauss had been the sole conductor of the orchestra and the main propagator of Straussian "Schmiss und Schmalz." But the name of Johann remained unforgotten, and to his undisguised disgust Eduard found himself repeatedly mistaken for his brother. Like all Strausses Eduard was a true musician who rose above the confining three-quarter time by including Beethoven, Mozart, Schubert, Wagner, and Weber in his programs. Neither cholera, rheumatism nor tornadoes could keep him from engagements which culminated in 1890 in a tour of seventy-three United States cities. But to his surprise, Eduard found that the Americans who cheered his waltzes could no longer dance them.

John Philip Sousa had overnight become America's idol. The waltz had been supplanted by the march, the salon orchestra by the band.

The two-step was soon to invade Europe with jazz not far behind. While Sousa's star rose, Eduard's personal fortunes dwindled due to unlucky speculations by his wife and sons. Once again in 1900, one year after Johann's death, Eduard went on another American tour to recoup his fortune. But monetary pressure rather than the spirit of music had prompted the exhausting journey and poisoned his joy in music. Upon return he disbanded the famous Strauss orchestra.

Sousa came to Vienna after triumphs in Paris, Brussels, Berlin, Warsaw, and St. Petersburg. When he asked, "Is the 'Blue Danube' still popular here?" he was told it would "endure as long as Vienna stands." He opened his concert with Austria's unofficial anthem and Vienna cheered the gesture. The magic remains. A few bars of "Tales from the Vienna Woods" or the "Blue Danube," and Vienna is conjured up in glowing grace. Every heart lifts to a Strauss tune in that three-quarter time which floated out of smoky taverns by the Danube to span the earth.

XV

The Critic

The conversation turned to Wagner, and the face of the dapper little man turned grim as he said: "He seems constantly on the verge of running out of breath." But as somebody in the crowd mentioned the name of Brahms, his eyes shone; "a national treasure," he remarked. The speaker was Eduard Hanslick, one of the foremost music critics of a time when Wagner and Verdi, Dvořák and Rimski-Korsakov, Tchaikovsky and Brahms, Grieg, Franck, Bruckner, and Johann Strauss created side by side. And through the eyes, ears, and pen of one of the great musicological minds of his day, these giants appeared even then in proper proportion.

Despite his study of the law, Hanslick was early drawn to a barely touched facet of musical culture—musical criticism, music appreciation, and the modern historical approach, a field opened by Robert Schumann. With his first critique in 1844 of Gluck's *Armide*, Hanslick started a custom he was to follow for fifty years: "I never criticized a composition that I had not read or played through, both before and after the performance." When he heard Wagner's *Tannhäuser* at a time when the opera was still unknown in Vienna, he set out to acquaint the Viennese with the work by writing an enthusiastic analysis which ran for eleven (!) installments in the *Wiener Musik-zeitung* and started him on his way.

Vienna's cultural life of the moment was at low ebb. "Musical life was dominated by Italian opera and the waltz," Hanslick later recalled. "This sweetly intoxicating three-quarter time to which heads as well as feet were abandoned, combined with Italian opera and the cult of virtuosity, rendering listeners steadily less capable of intellectual effort." Hanslick came to Vienna from Prague at a significant moment in the city's history.

The year 1848 marked the borderline between the old and the new Austria—not only in political and social matters but also in the literary and artistic life of the nation. The way had been prepared, partly in the nature of growing dissatisfaction with musical life as it was, partly in a growing sense of need for something more substantial and elevated . . . The public had not only grown tired of superficial bravura, it had also grown tired of its own enthusiasm. The intoxication it had indulged in for the better part of a decade under the stimulus of Liszt and Thalberg . . . could not be continued indefinitely . . . The brilliant but fleeting phenomenon of the Philharmonic concerts under Nicolai had made the darkness only more perceptible by contrast . . . No notice was taken of the new creative talent in Germany . . . Wagner was almost unknown. Mendelssohn was given only a belated hearing in Vienna after his "St. Paul" had been performed in the smallest provincial cities of Germany and even in America.

Before settling in Vienna, Hanslick had visited the capital and had met Liszt and composer-conductor Otto Nicolai. He had found the city still walled and unattractive, but social and musical contacts had proven stimulating. His favorable if lengthy *Tannhäuser* review established his name in musically petrified Vienna and started him on his vocation. This despite the doctorate of law which he received in 1849 and public service in the provinces. It was not until 1852, when he returned to Vienna, that he was able to combine a position at the Ministry of Finance with duties as music editor of the *Wiener Zeitung*, the official court newspaper, and a post with the university department of the Ministry of Education, a strenuous but rewarding routine. Somewhat later he made an important move to the newly founded *Neue Freie Presse*, destined to become one of Vienna's foremost newspapers.

Until the advent of the great newspapers, journalism in Vienna was a shoddy and shady business. Publishers sided with the party that paid the most, even stooping as low as blackmail. Debutantes paid a fixed price for "spontaneous admiration," and tenors were resigned to pay a set fee according to their fame for reports of "jubilant acclaim." Even men high in the government were not above paying to keep defamatory remarks (true or untrue), shown to them in proofs, from appearing in the papers.

Oblivious to the "revolver press," Hanslick devoted himself to studies in musical aesthetics which bore fruit in his famous discussion "Vom musikalisch Schönen" (The Beautiful in Music) which was to propel him into his famous lecture series at the Vienna University. Upon final appointment as professor extraordinary he was able to relinquish public service and devote all of his time to music criticism which covered most major events.

Hanslick disliked hurried reviews. To leave before the third act or before the final selection in order to make a deadline was unthinkable. Eventually he even refused overnight coverage because "such hastily conceived opinion could be arrived at only at the cost of objectivity." In the years to follow he devoted his time to the events of Vienna—the Imperial Opera, the Philharmonic concerts and the concerts of the Gesellschaft der Musikfreunde, and performances of the world's leading artists—and major events in Germany and Italy. He thus observed post-revolutionary Vienna and its atmosphere of spiritual and physical bloom. Vienna in turn witnessed the emergence of one of the most volatile champions of "absolute" music.

With his review of *Lohengrin* the early champion turned into an intelligently outspoken foe of Wagner. The feud was to reach a climax with Wagner's undisguised caricature of Hanslick in the figure of Beckmesser in his opera *Die Meistersinger*.

In many respects Hanslick was the ideal critic. With high principles, searching, capable of sound judgement and enjoyment and praise in his field, his views were clear-eyed and unobscured by the musical fashion of the day: Marschner's and Spohr's "creative span is finished. The fresh bloom of song has withered, the youthful fantasy grown old." Lortzing, the darling of Vienna, "is not for serious Grand Opera." Flotow "may yet accomplish something superior to his overrated 'Stradella'." One of his stings was reserved for Meyerbeer: "For years he has been carrying 'Le Prophete' in his suitcase between Berlin and Paris, possibly in an effort to determine whether prophets may travel duty-free."

Not only composers came under Hanslick's careful scrutiny. His critical pen also dissected the contemporary performing artists who paraded across Vienna's footlights: Vieuxtemps "is the greatest among contemporary violinists save Joachim," yet his concertos "do not rank with the truly great examples of instrumental composition." Clara Schumann "should be called the greatest living pianist . . . were the range of her physical strength not limited by her sex." One of his most painful barbs was launched at Franz Liszt:

> It was his desire that the composer should overshadow the virtuoso; it seems more likely that the musical world has suffered, in the virtuoso's abdication, a loss which the composer's succession can hardly replace . . . His piano compositions were consistently of such mediocre invention and execution that barely one of them could have claimed a lasting place in musical literature . . . Brassy noise interpreted as profundity . . . artificially distilled . . . Only those who do not know the works of Berlioz and Wagner [!] could mistake Liszt for a musical discoverer and reformer.

A fellow pianist and pupil of Liszt, Tausig, fared no better: "Not a single piece left a pure, satisfying, or even deep impression . . . he labors as if he had to chip frozen notes out of ice . . . Excited massacres are followed by long periods of indifference."

But when Schubert's "Unfinished" Symphony received its belated due after forty years of enforced slumber, Hanslick gloried: "Every heart rejoiced as if, after a long separation, the composer himself were with us in person . . . a crystal clear melodic stream where one can see every pebble . . . everywhere the same warmth, the same bright, life-giving sunshine . . . simple basic tone effects which no refinement of Wagnerian instrumentation can capture."

While he inevitably turned against Wagner, he continued to praise the German master whenever he felt praise was due: *Die Meistersinger* is "a remarkable creation, uniquely consistent . . . extremely earnest, novel in structure, rich in imagination and even brilliant in characterization, often tiring and exasperating but always unusual . . . its virtues cannot be denied." Other Wagner creations evoked his wrath: *Tristan und Isolde* "reminds me of the old Italian painting of that martyr whose intestines were slowly unwound from his body unto a reel."

As Hanslick withdrew from the neo-German camp it was inevitable that he should find solace in the champion of "pure" music, Johannes Brahms. He called the First Symphony

> one of the most individual and magnificent works of the symphonic literature . . . no composer approached the style of Beethoven as Brahms has done in this finale . . . he seems to favor the great and the serious, the difficult, the complex at the expense of sensuous beauty . . . having touched on minor reservations, I can continue in this jubilant manner in which I began. The new symphony of Brahms is a treasure of which the nation can be proud, an inexhaustible font of sincere pleasure and fruitful study.

Wagnerites saw their "god" as a dramatic giant as well as composer. The most zealous of Wagner apostles, Hans Paul Freiherr von Wolzogen, went so far as to proclaim that Goethe and Schiller had been surpassed by Wagner, his dramas having antiquated theirs. In the face of such hot-eyed partisanship, Hanslick attempted to retain a sense of fairness. When all of Wagner's *Ring des Nibelungen* was performed in August 1876, Hanslick reported:

> An extraordinary theatrical experience and much more. This four-evening long music drama is a remarkable development in cultural history . . . The descriptive power of Wagner's fantasy

. . . the astonishing feat of his orchestral technique and many musical beauties exert a magic power to which we surrender readily and gratefully.

Hanslick, however, was not the man of the grandly empty phrase. His intellect moved him to look deeper into Wagner's cycle. His review devoted four separate articles to it, entitled "Stage Festival," "The Theatre," "The Music," and "Production and General Impressions."

> [*Das Rheingold*] . . . deceit, prevarication, violence and animal sensuality . . . not a single ray of moral feeling . . . indigestible German, stammered and offered as poetry . . . This exalted god [Wotan] who never knows what is needed, never does the right thing, who gives way in the first drama to a stupid giant, in the second to his domineering wife and in the third to an impudent youth, should this unctuous pedent be revered as the godly ideal of the German people?

> [*Die Walküre*] . . . great dramatic and musical beauties . . . moral revulsion at so ecstatic an exhibit of incest.

> [*Siegfried*] . . . dramatically the weakest . . . the two principal figures border on caricature, the dragon fight on comedy . . . only the third act reaches dramatic heights . . . [Siegfried is] not a hero but a puppet . . . a magic potion which restores to this simpleton the memory of all the stupidities he had committed in his state of enchantment is a theme better suited for comedy. In tragedy, where a moral will must dominate, it becomes an absurdity.

> [*Götterdämmerung*] . . . genuine musical situations, forceful exposition and a steady stream of tension and suspence to the very end.

While he refused, to the howling of the Wagner clique, to be led up the primrose path, he readily succumbed to Wagner's "Forest Murmurs": "Here Wagner's virtuosity as a tone painter enjoys its most genuine triumph . . . a fidelity to nature achieved by neither Haydn nor Beethoven."

Yet he was only too glad to re-enter the field of "true" music. When Brahms' Second Symphony was premiered in Vienna in 1877 by Hans Richter, he reveled. ". . . radiant with healthy freshness and clarity . . . after the Faustian struggle in his I. symphony he has turned again to the blossoms of spring."

The subject of Wagner, however, was to occupy Hanslick critically for forty years:

> [In *Parsifal*] the composer seems perpetually on the verge of running out of breath . . . from tedious narration to sensuous ardor, from ardor to religious ecstasy . . . always in flight from everything beautiful and moderate in music . . . The episode of the flower maidens . . . belongs to Wagner's happiest inspirations . . . that is something one must see and hear for it achieves the purest effects through the simplest means . . . If we regard *Parsifal* as a festive magic opera, if we ignore . . . its logical and psychological impossibilities and its false religious pretensions, we can find in it moments of artistic stimulation and brilliant effectiveness.

No such kind words for *Tristan und Isolde*:

> From tragedy we demand above all that its characters act of their own free will . . . the origin of their fate must lie within themselves. Romeo and Juliet, Hero and Leander . . . needed no magic potion. The tragic fate of Tristan and Isolde had its source in a mistake for which neither is responsible. They are helpless victims—and thus the very opposite of tragic heroes.

Inevitably the word "moral" emerges as the key to Hanslick's critical aims. His was not bland appraisal or cursory examination. He searched for intrinsic values and standards. Thus the babble of pseudo-German alliteration, to which Wagner gave equal artistic importance with his music, was unerringly shown up as fabrication: ". . . stammering, stuttering language, murderous of thought and speech . . . bombastic monologue and dialogue, devoid of any sort of delicacy of feeling . . . appealing melodic buds, quickly drowned in the quicksands of declamation . . . Endless melodizing is no more equivalent to melody than thinking is to thought."

During the concert season to which Hanslick looked forward with the relish of a gourmet to a sumptuous repast, no facet escaped his scrutiny. He could glow or be biting with tongue in cheek:

> [Brahms' symphonies] never deny their kinship of ideals to Beethoven, a factor much more obvious with Brahms than with Mendelssohn or Schumann . . . It is like a dark well, the longer we look into it, the brighter the stars shine back.

> [Anton Rubinstein] played like a god; we do not take it amiss if, from time to time, he changes, like Jupiter, into a bull.

On the occasion of Verdi's triumphant *Otello* at La Scala, Hanslick again demonstrated his remarkable sense of integrity. Although he was present at the world-wide tribute to Verdi at the premiere, he preferred to withhold his appraisal until the glittering atmosphere of adulation had passed. "It was my intention to acquaint myself with the work, not to participate in a festival. The electric atmosphere is not conducive to the exercise of dispassionate judgment. To appraise the opera more objectively . . . I considered the twentieth performance better suited than the first."

But Hanslick's critical discipline deserted him in his dislike for the music of Wagner admirer Anton Bruckner. After the premiere of Bruckner's Eighth Symphony, he exploded into tirade:

> . . . tossed about between intoxication and desolation . . . dismal long-windedness—occasional flashes of genius . . . a model of tastelessness . . . a storm of ovation, innumerable recalls, laurel wreaths, etc. . . . for Bruckner the concert was certainly a huge success.

No touch of Wagnerian spirit escaped him, and Humperdinck's opera *Hänsel and Gretel* was no exception:

> The naivete of the fairy tale . . . resists the contrived Wagnerian style . . . an artificial orchestration . . . music directly derived from the "Ring" accompanies the children while they pick strawberries.

A special kind of wrath was reserved by the champion of "pure" music for the "program music" of young Richard Strauss, such as his tone poem "Don Juan":

> . . . use of purely instrumental music merely as a means of describing things . . . not to write music . . . a virtuosity in the creation of sound effects beyond which it is nearly impossible to go. Color is everything, musical thought nothing. Virtuosity in orchestration has become a vampire sapping the creative power of our composers . . . a tumult of brilliant daubs, a faltering tonal orgy, half bacchanalia, half witches' sabbath . . . exquisite skillfulness.

Wagner's death was deeply felt by Hanslick who, despite mental, moral, and musical reservations, had never denied Wagner's genius. In later years he felt a need for clarification of his views:

> I and others who share my views would probably have written more dispassionately about Wagner had our pulses not been agitated by the immoderate, often ludicrous excesses of our adversaries . . . I readily confess that in my case that may have happened from time to time . . . After having spoken my mind on Wagner for forty years, my task is finished . . . there is nothing new to be said on the subject. I would be as lacking in taste as the Wagnerites themselves if I were to make every pro-

duction of "Tristan" or "The Ring" the occasion for reopening the subject.

It was inevitable that Hanslick should comment on another genius of his time—Johann Strauss. Hanslick's words on Strauss' most famous composition, still warm our hearts: "A symbol of everything that is beautiful and gay in Vienna . . . a national anthem which honors the country and the people . . . a wordless Marseillaise of peace." Hanslick's verbal wreath at Strauss' bier is equally touching.

> Vienna has lost its most original musical talent. The sources of his melodic invention were . . . inexhaustible, his rhythms pulsated with animated variety, his harmonies and forms were pure and straightforward . . . We have lost not merely a brilliant talent, a herald of Vienna's musical fame . . . He was a last symbol of cheerful, pleasant times.

"A herald of Vienna's musical fame"—the words aptly referred also to the man who spoke them.

XVI

Vanishing Breed

While Strauss fiddled and Vienna danced, while Brahms philosophized and Goldmark invoked the intoxicating sounds of the Orient, there wandered through Vienna a man oblivious to all the gaiety and glamor, sensuousnes and decay. Wrapped in the cloak of music and the hood of religion, Anton Bruckner always remained a stranger to Vienna.

He was always hungry, for food in his early years, for kindness and recognition all his life. For six exhausting years he had traveled back and forth between the Lower-Austrian city of Linz, where he was cathedral organist, and the capital of Vienna. There he studied for untold hours the entire range of theory with Simon Sechter. The same Sechter who would have been the teacher of Schubert, shaped Bruckner's musical thinking just as Bruckner was destined to link Vienna's baroque traditions to the progressive thoughts of Mahler and Schönberg. Sechter became Brucker's first stepping stone into Vienna, but Vienna wanted no part of Bruckner. His petition for the position of court organist was rejected as was his application to the university for a chair of lecturer on composition. The hand of Hanslick could be detected in the latter rejection.

Sechter's death finally opened the door. Under conductor Herbeck's insistent prodding, Bruckner finally left the precarious shelter of the provincial capital to become Sechter's successor at the famous Vienna Conservatory. Herbeck also arranged for a five-hundred florin stipend from the Ministry of Education and a foothold at the imperial court as deputy organist. Such was the disinterest of the court that ten more years were to elapse before the composer was elevated to the position of first organist.

With typical peasant stubbornness Bruckner attempted again in 1874 to obtain a university appointment, and eventually the unpaid chair of lecturer on harmony and counterpoint was bestowed upon him, a position similar to Hanslick's first university chair. The appointment was made over Hanslick's strenuous objections. Bruckner's first fearful thought after hearing of the honor was "Hanslick will never forgive me."

Max Graf, one of Vienna's foremost music historians, once studied under Bruckner and has left us a description of his teacher: When Bruckner entered the classroom he bowed low and often, his face crinkling in delight over the solemn foot-stamping of the students, a distinctly Viennese mark of approval and applause. He repeatedly started his lectures by praising those who had made possible his early successes and displayed undisguised pleasure at reading his first favorable critiques. After one especially successful performance of his Te Deum in Berlin, he furtively whispered, "Just imagine, gentlemen, one of the honorable critics wrote I was a second Beethoven. Good Lord, how can anyone say such a thing," and he quickly made the sign of the cross as if to atone for the sin of self-praise. So deeply was he immersed in the faith of his fathers that when during a lecture a nearby church bell tolled the Angelus, he would kneel down amid the multitude of his students and pray amid their reverent silence: "I [Graf] have never seen anyone pray as Bruckner did. He seemed to be transfigured, illuminated from within . . . he looked like an aged Saint . . . His face humble and blissful, refulgent with celestial light." The prayer ended, Bruckner would rise and continue his lecture.

The university appointment coincided with Bruckner's first successes, particularly the Te Deum. When he had arrived in Vienna at the age of forty-four, he had already composed three Masses and one symphony. By then Brahms had also settled in Vienna and achieved his climactic triumph with the Requiem. Thanks to cliques and cohorts, the needless battle lines were soon drawn. Depending on who debated the issue, Bruckner either became "The apostle of divine inspiration" and Brahms the "dry formalist," or Brahms "heir to Vienna's classicists, the equal of Beethoven" and Bruckner "that mad Wagnerian."

Bruckner had first met Wagner in 1865 at the premiere of *Tristan*. He was immediately drawn to Wagner and his music, and visited Bayreuth no less than five times to see, hear, and speak to its creator. Flattered by such undisguised adulation, Wagner went so far as to praise Bruckner's symphonies. In later years, Cosima Wagner remembered her husband's favorable impression and honored Bruckner by inviting him to play the organ at the funeral of her father, Liszt.

In the gay, frivolous Vienna of the 1860's, Bruckner was an oddity. The stocky figure on short legs, the shambling gait, the bold large head, the face, criss-crossed by innumerable lines, was in odd contrast to the flamboyant dress of the military and the aristocracy. He was the antithesis of anything Viennese. Where the Vienna artist sported flowing beard and mane, Bruckner was close-cropped and his face smoothly shaven. A soft hat was his constant companion rather than the fashionable high hat, the snuff box instead of the "Virginia," the long slender cigar of Vienna. His clothes, particularly the trousers, were always too wide, flapping about his body. The picture of the grotesque, bowing and scraping provincial was completed by a tobacco-stained colored handkerchief protruding from the hip pocket and a perpetual look of innocent surprise in the deep-set blue eyes.

Unaware of, untouched by the Vienna of Johann Strauss, Bruckner continued in the deep-rooted ways of his youth with manners and beliefs unchanged. His time and his nature never met. Nor could he reconcile the sturdiness of his physique which withstood years of deprivation with his nervous sensitivity, or his pious beliefs with his constant amorous attempts which even old age could not diminish. Today Bruckner's behavior can be explained through the scientific approach of a fellow Viennese whose name has become a household word—Siegmund Freud. Grotesque, ridiculed, beset by an inferiority complex of vast proportions, Bruckner sought refuge in religion and music.

Although rockbound in musical beliefs, he was unsure in daily contacts and conversation, and completely naive in his approach to the opposite sex, although since the age of six he had been singularly attracted to maidens in their teens. Unlike Brahms, who avidly participated in the political, intellectual, and artistic exchanges of the day, Bruckner shambled through Vienna unaware of and unaffected by military and political events, human progress, or intellectual awakening. The clashes within his nature brought on several nervous breakdowns and once carried him to the brink of insanity. In that state he exhibited a morbid curiosity about corpses, widows, and crosses. He sought to view the remains of Maximilian of Habsburg after the body had been returned to Vienna from Mexico and insisted on being present when the body of Beethoven was exhumed for transfer to a grave of honor.

Aside from his questionable forays on the distaff side, Bruckner enjoyed the company of young people. It may have been his undisguised longing for the company of youth, coupled with his thorough knowledge and quaint delivery, which made him an immediate success as lecturer. (When Bruckner took his qualifying exam in 1861 at the Vienna Conservatory, Hellmesberger was so impressed that he exclaimed to Sechter and Dessoff: "He should have examined us. If I knew half of what he knows I'd be happy.") At concerts he was invariably among the students in the standing-room section, while

Brahms held sway in the director's box. Yet a large number of musical great were to proudly name Bruckner their teacher: great conductors Mottl and Nikisch, Franz Schalk and Ferdinand Loewe and the young Gustav Mahler among them.

The gulf which separates Bruckner and Brahms, aside from their different intellectual pursuits, may be found in their divergent basic religious beliefs as expressed in their music. While Brahms' "German Requiem" remained one of the few towering creations of the Protestant faith, Bruckner was the last composer dominated by the spirit of the Catholic Church. Just as Fux had been a lonely contrapuntal rock among the streams of Renaissance opera, so Bruckner remained a solemn crag enveloped by the incense clouds of a past era. "Bruckner originated in the sphere of influence of Emperor Franz . . . medievalism, grown grey, fearfully shut off from Europe, held motionless in intellectual stagnation," wrote Ernst Decsey. Jesuit influence still hindered creative impulses, and opposition to enlightened ideas was one of the reasons for the long delay in acceptance of Wagner's music in Vienna.

As late as 1885 only two major works of Bruckner had appeared in print. Even at his death, despite belated honors, two of his symphonies remained unpublished. This slow progress must be partly attributed to his timidity which carried over into his creative habits. After laboriously creating his gigantic epics over many years, Bruckner remained unsure of their final form. How diligently he labored is illustrated by the first version of his First Symphony in C minor, done in Linz at age forty-two, and the final version completed in his sixty-seventh year. Thus one is confronted with three versions of his Second Symphony and four versions of his Third. Sometimes disciples would take it upon themselves to "improve" the works, but sometimes a mere adverse newspaper review would send Bruckner scurrying back to his room and renewed revisions.

All those well-meant, ill-conceived "improvements" could not make Bruckner more palatable to the Viennese. Hanslick sneered that he composed "like a drunkard," and everybody took Hanslick's cue. In 1885 the composer withdrew his Seventh Symphony from the Vienna Philharmonic in order not to jeopardize his German successes by the inevitable criticism in Vienna by Hanslick and Brahms. Bruckner was dismayed but undaunted. Like Bach he considered music an instrument to extol the glory of God, and his Ninth Symphony is dedicated "Zum Lieben Gott" (To the Dear Lord). Blessed are the meek—in the end the humble master was to be vindicated.

In 1886 Emperor Franz Josef finally saw fit to honor Austria's great 62-year-old son. Suddenly honors were heaped upon the quaint man who had labored so diligently in the shadows. Although artistic appreciation beyond Johann Strauss was alien to the emperor, he underwrote publication of Bruckner's Eighth Symphony (the grateful composer immediately dedicated the symphony to his monarch), and the Austrian parliament bestowed an honorary stipend of four hundred gulden.

After much of the usual intrigue and red tape, Bruckner received the honor he coveted most, the title of honorary Doctor of Philosophy of the University of Vienna. It was the greatest moment in his recognition-starved life when the famous physicist Exner addressed him before the assembled faculty and student body of the second-oldest university in the world: "I, the Rector Magnificus of the University of Vienna pay humble homage to the former assistant teacher of Windhaag."

Overnight Vienna "discovered" Bruckner's gigantic creations and found them to its liking—long after Berlin, Leipzig, and Munich had acclaimed them. The change in Vienna, surprisingly, was brought about by a man who had helped delay Bruckner's recognition. Hans Richter, Vienna's musical power at that time, was at first openly allied with the Brahms camp. Even his occasional gestures in Bruckner's direction were so insincere as to border on the malicious. Bruckner called him "the generalissimo of deceit." After conductors Levi, Nikisch, and Ochs had scored triumphs with Bruckner's music, however, Richter had a change of heart. From then on his finest efforts went into Bruckner performances. The result was that between 1886 and 1894 he conducted the Vienna premieres of Bruckner's First, Second, Third, Fourth, Seventh, and Eighth symphonies and the Te Deum.

The years of privation and disappointment finally began to take their toll. In 1890 Bruckner fell ill and had to be relieved of his duties at the conservatory and the imperial chapel. He was partially compensated when he was made an honorary member of the famed Gesellschaft der Musikfreunde of which Brahms was a director. Innate peasant strength asserted itself, however, over and over again. While friends feared the worst, Bruckner summoned strength to continue work on his Ninth Symphony, rose from the sickbed to travel with Hugo Wolf to Berlin to hear a performance of his Seventh Symphony, and again he rallied to attend a performance of his Fifth Symphony by Mahler in Graz, and once more to celebrate his seventieth birthday at Steyr among friends and to receive the key to the city of Linz. Even after all outside activities had ceased, he continued his unceasing labor on his final symphony.

But his state of health was not the only bad news. Prolonged illness had sapped his meager savings. When this became known, Vienna rose to the emergency. The Ministry of Education presented a cash donation, and the emperor offered Bruckner free residence for life in a cottage on the grounds of the Belvedere Palace. The composer gratefully moved there from his candle-lit, fourth-floor walk-up apartment and doggedly continued work on the Ninth Symphony. But amid the newly won comforts of life, belated honors, and signs of devotion, Bruckner weakened physically and mentally. He suffered hallucinations and became less and less rational. Although constantly visited by his disciples, he was overheard to murmur: "Alone, all alone, no music anywhere." Funeral services were held in the magnificent Karlskirche, right under the windows of Brahms who was to follow Bruckner to the grave only six months later. A final tragi-comic gesture sheds light on Vienna officialdom. Hugo Wolf, Bruckner's devoted friend and disciple, was not admitted to the funeral ceremony because he could not present a ticket of admission or an invitation.

As a student at the Vienna Academy of Music, before hearing Bruckner's Fifth Symphony for the first time, this writer prepared by buying a second-hand copy of the score. Listening to a magnificent performance by the Vienna Philharmonic, entranced by the work's noble message, building to the awe-inspiring climax of the exalted finale, the writer turned page after page of the voluminous score. On the last page an unknown hand had written the words which sum up Bruckner's music and credo—"And the Heavens opened."

XVII

Songs at Twilight

One day old Josef Hellmesberger, the director of Vienna's famed conservatory received a note threatening him with assassination. It was signed "Hugo Wolf." It was the last school prank young Hugo was to play because it was the last school from which he was to be expelled. He had come to the music capital in 1875 because nothing but music interested him and also because his father had felt that the supervision of an aunt there would have a restraining influence. Nothing of the sort, for Hugo. His spirit was too soaring, his temper too short, and academic courses too dull. Mostly self-taught, he roamed the city and filled his mind with the creations of the opera and the court theatre.

His first gods, Meyerbeer and Schiller, paled before Wagner who came to Vienna in 1875 to prepare the production of *Tannhäuser*. Hugo Wolf was desperate to meet Wagner. But when he was finally received, the great man, resplendent in fur-trimmed housecoat, glanced at his music, condescendingly patted the youngster on the head, and advised him to return when he had gained more experience. This cool reception failed to dampen Wolf's Wagnerian ardor, but his parents were unimpressed, and the anxious father cited the fate of once famous Lortzing, composer of *Zar und Zimmermann*, who fell on such bad times that he had to play with wandering troupes of comedians to support his wife and six children.

Hugo was not to be warned although he had already gone hungry as he thirsted for music. At the conservatory he had made friends, young Gustav Mahler, the brothers Schalk, and his world was alive with the characters of Byron, Dickens, Grillparzer, Goethe, Hebbel, Heine, Rabelais, Scott, Mark Twain, and Schopenhauer in unordered profusion. His favorite became Kleist's *Penthesilea*, the Amazon whose heroic hysteria was akin to his own. After reading a few verses of *Penthesilea*, recalled his friend Bahr, "his hands shook, his eyes lit up, he gasped for air as if the doors had opened on an apparition of the heavens." Reading led to declaiming with his friends as audience, at night.

Tired from student drinking bouts we wished to rest when in the middle of the night the door opened from the adjoining room and there appeared Hugo Wolf, in his long nightshirt, a candle and a book in hand, pale, ghostly, in the gray shimmering light, odd to behold with his mystic, solemn motions . . . He would step into our midst and begin to read, mostly from *Penthesilea*. This had such power that our protests were silenced and we did not dare to speak . . . Never in my life did I hear such reading. [Hermann Bahr]

By day the slight young man with the Liszt hair and goatee roamed Vienna where every house exuded music for him. He fought the "Philistines" with Schumann and delightedly suffered the damnation of hell in Berlioz' "Symphonie Fantastique." In his garret he played, fought, declaimed, composed; the demons danced. He was a curious mixture.

Shy, confiding only in his friends, outwardly icy, inwardly raging. But the inner fire glowed in his eyes: "Only the eyes conveyed wonderful expression; dark stars, testing and searching, with lightning and fury in them, which could also smile, on occasion, look back into themselves with anguish," recalled one friend. "His deep, wonderful eyes, sharp, even hard of look, spoke of a reigning spirit," wrote another. "From his eyes looked the rebel, the observer, the painter; they were the weapon with which nature endowed him in his artistic battles," declared a third.

In 1884 two events brought temporary relief into Wolf's convulsive life. He met Bruckner and mutual Wagner admiration cemented a life-long friendship between the placid master and the explosive unknown. He also obtained, through friends' intervention, the position of music critic of the *Wiener Salonblatt*, a newspaper of limited circulation devoted primarily to the social events of aristocracy and the upper strata. This provided an outlet for Hugo's "Sturm und Drang" emotions, an opportunity to speak out against arty rabble and musical reactionaries, against prima-donna worship and tenor adulation at the cost of artistic considerations, against lack of rehearsals, against cuts in Wagner operas, against corruption and the pursuit of the eternal female in opera corridors. The prodding and probing of his conscience increased the circulation of the paper (everybody could be properly outraged) but not the esteem of his contemporaries. His antics earned him not fame but notoriety.

His sense of justice aroused, Wolf defended Bruckner against Brahms: "The true greatness of a composer can be seen in whether he can jubilate, rejoice; Wagner can rejoice, Brahms cannot . . .

[Brahms is] a man who, upon returning to his house after a long absence, turned the rusted key with much effort to view the cobwebs in his home." While Bülow rejected Wolf's songs as dilettante, Brahms, surprisingly, took notice of the reviews and commented on them thoughtfully. The Rosé Quartet of Vienna was not so fair-minded, however, and refused to play Wolf's Quartet in D minor.

Another painful blow was in the offing. The Vienna Philharmonic had accepted *Penthesilea*, but neither the orchestra nor Hans Richter, its conductor, had any thought of respecting the composer's intentions. They considered it the work of "an idiot, an insane person, a jester," and what was sounded at rehearsal was not Wolf's music but a howling, miaowing fiddling and scraping, lorded over by Richter with mock earnestness until the malicious parody broke up in the raucous laughter of the orchestra. As he had rejected Bruckner, Richter also rejected Wolf for his anti-Brahms attacks. Ashen and stunned, Wolf felt the insult deeply because the rape of *Penthesilea* had been perpetrated by one of Europe's foremost orchestras and conductors.

To add to his misery, Wolf broke a leg at this time. The infirmity added to his creative leisure, however, and his first important Lieder blossomed. His small circle of friends, realizing the importance of the songs, underwrote publication in 1888. The composer was gratified and inspired, but soon thereafter he received news of his father's death and a pall settled over him. He ended his work as a critic. To be alone became paramount. He moved to the summer cottage of a friend in a village near Vienna. In solitude he found himself and music ripened within him like melons in the sun. Nine songs in fourteen days. Ideas began to pursue each other on their way to being born. Another ten songs in fourteen days. Only after the first forty-three Lieder on poems of Möricke were on paper did the muse allow a breathing spell.

Wolf used the quiet to visit Bayreuth to hear *Parsifal* and left deeply moved. In autumn he returned to solitude at Lake Atter in Carinthia. While his "nose and ears were ready to freeze off," he created the balance of the "Möricke" Lieder. Fifty-three songs from February to October, a world of impressions captured in miniature gems. There was no more doubt. He had found his destiny and proceeded with the sureness and swiftness of inspiration. One of the great Lieder composers had begun to leave his footprints on the path of Schubert and Schumann.

Blind reaction in Vienna refused to acknowledge the master. New emotional expressions, new sounds were considered "painful" and "insulting" by those in the know, who ignored the new depth Wolf had imparted into the Lied. Spring saw him back in Vienna in a friend's suburban garden. Eichendorff's poems in hand, he created two volumes of his "Eichendorff" Lieder. Nearly seventy songs were born there, and his friends heard them first and basked in their glow. The warm summer breezes lured him farther out of the city to the village of Döbling—vintner's vines hugging the gentle sun-drenched hills, low-beamed houses tucked away in blooming gardens surrounded by crude stone walls over which cascading growth hangs a colorful veil. In the solitude of such dream-like surroundings, re-moved from the bustle and noise of the city, the fifty-one "Goethe" Lieder took shape in three-and-a-half months and the volume was finished in February 1889.

Another harvest began when Wolf was given the *Spanisches Liederbuch* of poets Geibel and Leuthold. The volume grew between October and April. Then, without warning, the well of inspiration ran dry, and no desperate effort could revive it. To fill the void he began to orchestrate his songs in the hope of recapturing fleeting inspiration, but not until the summer of 1890 did inspiration flow again when work on the *Italienisches Liederbuch* began. A com-mission from the Imperial Burg Theatre to write incidental music for Ibsen's *Feast at Solhaug* was a signal honor but, Wolf could not bring himself to write music to order and every line had to be wrestled from a recalcitrant muse. He cursed his lonely walls and his piano half in mockery, half in despair, and his songs suffered in consequence. But when nature froze in December, inspiration thawed and fifteen songs of the *Italian Songbook* completed the volume.

Vienna still ignored the new master of song and reserved its plaudits for Pietro Mascagni. Bruckner and Hugo Wolf had be-come known in Berlin but were still without honor in their own country. "We cannot find talent in them . . . this cannot be called music." But slowly friends rallied to his cause. Conductor Franz Schalk, singers Amalie Materna and Erik Schmedes included his songs in their concerts. Still the Vienna critics could not be pacified:

> He once wrote music critiques . . . after hearing his songs we amicably advise him to return to writing critiques.

> . . . vulgar . . . shocking coarseness, the shrieking of wild animals.

> Childish, thin sounding stuff in which emotions masquerade for spirit . . . banal melodies and ridiculous harmonious cramps.

Outwardly calm, seemingly undisturbed, Wolf continued despite catcalls and vituperation. He had become a well-known sight in

Vienna, with his shoulder-length ash-blond hair, goatee, well-worn velvet jacket and indispensable cigaret. His foes had to admit that in bearing and opinion he remained undaunted, even noble. Finally the prominent publishing house of Schott in Mainz expressed interest in Wolf's work; manuscripts were sent and composer Humperdinck was asked for his expert opinion. He was fascinated by the songs' strange charms. Wolf was obliged to travel to Germany. Stopping in major music centers en route he made a discouraging discovery. The public had changed. They no longer demanded new music for every concert as in the days of Mozart and Beethoven. A wave of mental laziness had descended upon the concert-going public. Their tastes harked back to classical times. In warming to the music of their day, their reactions were slow and negative. They had just "discovered" Liszt, Wagner, and Berlioz; they jeered Bruckner, distrusted Mahler, and had no time for the singer of songs with the burning eyes. Only the poet Liliencron raised a banner in his poem "To Hugo Wolf":

. . . . .

And while you sang gloriously,
The Germans outside passed by.
They carried in their pockets
Tickets to "Mamselle Nitouche"

. . . . .

Make way you rabble.
A young new German king arrives,
A king of our new art

. . . . .

But the Germans,
Horrified, fingered their pockets
For the tickets
Of "Mamselle Nitouche"

Autumn found Wolf back in Vienna again, enriched with newly found musical wealth, indelible memories, and the warm friendship of conductor Felix Weingartner and composer Humperdinck. At the same time his antipathy for Brahms deepened. Commented he to another composer: "If there remains with you a shred of sympathy for Brahms, then you are not ready for my music." Vienna was not ready either. His plight was also darkened by coughing attacks and throat infections, and only slightly improved by provincial successes. Undismayed friends devised a concert tour, first stop Berlin. Although Wolf proved himself as coarse as Beethoven, as explosive as Wagner, as inconsiderate as Brahms, he made friends.

Berlin enjoyed his songs "warmly" and he considered settling in Germany. But in March Wolf returned to Vienna and colds, fever, influenza. Another concert in Vienna, again disdain for the "unsingable songs."

The success of the first Berlin trip called for another, and during the second visit Berlin performed the tone poems "Feuerreiter" (Fire Rider) and "Elfenlied" (Song of the Elfs). The goddess of success finally seemed to beckon as Hugo was feted by his circle of newly-found friends. One of them, Bojida Karageorgevich, a Balkan prince, was, of all things, an expert in Spanish folk songs which he played and sang quite adequately. Wolf was captivated. He could not hear enough of them, and Bojida delightedly obliged and sang habaneras and madrilenas deep into the night. Spanish vigor released a secret desire of long standing, to write an opera. Not according to the beaten-to-death formula of drama, pathos, and death, but a comic opera of strumming guitars and moonlight nights, the clinking of glasses and lovers' sighs.

Reports of Hugo's success had filtered back, and the first performance in Vienna on December 2, 1894 of his "Feuerreiter" and "Elfenlied" shared the program with works by the popular composer-conductor Eugene d'Albert. Success, success—Brahms attended, applauded; even Hanslick relented: "Undoubtedly a man of spirit and talent." Germany clamored for him again, and music-loving aristocrat Baron von Lippenheide offered Wolf a stipend to enable him to work unhampered by financial worries. For once reticent Hugo was not insulted. On the contrary: "It's high time that someone had the idea. Actually it is the damned duty and debt of the state to support its musicians and poets."

Another puzzle piece fell into place early in 1895. The elusive opera libretto presented itself with "moonlit feasts and guitars." The Vienna poetess Rosa Mayreder adapted the libretto of *The Corregidor* from Don Pedro de Alarcón's book *The World of the Three-cornered Hat*. The libretto was pedestrian, without build-up or proper identification of characters; the action slow, the sentiments untrue, the motives contrived. But Wolf reacted with enthusiasm. Here was the world of Spain he had longed for plus a musical comedy of errors with brash, broad comedy lines. His mind aflame, inspiration flowed and *The Corregidor* took shape rapidly. Already in April he was able to play the first parts of the opera to his friends. In the precious solitude of Baron Lippenheide's castle he raced towards completion, waiting impatiently for the verse to issue from the poetess' pen: "Hurry, hurry, for the love of God, hurry."

In May the second act was ready, in June the third, the opera completed in July. He could not explain the desperate drive, could only comply with its dictates or rave impotently when the flow temporarily subsided. With the piano draft completed, he threw himself into orchestration as if possessed. In December the last note was written. The proud father was confident that his child would succeed, desperate that it should. But Otto Jahn, director of the Imperial Opera in Vienna, after looking over the score, hesitated, returned it; discussions with Berlin and Prague led nowhere. Finally Mannheim, which had given Wagner and Schiller early triumphs, accepted the opera for performance in May 1896.

Suddenly another creative well gushed up in Wolf. He disappeared into his "work room" in the suburbs, and there within a month the second volume of the *Italian Songbook* was completed. But unrealized by Wolf, his never strong constitution and with it inspiration began to fail. Thus the second *Italian Songbook* is as a curtain descending. But fate was compassionate. In a short span of time it had allowed genius to bring forth the creations otherwise allotted to a full lifetime.

Rehearsals had meanwhile started in Mannheim, and the composer's presence was needed for interpretation and to correct the copies which had innumerable mistakes. Wolf arrived exhausted, irritable. A bad situation was compounded by his ineptitude, lack of stage-craft knowledge, and ignorance of singers' foibles and vanities. He could barely suppress his angry impatience which threatened total disruption of rehearsals. After innumerable postponements, the fateful evening arrived. Wolf hid in the highest gallery of the opera house, hollow with despair. When the poetess finally located him, he silently rose, embraced her, and cried on her shoulder. But under no circumstances would he take a bow; no, no, absolutely not. When the librettist's gentleness finally persuaded him to relent, he stood at the footlights, "melancholy and somber," as she recalled, "the pale face showing traces of the emotional upheaval under which his soul trembled."

He still held high hope for performance in Vienna. Gustav Mahler, his friend since student days, now in charge of the Imperial Opera, had tentatively agreed to consider *The Corregidor* for the 1897–98 season. That winter brought many new works to Vienna, Smetana's *Dalibor*, Tchaikovsky's *Eugene Onegin*, Puccini's *La Bohème*, Bellini's *Norma*, Verdi's *Masked Ball*, but *The Corregidor* was not among them. After studying the score, Mahler decided against performance of "the opera of songs." It meant the death knell for

Wolf's hopes, and he suddenly saw the entire world, in the person of the Imperial Opera Director, bent on destroying him and his work.

Yet all seemed serene on the surface. For the first time Hugo had an apartment of his own, and in its quiet the Michelangelo poems inspired him. On February 22, 1898 his somber, Christ-like head bowed for the last time from the concert stage. Applause, applause, congratulations, honors, flowers, success, inspiration. The future would have glowed with a rosy light had not, from time to time, a dark hand clamped itself about his mind, shutting out light and inspiration, thrusting him into unnamed darkness and horror. As early as the second stay in Germany, Wolf's friends were becoming disturbed by his increasingly odd behaviour and aggravated nervousness. At one informal dinner given in his honor, such unnamed dread began to fill him in the midst of the gay party that he fled from the table and left the same night. Only when the seizures abated, did music flow in spurts of creative activity. The Michelangelo Lieder progressed, their inward listening a dark omen; what the "Requiem" was to Mozart they were to be to Wolf. They were to be his last will and testament, surprisingly detached and resigned, oddly tinged with bitterness at his age of thirty-seven.

Mahler's final refusal to stage *The Corregidor* was the blow to destroy the already weakened pinions of his being. Delusions tore at his mind. Excitedly and almost convincingly, he told his friends that he—Wolf—was now imperial court director, that he would reward his loyal friends with positions, that he was to perform his own opera. A private world closed in, reality became unbearably hostile, dreams soothing reality. Insomnia began to drive him from friend to friend, by day, by night, proclaiming his might to one, his misery to another. Only when he was able to immerse himself in music was Wolf still capable of keeping a clear mind.

During a private performance among friends, he suddenly rose and delivered a tirade against Mahler. But his voice became incoherent and those present were aware that Wolf had stepped across the fine line which separates genius from insanity. A ruse of his friends made him sign commitment papers. Although his delusions increased, he still composed during brief spells of lucidity, and to his friend's stunned disbelief he was released in January 1898 as "cured and healthy." Despite hatred of Vienna (the city which lets its children die in an insane asylum) he raced there. Old friends, old haunts brought no relief. On he went to the mountain resort of Semmering near Vienna, on to his native Styria. The green hills furnished no opiate to dim the ever-hovering terror, and he fled from there to Cilli, to Hochenegg castle; and on and on, to Trieste, Pirano, Abbazia. The nightmarish drive did not abate under Italy's sun; no peace could calm it, no rest relax it, there remained only flight from ghostly horror. Like an animal pursued he raced back to Salzburg, to Vienna, to Traunkirchen. No escape. Desperately he turned to music. No escape. An unrelenting fate caught up with him in October, and he attempted suicide in Traun Lake. The coldness of the water revived his senses. With momentary restoration also came full realization, and, like Schumann, he requested confinement. As he lingered in four years' darkness, the world discovered the light of his music.

It was the pre-Lenten Fasching again and Vienna danced. Masked merrimakers looked on dumbly as the cortege bearing Wolf's body passed and a choir intoned the dead master's "Ergebung" (surrender)

Oh mit uns Sündern gehe	Lord with us sinners
Erbarmend ins Gericht	Have mercy and be just
Ich berg in tiefstem Wehe	We hide in deepest sorrow
Zum Staub mein Angesicht.	Our faces in the dust.

XVIII

Ten-Year Glory

The bold head of Bruckner and the sharply chiselled face of Gustav Mahler were bent over the score of Bruckner's Third Symphony in absorbed discussion. The old master, bestowing a signal honor on Mahler, had entrusted the younger man with the preparation of the piano arrangement of the symphony. A letter by Mahler dated April 1892 shows that Bruckner's trust was well placed:

> Honored Master and Friend: Yesterday . . . I conducted your splendid and powerful Te Deum. Not only the entire audience but also the performers were deeply moved by the mighty architecture and truly noble ideas and at the end of the performance I witnessed what I consider the greatest personal triumph. The audience remained silently seated . . . and not until the conductor and the performers had left their place did the storm of applause break loose.

In later years, however, Mahler spoke less highly of Bruckner as well as of Brahms.

> . . . It is seldom that he can make anything whatsoever of his themes, beautiful as they often are . . . Now that I have worked my way through Brahms, I have fallen back on Bruckner again. An odd pair of second-raters. The one in the casting ladle too long, the other one not long enough. Now I stick to Beethoven. There is only he and Wagner. [Gustav to Alma Mahler]

Brahms and Bülow, on the other hand, admired Mahler as a conductor but refused to acknowledge him as a composer of stature. Brahms dismissed Mahler's creations as "Kapellmeister Musik" (conductor's music) or as "incorrigibly revolutionary." Mahler disagreed: "I am not speaking of my activities in opera or as a conductor; they are after all of an inferior nature." Yet Mahler's initial lack of success with his First Symphony in Budapest and Hamburg seemed to bear out Brahms' and Bülow's opinions.

Mahler had met Bruckner at the Vienna University where the older man was his instructor in counterpoint. Despite an age difference of thirty years and the vast contrast between Jewish nervous intellect and Catholic peasant placidity, a lasting friendship developed, although their musical approaches also differed widely. While Bruckner wallowed in nineteenth-century romanticism, Mahler's ancestral heritage and his concern with the intellectual crisis of his time, took him far afield from their common background of Beethoven and Schubert. Even in their approach to their idol—Wagner—the two men differed. Bruckner unquestioningly adopted Wagner's musical speech in his symphonic creations. Despite admiration and superlative re-creations of Wagner's operas, Mahler remained unaffected by them. He proceeded from the outset on his own way and thus prepared the approach to a new musical era in Vienna. The awesome finale of his Second Symphony, inspired by Klopstock's ode "Aufersteh'n" (Resurrection), hinted at the impending collapse of the symphonic structure of old.

Mahler's first forays into the world of practical music were sheer drudgery. Early signs of musical ability had sent him in 1875 to Vienna's famed conservatory and to the university in 1877. After his graduation, he gave music lessons to a Hungarian nobleman, and conducted operettas in an Austrian spa. Of all the compositions of that period, only his cantata "Das klagende Lied" (The Plaintive Song) remains. Although it foreshadows his later mature "Lied von der Erde" (Song of the Earth) it failed to win the Beethoven prize in Vienna for which he competed. His Wagner admiration and Bruckner friendship may have adversely swayed the jury which included Hanslick and Brahms. In 1881 Mahler conducted in Olmütz and Laibach but soon left to take charge of the Royal Prussian Court Theatre in Kassel. He soon became impatient with the pedantic Prussian atmosphere and naively complained to the mighty Bülow. Bülow maliciously turned the letter over to the Kassel intendant, making Mahler's position there untenable. But Prague and Leipzig beckoned. In Leipzig Mahler made the acquaintance of Carl Maria von Weber's grandson who invited Mahler to weld the sketches of "The Three Pintos," left by his grandfather, into an opera. While working on the sketches, Mahler fell passionately in love with attractive Frau Weber, several years his senior. The lady reciprocated and they made plans to leave her husband and go away together. Mahler had secret doubts as to the wisdom of such a step but felt honor-bound to carry it out. Great was his relief when at the appointed hour, his paramour failed to make an appearance. His work on Weber's sketches remained Mahler's only foray into opera composition.

In Leipzig Mahler had begun work on his first important compositions, the First Symphony and "Lieder eines fahrenden Gesellen"

(Songs of a Wayfarer). Soon preoccupation with his creations began to crowd his theatrical duties, and he resigned under pressure. It was the last time Mahler permitted such a conflict to arise. The first big opportunity offered itself soon thereafter. In a carefully drawn-up contract which took even the shifting political winds into consideration, Mahler was put in complete charge of a major opera house—Budapest. Although his tenure was a spectacular success, politics and his radical innovations (such as opera in Hungarian), blew him out of office after two years. But solid achievement and a generous financial settlement eased the blow. Soon he again crossed the continent to Hamburg where he was to remain with the opera for six years. By this time Brahms had testified in his native city to Mahler's inspiring leadership. Bülow had also praised his conducting: "Recently I heard *Siegfried* under Mahler's direction . . . sincere admiration has filled me for him, when, without an orchestra rehearsal, he compelled the musical rabble to dance according to his whistle."

The overwhelming reception of his Second Symphony in Berlin in 1895, however, was the opening wedge as a composer. Panted Mahler after the performance: "One is beaten to the ground only to be lifted again by angel's wings to the most exalted heights." Some of the recognition he attained at this time was due to Richard Strauss who performed Mahler's First Symphony in Weimar. Mahler reciprocated later by introducing Strauss' early opera *Feuersnot* (Fire's Threat) to Vienna.

With finances improved, Mahler allowed himself a trip to Italy and an Austrian vacation at beautiful Lake Atter near Salzburg. The idyllic loveliness of the lake and the villages nestled close to it are in stark contrast to the majesty of the Austrian Alps which present so awesome a view that certain peaks are dubbed "Höllengebirge" (Mountains of Hell) and "Totengebirge" (Mountains of Death). In those contrasting surroundings, Mahler composed his Third Symphony. The material was neither fresh nor strange. What gave it power was the composer's ability to bestow depth and emotion on what, in lesser hands, would have appeared commonplace. But certainly in the grandeur of conception of his compositions Mahler paralleled his idol Beethoven:

> My symphony will be something that the world never heard the like before. All nature is endowed with a voice in it.
> . . . Imagine the universe beginning to ring and resound. It is no longer human voices. It is planets and suns revolving . . .
> Each symphony is a separate world with a law and order all its own. [letter to Willem Mengelberg]

Three years later Mahler realized one of his loftiest goals. He moved to "the God of Southern Zones"—Vienna. At that time, as his biographer Ernst Krenek wrote, the city "offered splendid potentialities for the highest accomplishments as well as the most stubborn resistance to their realization." Shortly before Mahler arrived in Vienna, he became converted to Catholicism. His other biographer, Engel, maintains that opportunism prompted the step, while Krenek cites philosophical outlook. The actual reason may have been a third factor—artistic drive. The Imperial Opera in Vienna was Mahler's goal. In striving for it he must have been aware of the unwritten law that no non-Catholic could hold a position at court. Mahler, although born of Jewish parents, had never practiced the parental religion but had formulated his own religious concepts. He therefore had no conflict with his conscience or integrity in shifting from one creed to another. The step was significant only in the light of fulfillment of an artistic mission.

Nevertheless the Jewish question, constantly smoldering in Vienna under the surface of public acclaim, was much on his mind. Mahler never denied his origin and background. He was aware of his strong Semitic features and realized that others were also. The deepest cut was Cosima Wagner's efforts to have him barred from the Imperial Opera because of her inability to see a Jew at the helm of that institution. But her antagonism did not keep her from approaching Mahler (after he had attained world renown) to ask to have the mediocre operas of her son, Siegfried Wagner, performed in Vienna.

On May 11, 1897 Mahler appeared for the first time on the podium of the Vienna Imperial Opera conducting Wagner's *Lohengrin*. So immediate and deep was his impact that in October of the same year he became director of the world-famous institution. At thirty-seven, in the prime of his life, he had reached an artistic pinnacle; his eminence and dominance grew and remained unchallenged for ten years despite the inevitable intrigues and controversies over his compositions and interpretations. Those who mocked him and plotted against him, eventually became his admirers. The singer Theodore Reichmann, who first nicknamed him "Jewish monkey," was later to call him "the God Mahler." Even the man in the street referred to him in awesome whispers as "Der Mahler" when, hat in hand and black mane flying, he would hurry along the Ring boulevard on his way to the opera. Austria was a paradox It was viewed as a den of reactionary political iniquity, yet possessed a peculiar liberal spirit which enabled a baptized Jew to wield a near-absolute baton for ten years at the world's foremost musical institution.

In many ways the easy-going manners of Vienna always remained alien to this fierce, brilliant creator. His insight and fanatic loyalty to a composer's intentions, coupled with his own inspiration made every performance fresh and unhackneyed, lifting a masterpiece from patinaed routine to artistic rediscovery. Just as Mozart had aroused the ire of his contemporaries by reorchestrating Handel's music, so Mahler did not hesitate to do the same with Beethoven's. His changes were severely criticized but he brushed them aside: "Your Beethoven is not my Beethoven." It was he who inserted the "Leonore" overtures between the acts of *Fidelio*, presenting the monumental "Leonore III" before the final act. That Mahler innovation has become tradition, but many a hoary Vienna opera "tradition" vanished. The claque was abolished, worn-out voices put out to pasture, cuts in Wagner operas restored. Tradition is "bloss Schlamperei" (only sloppiness). He was feared and respected, but his driving ways and searing tongue hardly made him the most beloved artist in Vienna. When he cuttingly informed a baritone during rehearsal, "Sie sind so blöd wie ein Tenor" (You are as dumb as a tenor), he did not endear himself to either baritone or tenors. If music bored him while a guest, he would leave regardless of hurt feelings, and when conversation in Vienna's salons wearied him, he departed without a word of apology or explanation, completely unaware of and unconcerned by the consternation he caused distraught hostesses.

Four years after Mahler arrived in Vienna, young conductor Bruno Walter joined him. Walter, some years earlier, had accidentally become Mahler's assistant. He had been listening in at a rehearsal at which the accompanist proved unsatisfactory to the conductor. Walter, on impulse, offered his services on the spot. The two men understood each other so well that Walter soon became Mahler's close associate and spent two years with him in Hamburg. Walter's impression of Mahler was one of "demoniac obsession . . . the orchestra would remain in hypnotic silence under the spell of a master who, himself spellbound by the intrinsic conception of a work of art, seemed urged by compelling force to make his co-workers comply with the irresistible dictates of his inner self."

In 1902 Mahler met and married vivacious, talented Alma Schindler,* a pupil of composer Alexander Zemlinsky and a talented musician in her own right. Through Alma, Mahler was introduced to the Viennese circle of painters which was also in ferment at the time. Led by Gustav Klimt and Egon Schiele, they had broken away from the staid "Künstlerhaus" (Artist's House) and had aptly named

---

* After Mahler's death she became the companion of Kokoschka, then the wife of architect Walter Gropius, and later the wife of novelist Franz Werfel.

their new artistic home "Secession." Its motto: "To each time its Arts, to each Art its Freedom." Their building was itself a radical break with the past: basically a cube surmounted by a golden globe of leaves, promptly nicknamed by the Viennese "the Golden Cabbage Head." Associated with the group were a number of persons destined for greatness: the painter Oscar Kokoschka, architect Adolf Loos, the hunchbacked writer and satirist Karl Kraus, poets Schnitzler and Altenberg, and the writer and critic Hermann Bahr, husband of famed Vienna opera singer Anna Bahr-Mildenburg. So was Hugo von Hoffmannsthal who injected an aristocratic element whenever he raised his voice in the typical drawl of highborn Viennese dialect. Among the musical members of the group were composer Zemlinsky, conductor Artur Bodanzky, music critic Max Graf, and later Arnold Schönberg.

After four years Mahler was in complete control of every phase of the Imperial Opera and Emperor Franz Josef congratulated him on having made himself "master of conditions." Whenever he appeared the atmosphere became charged: "A demonic man from whom streams of nervous energy emanated and pervaded stage, orchestra and audience," wrote Max Graf. "When the house grew dark, the small man with the sharply-chiselled features, pale ascetic looking, literally rushed to the conductor's desk . . . He would let his baton shoot forward like the tongue of a serpent . . . He would stare at the stage and make imploring gestures at the singers. He would leap from the conductor's chair as if stung. Mahler was always in full movement like a blazing flame."

The artistic climate of Mahler's Vienna and the success of his energy-charged interpretations was not comfortable for the older generation, and this was the reason why Hans Richter departed from the Vienna scene. No greater contrast could be imagined than the blond, powerfully built, bearded Richter and the slender, tense, clean-shaven Mahler. Their respective interpretations were equally poles apart. When Max Graf took exception to Mahler's tempi in *Die Walküre* and pointed to the slower speed of Richter, Mahler snapped: "Richter has no idea about the tempi." Graf countered that Richter had conducted the Bayreuth premiere and should know the tempi as intended by Wagner. Mahler scoffed: "Maybe he knew the right tempi then. Since then he has forgotten them." When Graf had occasion to discuss the same performance with Richter, his resigned reply revealed the abyss which separated the viewpoints of the two men: "The 'Feuerzeuber' at the end, that was brought out very well by Mahler. But that this end is a transfiguration and a painful resignation—of that Mahler has no idea." Yet there was no clash of personalities. Each respected the other's integrity and avoided public criticism, and, with London beckoning, Richter left silently.

Neither the tremendous mental and physical demands made on Mahler, nor the storm of applause which greeted his performances, could prevent him from forever questing for the new, be it in Mozart or Wagner, Gluck or Pfitzner, Offenbach or Charpentier. During his ten-year tenure at the Vienna Opera, despite grinding administrative duties and tortuous artistic problems, he still found time, energy, and inspiration to write his Fourth and Fifth Symphonies in 1902, the Sixth in 1904, the Seventh in 1905. As he staged a gem-like *Figaro* in Salzburg in 1906, his mind was crowded with the most grandiose of all his works, his Eighth "Symphony of the Thousand." Arnold Schönberg, who so often had been at artistic loggerheads with Mahler, was moved to say: "The impression made on me by the Seventh and before that, by the Third are permanent. I am really and entirely yours . . . I have put you with the classical masters."

Mahler's triumphs as conductor outshone the successes of his symphonic creations. Yet the varying winds of critical acclaim or rejection left him surprisingly unmoved: "The 'Frankfurt Börsen Courier' . . . denies me in a few words all talent whatsoever. I cannot even orchestrate . . . The hard knocks I have to put up with from all sides only stimulate me. The Berlin critics are almost unanimously contemptuous" (to Alma Mahler).

Willem Mengelberg, famed conductor of the Concertgebouw Orchestra, single-handedly turned Amsterdam into a "Mahler City." His efforts culminated when Mahler's Fourth Symphony was performed twice on the same program, with Mengelberg conducting the first rendition and Mahler the second. Vienna was not as generous. At the premiere of the same work, friends and antagonists nearly came to blows.

The inevitable break with youthful romanticism came with Mahler's Fifth Symphony. Like the deep chasm which separates Beethoven's Second and Third Symphonies, so a new expressive world separates Mahler's Fifth from its predecessors: "The routine I had acquired in the first four symphonies deserted me altogether as if a totally new message demanded a new technique . . . It is the sum of all the suffering I have been compelled to endure at the hands of life." A new wave of polyphonic invention combined with a "ruthless contrapuntal technique" (Mahler's main contribution to a new era which produced Schönberg) reached its culmination in his Eighth Symphony and "Das Lied von der Erde" and the lucent transfiguration of his Ninth Symphony. Like Schubert and Bruckner before him, Mahler was attracted to Austrian folk melodies which often sparkle in his symphonies. Nowhere else is Mahler's inventive spirit more manifest, however, than in the Scherzi of his symphonies. "The Scherzo of his Second Symphony undoubtedly represents a culmination point in the entire realm of symphonic scherzo literature," declared Bruno Walter.

> How droll and at the same time graceful is the inventive element in the Scherzo of his Third . . . How mysteriously exciting . . . that of the second movement of his Fourth. That central idea of the Scherzo of the Fifth is not humorous but a striking expression of vital force. The Trio of the Scherzo of his Sixth is remarkable for an indication of the most singular charm of invention which is quite Mahler's own. The Scherzo of his Seventh is a spook-like nocturnal piece, while in his Ninth with symphonic mastery and exquisite charm he makes use of the Austrian slow country waltz.

After ten glorious years, Vienna's never-to-be-equalled "Mahler Era," the conductor resigned. Despite constant sniping from lesser musicians, support from his superiors, Princes Liechtenstein and Montenuovo, had never flagged. Over the years, however, Mahler's position became perceptibly more difficult. When Prince Montenuovo finally objected to high costs and to liberties taken by Mahler's associates, harsh words and tart replies were exchanged. The princely intendant did not forget nor did Mahler relent. "My cycle at the opera is completed." The composer could not spare the time and energy for administrative duties and bureaucratic squabbles. He had to steel himself for a final assault on his most important creations in the face of a detected heart ailment. But Prince Montenuovo's personal feelings did not influence his actions. Due to his efforts, the parting from the opera was without outward ill feelings, and the emperor rewarded Mahler financially far beyond the conductor's expectations. Also thanks to the prince's tact, the transition from Mahler to his successor, Felix Weingartner, was smooth. In October 1907 Mahler presided from the pit over his last and most memorable production—of *Fidelio*—and November saw his last appearance with the Vienna Philharmonic. His Second Symphony was his Vienna swan song, but his influence in the city of his greatest triumphs and his greatest love was to be felt for decades to come.

In December of the same year, Mahler went to the United States to lead the Metropolitan Opera; he had decided to spend half of each year in America, the other half in Europe. The premieres of his works, however, were still reserved for Europe. Mahler was quite taken with the Americans. Their open-hearted ways, their hospitality soon made him feel comfortable despite the language barrier. He also gloried in the wealth of great voices at the Metropolitan Opera. Vienna had the better ensemble, the peerless Vienna Philharmonic in the pit, and an unexcelled chorus, but collectively the voices at the Metropolitan were unsurpassed anywhere—Caruso, Chaliapin, Scotti, Eames, Melba, Farrar, and Lilli Lehman. When Toscanini was called upon to conduct at the Metropolitan and conflict loomed between the two great interpreters over the performance of *Tristan*, Mahler resigned. The moment was propitious because a group of New York distaff social leaders had offered him the post of conductor of the New York Philharmonic Orchestra, America's oldest. Mahler accepted, welcoming the change.

While Mahler was honored, feted, and applauded by the musical literati of America, the American mind was largely closed to his creations due to preoccupation with the works of one of his contemporaries, Jean Sibelius. "I heard some pieces by Sibelius, the Finnish national composer, who makes a great stir not only here but throughout the world of music," Mahler wrote his wife. "In one of them, the most hackneyed cliches were served up, with harmonizations in the 'Nordic' style, as a national dish."

The Munich premiere of his Eighth Symphony was more than the major European event of 1910, it was the last climax of Mahler's life. For it he summoned in his faltering heart all the memories of strength and vigor. No detail was overlooked in preparing the gigantic work whose very proportions seemed to pose unending problems. Bruno Walter was called upon to select and coach the soloists. Mahler's unexpected gentleness overwhelmed all. He was rewarded with a performance and a triumph to surpass all others. "As Mahler entered the stage he received a standing ovation," recalled his wife. "Mahler, god or demon, turned those tremendous volumes of sounds into fountains of light. The experience was indescribable. Indescribable too, was the demonstration which followed. The entire audience surged toward the platform."

Aside from parting from his beloved Vienna and the disquieting heart trouble, another blow had come with the death of Mahler's older daughter at the age of five. All this brought the hovering thought of death ever closer. It had a profoundly darkening and mellowing effect. The melancholy spirit of farewell, of dark fears, which had entered his life early with the suicide of his younger brother and Wolf's insanity, was now given expression in his final masterpieces, the Ninth Symphony and "Das Lied von der Erde." There is purposeful illogic in the numbering of Mahler's last symphonies. "Das Lied von der Erde" was to have been his Ninth ["Song"] Symphony but he feared the number which had marked the final symphonies of Beethoven, Schubert, and Bruckner. He therefore left it unnumbered and simply called it "A Symphony of Songs." Eventually another symphony numbered nine could not be delayed or avoided, and it did mark Mahler's creative end.

But time was running out. Despite the necessary relaxing of rigid demands for perfection and abandonment of strenuous activities, Mahler's worsening heart condition aged him so noticeably that strangers often mistook him for Alma's father rather than her husband. Back in Austria for the summer, he was deprived of his long-loved walking and climbing. As the danger signals multiplied, Mahler, racing against time and toward death, was forced to curtail his American commitments drastically. But disaster had become inevitable, and in February 1911 Vienna was shocked to hear of Mahler's collapse in New York. He returned to Europe for emergency treatment in Paris. "There he lay tortured victim of an insidious illness," wrote Bruno Walter, "his very soul affected by the struggle of his body, his mind gloomy and forbidding, only when his visitors spoke of Vienna did his eyes light up and his attention rise from the depth of gloom." He expressed only two desires, "to take enough digitalis to support my heart . . . and to go home." Home was Vienna, and upon his repeated requests he was moved to the city he loved best of all. He reached it in time to die. He was buried next to his daughter in the shadow of the vine-covered hills he had loved so much. A tombstone gravely inscribed "Mahler" marks the site. He had insisted on such brevity. "Those who are looking for me know who I am, the others need not know."

The drum and trumpet were among the main tools of Mahler. They relate the story of struggle and battle, and Mahler, enigma, dynamo, demon, creator and innovator, was first and foremost a fighter. One must wonder how the guns, the drums, the trumpets of the holocaust of war would have affected Mahler and his music.

THE DYING CITY

XIX

Danse Macabre

Signs of dissension within and threats from without mounted. But if dissension from within was real, threats from outside were deliberately exaggerated or trumped up. No doubt Austria's brazen annexation of Bosnia and Herzegovina and its Balkan policies in general had made enemies. But now the jingoes, the political dilettantes, the Sunday warriors suddenly saw threats in Serbia's aspirations and protests against the treatment of its subjects, as well as in the building of fortifications by Italy on Austria's southern border. Austria had no policy beyond day-by-day makeshifts. Those in power in the cabinet of the moment either resignedly shrugged their shoulders or began to speak in voices ranging from sepulchral whispers to hysterical shrieks of dealing with the "aggressors" by a punitive war, hoping thus to divert attention from indecision and decay.

Archduke Franz Ferdinand, heir to the throne of Austria, a reactionary, arrogant and absolute in outlook, came into ever sharper conflict with the policies of irresolute Emperor Franz Josef and began to conspire against the court and its ineffective, patchwork cabinet. Amid mounting pressure from Foreign Minister Count Berchtold, Chief of Staff Conrad von Hötzendorf, and Archduke Franz Ferdinand, the emperor tenaciously clung to his half-century-old motto: "My policy is that of peace." But with threats, imaginary and real, mounting, a show of force was clamorously sought. "The honor of Austria demands it." Finally Franz Josef acceded and maneuvers were ordered in June 1914 in Bosnia on Serbia's border while two mighty warships of the Austrian Navy would patrol the Adriatic. Both actions would serve as a warning to Serbia and Italy that the might of Austria was not to be challenged with impunity. To lend additional weight to the show of force, the heir to the throne was to personally command the seventy-thousand men assembled in and about Sarajevo for maneuvers.

On June 28, 1914 a blazing sun shone on flag-draped Sarajevo. People in festive mood lined the streets, windows, balconies and rooftops, laughing, waving, gawking. They had come to mingle with the soldiers, partake in the holiday atmosphere, and see the second-highest dignitary of the realm arrive and open the "festivities." Archduke Franz Ferdinand and Duchess Sophie, riding in an open automobile, were pleased and surprised at the friendly atmosphere as they slowly proceeded to the town hall for the official ceremony of welcome.

Suddenly a muffled roar dispelled the gay atmosphere. The cars of the archduke and his entourage shuddered under the blast of a bomb thrown from the crowd. An adjutant hurriedly made his way along the cars and advised them to proceed as quickly as possible. No harm had come to the ducal pair, but a member of the staff in the second car had been wounded. Franz Ferdinand was outraged. Upon arriving at the city hall, he brusquely ordered the mayor to hold speeches to a minimum, then sarcastically invited him to lead the way to the hospital where he wished to visit his wounded aide. The cavalcade proceeded in ghoulish somberness amid the laughing throngs with the mayor's car in the vanguard. Suddenly the mayor's car took a wrong turn; during the delay that followed a crackling noise was faintly heard above the noisy crowd. The body of the duchess slumped limply against the archduke from whose mouth blood had begun to flow. The assassin, a Serbian sympathizer, had aimed well; both were already unconscious. Wending their agonizingly slow way through the crowd, the cars finally arrived at the hospital. The duchess had already succumbed, and Franz Ferdinand died shortly after arrival without regaining consciousness. The trumpets sounded. The maneuvers ended. The war began.

The youngest veterans of the last major European war were in their sixties, and hardly anyone could envision the horror of the holocaust which would engulf most of Europe. It was to be a "punitive expedition," a "cleansing bath of steel," an "heroic pilgrimage of arms." The clergy invoked God's blessing on the arms of their particular army, and generals and politicians exhorted their people to "fight to the death" or "fight for the glory" of this or that country and "avenge" this or that shame or insult. Nobody really wanted a war of global proportions, least of all Serbia. Germany, although bound to Austria by treaty, was reluctant at first; so was Russia, and sober Englishmen warned all who wished to listen against any large-scale armed venture.

The most reluctant was Emperor Franz Josef. Despite cries that "Serbia must be punished," despite a harsh ultimatum, he wished for peace. Finally, nearly thirty days after the assassination, a ruse forced his hand. Count Berchtold informed the monarch that Serbian troops had attacked a unit of the Imperial Army, and Franz Josef had no choice but to sign the declaration of war his foreign minister had prepared and put before him. Not until three days later, with the declaration of war well on its way, did Count Berchtold send the emperor a "small amendment": "As the report of an engagement at Temes Kubin has not been confirmed, I have taken it upon myself, in anticipation of your Majesty's subsequent approval, to omit from the declaration of war the sentence referring to an attack by Serbian troops."

Germany, in the words of Emperor Wilhelm II, "stood in shining armor" by the side of its comrade-in-arms. Austria was being whipped into a frenzy of patriotic fervor. Men who had been pressed into military service returned home briefly with fancy little bouquets on their hats indicating that they had been mobilized. They returned to say goodbye or get dismally drunk before moving to the front after a minimum of training. Regiments marched into battle in dress uniforms with flowers bound to their rifles and with their regimental bands blaring Austria's famous marches within sight and range of the enemy. Cavalry in colorful uniforms attacked machine guns with lances. And such tragic ignorance was by no means limited to Austria.

They had all marched off, their young faces shining, with "Tipperary," "La Marseillaise," or "Die Wacht am Rhein" bursting from brave lips. But it became a war of attrition with millions of lives flung into death's cauldrons, a war of global proportions in which gains were measured in yards. At one point on the Western Front the gain of a few trenches was achieved at the cost of twenty-thousand men.

Enthusiasm, patriotism, bravery were not enough. With treaty-bound Italy deserting Austria, with Japan declaring war on Austria and Germany, and finally with the entry of the United States on the side of the Allies, the tide took a decisive turn. The downfall of the Central Powers became only a matter of time. Emperor Franz Josef was spared the grim spectacle of the dismemberment of the Habsburg empire. The beloved monarch passed on in November 1916, two years before the end. The dramatist Franz Theodor Csokor graphically depicts the fate of Austria in his play *Third November 1918*: The scene—a farm house high in the Austrian Alps. The son has returned from the war, and the isolated family gathers about to hear his account. The son takes his bayonet and steps to a map on the wall. He slashes at the south: "Southern Tyrol went to Italy. Bosnia went to Yugoslavia." He slashes at the north: "Bohemia and

Moravia went to Czechoslovakia." He slashes at the east. "This went to Hungary, this to Poland, this to Rumania." As he turns to the stunned family there remains on the wall an odd, unwieldly shape, an alpine patch of eight million people with a capital of two million, a head too large for its rocky body. It is the remnant of a once proud empire, too small to live, too large to die, forthwith to be known as "The Republic of Austria."

XX

The Madman

"I consider the final undertaking of my artistic plans, to which I am now turning, to be the most decisive moment of my life . . . there lies before me a stormy but also . . . a fertile world. I had to clear my entire past, had to bring to consciousness everything that was dawning within me." Richard Wagner spoke these words but they could also have been, word for word, Schönberg's view of his artistic fortunes.

Arnold Schönberg early combined the romantic sensuality of Wagner with the controlled intellect of Brahms. Although demonstrating an early talent for composition and an analytical mind, his study of the violin and viola was accomplished without help. Later he took brief instruction in counterpoint from Alexander Zemlinsky who had achieved something which Schönberg, only two years younger, might have envied. He had so impressed Brahms that the old master went out of his way to have Zemlinsky's music published. Alma Mahler was not so charitable in a diary entry of January 1905: "Concert yesterday. Zemlinsky–Schönberg . . . Zemlinsky, despite many charming little inspirations and imposing knowledge, has not the strength of Schönberg, who, for all his wrong-headedness is a very original fellow."

Although Schönberg and Brahms shared Vienna for twenty years, they never met because of Brahms' aloofness and Schönberg's fear of the master's acid comments. Hans Rott, young Mahler's sensitive friend, had once had the temerity to show his compositions to Brahms. The opinionated master, knowing Rott to be a Bruckner admirer, scathingly denied him any talent and brusquely advised him to abandon music. Already weakened by poverty and hunger, Rott went insane.

The words of one of Schönberg's early songs forecast his tenets. "I stand alone, yes, all alone, / Even as a roadside stone. / Lightning, write upon the stone, / Would you go free, walk alone." Those early Lieder were premiered with Zemlinsky at the piano. Vienna was scandalized and the scandal continued for some time. Actually

Schönberg was not to appear fully in the Vienna musical arena until the premiere of "Verklärte Nacht" (Transfigured Night) after a poem by Richard Dehmel. In it Schönberg scored a "first" by creating a symphonic poem for a chamber group. Soon thereafter his exuberant mind started on the eleven-year task of his "Gurre-lieder."

It was a time when Vienna's life, pessimistically, cynically, irresolutely followed its rutted path to decay and destruction. Social life blandly, blindly, continued at a placid pace in its traditional agora of leisurely contemplation, the café. But even there the finely drawn distinctions of a feudal society were observed. Aristocrats, diplomats, ministers gathered at the Café Daum. Government officials below such exalted rank relaxed and discussed affairs of state at the Café Pucher, while fashionable society fussed over the latest balls and scandals at the Café Fenstergucker. At the "Imperial" the world of horses was the main topic, while the subdued atmosphere of the Café Central served as the meeting place of the intellectual, the journalist, the chess player. There a Russian was frequently seen who was to make history as Leon Trotsky.

A different atmosphere, noisy, of heated debate, pervaded the smoke-filled Café Griensteidl, the rallying point of the avant-garde: Bahr, Schnitzler, Altenberg, Hoffmannsthal, Karl Kraus, and others. Its atmosphere was also conducive to the young musical minds and a table was reserved for Zemlinsky, Max Graf, Bruno Walter, violinist Bodanzky, and Schönberg. One day Schönberg showed Graf his string sextet, "Verklärte Nacht": "The music sounded new, the harmonies unusual," Graf recalled. "Since I did not trust my judgment I gave the score to Mahler . . . Mahler wavered in his opinion . . . and asked Rosé to play the sextet with his musicians in Mahler's office. He invited me to come to this private performance, and we both were enthusiastic. Mahler said to Rosé: You must play that, and Rosé played it at the next chamber-music evening, to the great displeasure of the Viennese public who hissed loudly."

On October 7, 1901 Schönberg married Mathilde Zemlinsky, the sister of his friend and mentor, and they moved to Berlin. Berlin's sarcastic literary stages, their sharp-tongued satire, attracted the intellectual. There he met Dehmel whose poem "Verklärte Nacht" he had set to music, the dramatist Frank Wedekind whose *Lulu* was to inspire Alban Berg, and Albert Giraud whose *Pierrot Lunaire* was to serve Schönberg as well as the more conservative composer Josef Marx; and also Ernst von Wolzogen, whose libretto *Feuersnot* became a Richard Strauss opera. Berlin was a relief to Schönberg after the meager income he had earned in Vienna by orchestrating about six thousand pages of the music of others. By contrast, in Berlin the influential Richard Strauss provided a scholarship and a conservatory position. He also encouraged Arnold to compose the tone poem "Pelleas and Melisande," using a text on which Debussy wrote an opera at about the same time.

In the "Gurrelieder," on which he resumed work, the mammoth orchestrations of Wagner and Mahler are still evident. In "Pelleas" Schönberg's own personality emerges with a surprising dash of Viennese flavor, an incongruous ingredient in a story laid in France. It is this obvious flavor which marks Schönberg as a Viennese master. Actually no other national or racial influence ever swayed him. Despite his Berlin residences, Teutonic influence was fleeting. He had not become sufficiently acquainted with Debussy's France to come under its spell. Nor did religious concepts sway him until the dark hours of 1938. Thus, while his art became universal, it had its unmistakable roots in Viennese tradition.

The year 1903 saw Schönberg back in Vienna. In youthful heedlessness, the younger man had called Mahler incompetent, but when the two met at a rehearsal of the "Verklärte Nacht" by the Rosé Quartet they became close friends. "Schönberg was inspired by a youthful rebelliousness against his elder whom at the same time he revered," wrote Alma Mahler. Schönberg and Zemlinsky

> used to come in the evening. After one of our . . . simple meals all three went to the piano and talked shop—at first in all amity. Then Schönberg let fall a word in youthful arrogance and Mahler corrected him with a shade of condescension—and the room was in an uproar . . . Schönberg leaped to his feet and vanished with a curt good night. Zemlinsky followed shaking his head. As soon as the door had shut behind them Mahler said: "Be sure never to invite that conceited puppy again." On the stairs Schönberg sputtered: "I shall never again cross that threshold." But after a week or two Mahler said: "By the way what's become of those two?" I lost no time in sending them an invitation; and they, who had only been waiting for it, lost no time in coming.

When the Vereinigung schaffender Tonkünstler (Society of Creative Musicians) was formed by Schönberg and Zemlinsky, Mahler became its honorary president. The premiere performance of the "Society" could not have been more promising. Mahler conducted, and the program included Richard Strauss' "Sinfonia Domestica." A second concert was devoted to Pfitzner's piano trio and songs by

Kurt Schindler and Rudolf Hoffmann. The third concert provided the fireworks. The powder keg—"Pelleas and Melisande" by Schönberg with the composer on the podium. As one of those present recalled, "A sort of rage came over the audience. Many simply left ... many more created disturbances. A few felt the promise of new music, had some inkling of its message." The tenor of the press was predictable:

> The three leaders of the Verein schaffender Tonkünstler ... devoted an entire evening to their cause. The most talented of them, Schönberg, was the most unpalatable. Fully fifty minutes were needed for his continuous symphonic poem, Pelleas and Melisande. Here and there a speck of common sense. Otherwise, for the entire fifty minutes one deals with a man either devoid of all sense or one who takes his listeners for fools ... Schönberg's opus is not merely filled with wrong notes ... but is itself a fifty-minute-long protracted wrong note. This is to be taken literally. What else may hide behind this cacaphony is impossible to ascertain.

Surprisingly, Schönberg seemed undisturbed by the hissing and the catcalls. Even more surprising was the attitude of the conservative Rosé Quartet. They who had rejected Wolf's chamber music, stirred to Schönberg's sounds. One evening, when the audience expectedly displayed its turbulent dismay with "Verklärte Nacht," the players rose, smiled, bowed—and sat down to repeat the work as if impelled by a clamorous ovation. The catcalls had become a badge of honor.

The summer of 1904 found Schönberg busy at his First String Quartet in D. He clearly patterned it after Beethoven's last quartets, a telling proof of its Vienna tradition. Again the devoted Rosé ensemble performed it although forty (!) rehearsals were needed to master its complexities. Vienna of course rejected it out of hand and Berlin called it "a pitiful negation of all art." His "Chamber Symphony" strained tonality even farther, and was promptly dubbed "Horror Chamber Symphony" by the Viennese.

Despite their divergent approaches to music, Mahler and Schönberg drew closer, and finally the younger man was mature enough to acknowledge Mahler's stature: "I have felt your symphony: I have sensed the battle for ideals; I have experienced the grief of the disillusioned one, saw the forces of good and evil struggling with each other. I saw a man deeply troubled, fighting for inner harmony; I have perceived a man, a dream, truth with no restrictions." (Schönberg to Mahler, July 1906.) Schönberg eventually counted Mahler among the classic composers, and this reveals his view of the two musical worlds of his time, the classic, Mahler's, and the modern, Schönberg's.

"I feel the breath of other planets blowing," declared the younger man. The last tonal frontiers are left behind. Appropriately a musical development which broke so sharply with the past went hand in hand with the crumbling of an empire which had outlived its usefulness. There is a spanning of two worlds as Schönberg observed classical structure in his Second Quartet. And a further reminder of Vienna's background is offered in the quotation of "Ach du lieber Augustin" in the quartet. The bitterness, the irony of the quotation reveals an awareness of decay by composers long before politicians or writers had realized the steep downhill course of affairs. "We mistook the dying afterglow for the first blush of dawn, and the smiling death of Austria for a holy springtide," wrote Hermann Bahr. When Schönberg arrives at the words "Alles ist hin" (all is lost) in his "Augustin" quotation, the acid counterpoint of the simple melody provides its own meaningful commentary. This was underlined by the composer's comment that it was of "real emotional significance and not ironically meant." The last movement of the quartet is the deliberate step across the threshold of atonality. Schönberg sheared his art of the time-honored symbols of the past to create a new orchestration devoid of all previous points of orientation. The challenge was great, reaction violent.

By then all phases of musical life had been touched by atonality except opera. Opera composition is a highly specialized field. Beethoven had grandly failed in it as had Schubert. Bruckner, an ardent Wagner admirer, had ignored the form as had Mahler. Schönberg had no such qualms. His one-act, one-character monodrama *Erwartung* (Expectation) is one of the longest steps away from convention. Only the basic drama is akin to Tristan's *Liebestod*. This may have been Schönberg's intention. Musicologist Paul Bekker commented on that similarity at the premiere in 1928, nineteen years and one world war after its creation and, incidentally, gained the proper perspective for the work: "Even including the most striking creations of the young generation, Hindemith's 'Cardillac,' Krenek's 'Orpheus' and 'Jonny,' Berg's 'Wozzeck,' nothing has yet been written that . . . was not already contained in Schönberg's 'Erwartung.' This work is one of the fundamental manifestations of modern operatic composition." Schönberg's journey into the unknown did not end with *Erwartung*. While Stravinsky outraged and delighted his audiences with *Sacre du Printemps*, Schönberg put the finishing touches to "Pierrot Lunaire." This crowning achievement of Schönberg's work in the 1920s brought total elimination of the tonal system. The classical pillars had fallen.

What was to uphold musical structure, to bind and unify, provide body, form? The old had been abandoned, the new not yet achieved. "Progress" thus far had been merely negative, abandonment, destruction. Schönberg provided the answer. Shortly after his fortieth birthday he handed bewildered Vienna the thread to lead it out of the labyrinth of atonality—the twelve-tone row. As Bela Bartok has pointed out,

> the decisive turn to atonality began when one realized the necessity of equality of the individual single tones of our twelve-tone system; when one tried to arrange the twelve tones, no longer according to specific scale systems . . . but to use the individual tones in any combination . . . at one's discretion . . . In this procedure, certain tones . . . do acquire a relative preponderance; but this difference . . . is no longer based on this or another scale system, but is the result of the actual combination. The possibilities of expression are increased by the free and equal treatment of the individual tones in a measure hardly yet to be gauged.

Silence accompanied the birth of the "row." With it Schönberg had found the means "to organize the chaos of atonality." It stands today as his major contribution to modern music but did not "deal the death blow to the tonal universe" as predicted. Actually the tone-row wasn't fully used by its creator. It was left to his disciples, Webern and Berg, to apply it, to carry Schönberg's torch and lead music in new directions.

To Vienna Schönberg remained an enigma, a disturbing thorn in the placid Viennese ways of enjoying the music of the past. Richard Strauss, who occasionally prided himself on inserting a speck of atonality into his music, half mockingly, half seriously asked Paul Hindemith: "Why do you write atonally? After all, you have talent." Even Mahler professed: "I don't understand his [Schönberg's] work, but he is young and he may well be right. I'm old and perhaps don't have the ear for his music." Yet when Mahler established a fund which should benefit one promising composer each year, Schönberg was the first recipient. Schönberg dedicated his *Harmonielehre* (Harmony Manual) to the memory of Mahler. The manual, again, reflects Schönberg's Vienna ties. It starts from the teachings of Simon Sechter who was himself a link with the music of Schubert and Bruckner. Guido Adler, the renowned musicologist fully realized Schönberg's ties to Vienna's past. He invited him to collaborate in his monumental *Denkmäler der Tonkunst in Österreich* (Monuments of Musical Art in Austria).

As if he had found new strength by formulating his theories, Schönberg progressed to new creations. Yet Vienna was not willing to follow. They had barely hurdled Bruckner and Mahler and were mentally too breathless to keep pace with Schönberg. He had veered too abruptly, leaving no bridges or markers to guide the bewildered Viennese who refused to be led from verdant valleys, placid and familiar, onto arid wastelands. The historic concert of March 31, 1913 featured Mahler's "Kindertotenlieder," Berg's "Picture Post Cards," orchestral pieces by Webern, songs by Zemlinsky, and Schönberg's "Chamber Symphony." With Berg's Lieder, the noise-making became so loud that it drowned out all music in an unprecedented anti-Schönberg demonstration and one of the worst musical scandals in Vienna's annals.

> The audience was quietly and by tacit agreement taking it as a great joke until one of the critics present committed the unpardonable blunder of shouting for the performers to stop. Whereupon a howling and yelling broke out such as I have never heard before or since. One man stood up in front and hissed Schönberg every time he came apologetically forward to make his bow, wagging his Semitic head, so like Bruckner's, from side to side in the embarrassed hope of enlisting some stray breath of sympathy or forgiveness. Mahler sprang to his feet . . . a man raised his arm as if to strike Mahler . . . Moll saw this and . . . forced his way through the crowd and collared the man . . . He was hustled out of the hall without much difficulty. But at the door he plucked up his courage and shouted: Needn't get so excited—I hiss Mahler too. [Alma Mahler]

> People began to push their chairs back noisily halfway through the concert, and some went out in open protest. Mahler got up angrily and enforced silence. As soon as the performance was over, he stood near the front and applauded until the last of the demonstrators was gone. [Max Graf]

Meanwhile Schönberg had again sought the seemingly more permissive atmosphere of Berlin and there began work on Giraud's "Pierrot Lunaire." In it a new expressive device, "Sprechstimme" (speaking voice), neither speech nor voice but of predetermined pitch, is fully employed. "Inexhaustible fund of healthy melody . . . rhythm so varied and pulsating with so much life . . . harmony so refined, so bold and yet so clear and transparent," declared Berg, but the world held its ears in amusement and exasperation. The work was completed in September 1912 and after forty (!) rehearsals had its Berlin premiere. As one critic described it:

> At first, the sound of delicate china shivering into a thousand luminous fragments. The welter of tonalities . . . made the ears bleed, the eyes water, the scalp freeze . . . Schönberg mingles with his music sharp daggers at white heat . . . What kind of music is this, without melody . . . without a harmony that does not smite the ears . . . and rhythms that are so persistantly varied as to become monotonous—what kind of music is this that can paint the blackness of prehistoric night, the abyss of a morbid soul, the faint sweet odours of an impossible fairyland . . . There is no melodic or harmonic line, only phrases that sob and scream, despair, explode, blaspheme.

But the masochistic desire to hear that "outrageous music" spread. In September 1912 Sir Henry Wood presented "Five Orchestral Pieces" in London. Zemlinsky performed "Pierrot" in Prague. In Amsterdam Mengelberg rehearsed it, and Schönberg conducted a rousing performance. Milhaud presented it in Paris. Even St. Petersburg received it well, but Vienna cold-shouldered it and a Berlin critic prescribed certain objects to be brought to a Schönberg concert: "Some door keys in good condition (to whistle on), a few handy missiles, and a small collection of money to pay for the return to Vienna of this charlatan and humbug."

After eleven years and upon Webern's insistence, "Gurrelieder" received a hearing in Vienna on February 23, 1913. The audience followed the unfolding of the work with mounting excitement. When at the climax the chorus reverted to the doubly brilliant key of C major in their jubilant outcry "Behold the Sun," the audience rose and remained standing until the finale. The analogy with another occasion 125 years earlier, when Haydn's "Creation" burst into "And there was Light," was inescapable. Schönberg had scored his first triumph in Vienna. When he was finally induced to take a bow he received a standing ovation. Ignoring the audience, he bowed to the conductor and the orchestra and left the stage without a glance at the audience: "For years, these people who cheered me tonight refused to recognize me. Why should I thank them for appreciating me now."

In lavish orchestration the score of "Gurrelieder" outdoes almost anything Wagner, Strauss, or Mahler might have envisioned: Recitator, 5 solo voices, 3 male choirs, one mixed choir, 3 piccolos, 4 flutes, 3 oboes, 2 English horns, 5 clarinets, 2 bass clarinets, 3 bassoons, 2 double bassoons, 10 horns, 6 trumpets, 1 bass trumpet, 5 trombones, 1 bass trombone, 1 double bass trombone, cymbals, triangle, glockenspiel, side drum, tenor drum, xylophone, gong, 4 harps, celesta, a brace of iron chains, and a huge body of strings. All this permitted effects unheard of before and never equalled since. For a complete annotation, the Vienna printers of the score were obliged to cut and print a special 48-line music-sheet, twice the size used by either Mahler or Strauss.

Contacts and friendships with avant-garde painters Paul Klee and Vasili Kandinski in Berlin, Egon Schiele and Oskar Kokoschka in Vienna, added new dimensions to Schönberg's art. Wedekind and Giraud, Stefan George and Dehmel, also played significant roles in the artistic growth of Schönberg when words and music were fused with color in "Die Glückliche Hand" (The Fortunate Hand). An impression of wind which gradually rises in intensity corresponds with a display of color, from pale rose through brown to grayish green, blue green, dark blue, purple. As the music and wind gain there is a moment of dramatic darkness, then the colors flash on in renewed intensity, to deep red, brighten into glaring red, orange, rise into blinding yellow and finally a glaring white, with the trumpets at lung-bursting power. Slowly color and music subside to light blue, the tinkle of the celesta, woodwinds and solo violin. Superimposed upon the spectacle is the "Sprechstimme," used for the first time in choral application.

"Jacob's Ladder" which followed was never finished because of Schönberg's induction into the Austrian Army. Despite its title, "Jacob's Ladder" is not a religious work in the ordinary sense because religion in its external aspects held little interest for Schönberg. Like many of his Austrian coreligionists he had joined the Catholic faith. Only the persecution by Hitler made him again aware of his heritage and prompted him to solemnly reaffirm his Jewish faith in 1938. The opening words by Gabriel in "Jacob's Ladder" are also a re-affirmation of his artistic faith: "Whether right or left, whether forward or backward—one must always go on without asking what lies before or behind one." A mellowing Schönberg concedes, however, that "a longing to return to the older style was always vigorous in me; and from time to time I had to yield to that urge."

Resistance to his music, from one quarter or another, ceased at no time, but Schönberg and his disciples were not to be deterred. The end of World War I saw the founding of the unique "Verein für musikalische Privataufführungen" (Society for Private Musical Performances) in Vienna, complete with card-carrying members but with neither programs nor critics. It was founded by Schönberg during most trying times. Vienna, shorn of its imperial splendour, Austria fighting for its life. How could men and women attend such concerts at a time when their waking hours had to be devoted to standing in breadlines or hunting for coal, flour, soap, potatoes? But Schönberg's ideals and Vienna's musical urge overcame all obstacles of post-war life. Vienna heard such divergent music as Mahler, Reger, Strauss, Ravel, Debussy, Bartok, and Kodaly side by side with Schönberg, Berg, and Webern. Alban Berg was the musical director, and his devotion and enthusiasm matched that of Schönberg.

With such a new spirit pervading Vienna after World War I, it was logical to find Schönberg's "Gurrelieder" and "Pelleas" in splendid performances during the "Wiener Festwochen" (Vienna Festival Weeks). Amsterdam was also in the forefront again. The Mahler city and its great orchestra under Mengelberg included Schönberg in its Mahler Festival of 1920 and elected him president of the newly-founded International Mahler Society. Austria, though at the brink of starvation, was determined to make music no matter what the sacrifice. Thus a new festival, destined to become the most famous, came into being in Salzburg in August 1922 only four years after World War I. There again the world heard Mozart and Beethoven side by side with Wellesz, Webern, and Schönberg. The Vienna wave of new music was rising to its crest.

The crest was reached in 1924 when Vienna acknowledged Schönberg's music on his fiftieth birthday. To its own surprise, the city went all-out to honor the composer—with a ceremonial address by the mayor and the opera chorus singing "Friede auf Erden" (Peace on Earth) by the man so honored. Within a decade Schönberg had become recognized in Vienna, an unheard-of feat in the annals of the city. A special collection of essays in his honor was issued. It contained a contribution by a mellowed Schönberg who admitted "I cannot hate anyone the way I used to and, worse yet, I can now sometimes understand things without holding them in contempt."

In 1925 Schönberg was again invited to Berlin, to replace Ferruccio Busoni who had died the previous year. Forgotten were the days of near starvation. He was honored, recognized, secure. In September 1927 the Kolisch Quartet premiered in Vienna his Third Quartet, his finest chamber work in the twelve-tone technique. In December Furtwängler conducted the orchestral version in Berlin. On January 30, 1933 Adolf Hitler ascended to power. Schönberg promptly lost his Berlin position, but America beckoned. He arrived in New York in October 1933, sick, weakened, unable to keep an appointment with the Boston Symphony. Not until March 1934 was he able to lead them in "Pelleas and Melisande." But the Eastern winter had proved too severe, and he sought the balmier climate of California.

While Mahler strenuously avoided the number "9" in his symphonies, Schönberg's concern centered around the number "13." "It is not superstition," he declared, "it is belief." He had been born on December 13 and considered the date a bad omen. He was afraid that he would die in the year of his 65th birthday because that number was a multiple of "13." He was upset when an astrologer-friend warned him of the danger inherent in his 67th birthday because the two numbers added up to "13." "If only I can pull through this year I will be safe." He always numbered the bars of his compositions and staunchly believed that it required his greatest efforts to proceed past measures "13" and multiples. In later years like Mahler he actually tried to circumvent what he considered his fateful number by marking measures "12," "12a," "14." He died on July 13, 1951 at the age of 76.

XXI

The New Breed

To Alban Berg the number "23" had special significance. The first attack of asthma, which troubled him all his life, occurred on July 23, 1900. He wrote all important letters on the 23rd and often pointed out that he received all important news on that date. He arranged work on his music in such a manner that the first draft was always finished on the 23rd. During his mortal illness he was always aware of that date. His death throes began on December 23. He moved his pupil and biographer, Willi Reich, who published an avant-garde music magazine in Vienna, to call it *23*, even designed the title page, a large "23."

In this connection, however, the "23" had a different connotation. It was the paragraph of the Austrian press law by which one could force correction of an incorrect announcement in a newspaper. Through the magazine *23*, Reich and Berg hoped to fight and correct what they considered in need of correction in the realm of music in Vienna. "I would not wish to look into the souls of people who enthusiastically applaud a Bach concerto, the last Beethoven quartets, or even a Mozart aria, although they are actually bored by them. Brahms . . . bores people to death and now shares the fate of Bach, Beethoven, Schubert, etc. They only act enthusiastically." Such was the opinion of Alban Berg of the Vienna concert-going public. The distrust was mutual. Whenever the music of Berg, Webern, or Schönberg played the audience left in droves.

Alban Berg and Anton [von] Webern, two disciples of Schönberg who were to surpass their master, were eleven and nine years younger than Schönberg and, consequently, did not assert themselves until after the first great world conflict. It was Alban's brother who showed Berg's early songs to Schönberg. He was impressed and accepted Berg as a pupil. Webern met Schönberg at about the same time through musicologist Guido Adler with whom the younger man had studied counterpoint. He and Berg continued to study with Schönberg, and a close friendship developed among the three. Music publisher H. W. Heinsheimer recalled Berg as unusually tall but always slightly stooped, as if bowing in humbleness and grace to the world . . . He had a beautiful face, a smiling, almost mocking mouth. He had great warming eyes that always looked straight at you, knowing penetrating eyes that would demand the truth—and always get it . . . But he wasn't a saint or a hermit. He was full of life and he loved to tell jokes, and when he told one of his doubtful stories, he would roar with delight.

Berg's first major compositions were created under Schönberg's watchful eye. Their first performance in November 1907, in a concert of eight Schönberg pupils, predictably outraged Vienna. Few had the courage, conviction, or foresight to proclaim a new generation of Vienna composers. "Eight different talents—all united in unusually serious efforts," wrote music critic Dr. Elsa Bienenfeld. "The mechanical aspects of composing technique, the laws of harmony, the polyphonic voices are handled with sureness and by some even with virtuosity . . . respect for art, purity of feeling, security of style, is the remarkable result of good upbringing. It is wonderful how the strong and original personality of Schönberg strongly and securely guides the talents of his pupils."

Asthma kept Berg out of active military service. While serving in the War Ministry he wrote the libretto to *Wozzeck* after the fragmentary play of an obscure nineteenth-century poet, Georg Büchner. Between 1917 and 1921 he scored it and had it printed with the help of some friends. Four years later, on December 14, 1925, after one hundred (!) rehearsals, conductor Erich Kleiber undertook the formidable task of a full production at the Berlin opera. The impact was that of a thunder clap. Musical history had been made; a new vista in operatic history had been opened. The music awed and outraged, and a new term was born—*Kulturbolschewism* (cultural bolshevism), a dangerous expression in dangerous hands. Berg had arrived. Whether people admired or despised his work, his name was engraved in music history, was carried to Amsterdam, Zurich, London, New York, Philadelphia. Although he was now famous or notorious, although fist fights broke out whenever and wherever his music was performed, he continued serenely on his path.

Both Webern and Berg were products of their time, haunted by Austria's postwar frustrations and struggle for survival. In Berg's music, the hopelessness of his time and its bleak effect on art makes him a key figure in the postwar expressionist movement. His path was smoothed by Schönberg's accomplishments, and he was spared the latter's creative growing pains. He overtook the older master by a

quicker grasp and bolder utilization of the tone row. His Chamber
Concerto and "Lyric Suite" prove the point. The headings of the
"Lyric Suite," worthy of Berlioz, indicate Berg's romantic Vienna
notions, such adjectives as "gioviale," "amoroso," "appasionato,"
"delirando," "tenebroso," and "desolato."

Berg's operas were to surpass his instrumental creations. Büchner's
morbid drama became a masterpiece only through Berg's lavish music.
Its psychological implications, on the other hand, could not fail to
have an enormous impact on the Vienna of Siegmund Freud. The
total integration of Büchner's drama and Berg's music, with the music
greatly intensifying the drama, raises the opera to a place among the
greatest operatic masterpieces created in Vienna. "Peter Altenberg–
Gustav Mahler–Arnold Schönberg–Adolf Loos–Karl Kraus. Those
five names were the stars of his [Berg's] world," declares Soma Mor-
genstern. "He did not admire them in far-off heavens, they were his
house-gods and he lived in their nearness, too modest to be aware
that among those stars he was a star of equal magnitude."

Webern's progress was never as spectacular as that of his master or
his friend. In composition and as a conductor he labored inconspicuously for twelve years as the guiding figure of Vienna's Arbeiter
Symphonie, the workers' symphony orchestra (socialist leanings also
prompted him to drop the "von" from his name), and earned a living
as proof reader for a Vienna music publisher. Webern did not seem
to resent such an uneventful life. His devotion to music and flowers
sufficed the modest, retiring man whose small output of miniature
gems reflect the gossamer quality of his being and inspirations. Musicologist Willi Reich considers his songs "of a wonderfully pure
tenderness completely retired within themselves, as if at the edge of
hearing . . . Nearly too gentle for the ear which serves the daily noises,
always expressing the innermost, the most urgent things, which are
here for the moment without a past or a future. Thus their brevity,
their renunciation of theme and development."

Ironically the dramatic death of so gentle a genius, who almost
sought obscurity, caused a ripple of belated recognition and led
people to recall him who had so unobtrusively lived and created
among them. On September 15, 1945, absentmindedly ignoring the
curfew while lost in thought, he was shot by a suspicious member of
the American Military Police.

Compared to Schönberg, the creative output of Berg and Webern
is exceedingly small. Aside from the opera *Wozzeck* (dedicated to
Alma Mahler), Berg's major work consists of his Chamber Sym-

phony, his "Lyric Suite" for String Quartet and his Cantata "Der Wein." His last work, the Violin Concerto, is often called his Requiem. Like Mozart he received a secret commission. It coincided with the death of Manon Gropius, daughter of the architect and Alma Mahler. Thus the dedication "to the memory of an angel" and the inclusion of a Bach Chorale. The Requiem was also his own. The concerto seems to have been uppermost in his mind. The usually slow Berg wrote it in six weeks, interrupting work on his opera *Lulu* which remained unfinished despite six years' work. Like Mozart he heard neither his concerto nor his opera.

Compared again with Schönberg, the romanticist, his two most famous disciples are cut from different cloth. Berg storms and rages, catastrophies explode in his music and shake the universe and, against seemingly insuperable odds, strive for redemption. Webern, the extreme introvert, is equally shaken and equally striving. But implosions, not explosions, are the means of visualizing his tragedies and ecstasies. Yet both drew their strength and inspiration from their ideal and teacher, Schönberg. Never did he attempt to shape their talents according to his own visions. He showed the way, the direction, and let them mature according to their own lights.

Although the list of Webern's works is much longer than that of Berg, there is actually much less music because Webern was the master of the minuscule composition. Despite their elaborate orchestrations, neither Schönberg nor Berg were as acutely aware of the value, the very meaning of sound as was Webern. Tone, in the sense in which it had been first employed by Debussy, was Webern's main way of expression and communication. Neither the lasting friendship between Berg and Webern nor their ties to Schönberg insured unanimity in their aims and creations. "Schönberg and Berg," declares Pierre Boulez, "belong to the twilight years of the great Germanic tradition which they brought to its peak in such luxuriant flamboyant works as 'Pierrot Lunaire' and 'Wozzeck'; whereas Webern reacted strongly against all forms of inherited rhetoric in his effort to rehabilitate the power of sheer sound."

By happily wedding Debussy's tone color and Schönberg's "Klangfarbenmelody" (sound-color-melody) Webern created and attained a mastery of twelve-tone sound seldom approached by Schönberg or Berg in its sensitiveness. Like Debussy he was in love with sound for its own sake. In response to that love, he also went beyond Schönberg and Berg in ignoring all time-honored musical forms. Instead he strove to capture a new world of sound in extremely concentrated, painfully short orchestral sound patterns, some of less than a minute's duration. If one does not listen to every note one might miss the entire piece.

In attempting to formulate a new language, attuned to his particular genius, Webern could cope with its inherent problems only in miniature sound patterns and portraits, adhering to an amazing discipline of his own. He thus achieved a refinement of orchestral color never before accomplished in which even silence took on a deliberate meaning. Such evocative, challenging music demands total absorption by executant and listener alike. Yet Webern, too, seemed to have been reluctant to cut all ties with the past and continued to probe in both directions, weighing the inherited old against the new he strove for.

XXII

Kaleidoscope

In Vienna immediately after World War I, one could see women rushing a bread wagon, pulling down the driver and forcing him to open the doors; men, women, and children sitting on the curb, devouring the bread they had just taken; hungry mobs breaking open milk wagons, and milk coloring the granite pavement a whitish grey as bottles fell and broke among the starving people fighting over them; infants near death from watered-down milk and lack of citrus fruit; old women and children following horse-drawn coal wagons through the wintry streets and gathering in their aprons or on primitive home-made sleds the chunks of coal which tumbled from the wagons as they lumbered along the pavement. The Cassandras, the prophets of doom predicted that Vienna, shorn of its empire of fifty-five million souls, would revert to an overgrown provincial city; grass would grow between the granite cobblestones, and cows would pasture on the Ringstrasse. As hunger stalked the land, there were outcries that the young republic should sell the art treasures of the Habsburgs to keep its people from starvation.

People ate bread which soon turned to stone, used homemade soap which barely lathered, pulled little carts for miles for a bag of coal, stood in line for hours for a bag of flour. But they also stood in line to hear music. The young republic realized that music was one of its great treasures, and, despite scarcities, the opera continued to be subsidized by the government. Music not only survived, it flourished. With inflation rampant and little to buy, the Viennese went to operas and concerts as never before. So great was the clamor that in 1921 each subscription concert of the Philharmonic had to be given three times. In the "State" Opera (gone was the double eagle of the Habsburgs) the singers were still the ones of the famous Mahler ensemble. Gone were the brilliant coloratura Selma Kurtz and the tenor Erik Schmedes whom the older generation had glowingly recalled. But still to be heard were some of the greatest voices: gigantic tenor Leo Slezak, regal Madame Gutheil-Schoder, and the incomparable Richard Mayr.

When Mahler resigned from the opera, there set in a period of stagnation under elegant, archconservative Felix Weingartner. Weingartner could not repeat in the opera his brilliant successes with the Philharmonic. The man to follow Weingartner at the opera was not even a musician. Concerned about falling box-office receipts, the administration appointed a theatrical business man, Hans Gregor, as opera director.

Neither period was devoid of great events, however. Weingartner staged Strauss' explosive opera *Electra*, d'Albert's passionate *Tiefland*, and bowed out with an acclaimed production of Berlioz' *Benvenuto Cellini*. Gregor's daring production of *Pelleas and Melisande* by Debussy won him praise. Other events reflected favorably on his administration. The production of *Der Rosenkavalier* (which Weingartner had acquired) was one, giving the role of Baron Ochs von Lerchenau to Richard Mayr another. Tall, plump, and jovial, Mayr looked the part of the easy-going, lecherous aristocrat. He made the role so completely his own that every artist to follow modelled himself after Mayr's inspired original. He gave the basically obnoxious character a depth and charm which drew praise from Strauss and Hofmannsthal alike. Another Gregor coup was his discovery of soprano Maria Jeritza at the Volksoper, Vienna's second opera house. Her brilliant, sensuous voice and personality filled the theatrical and gossip columns with fascinating accounts. Gregor's most lasting appointment was Franz Schalk, the Bruckner and Wolf disciple, as music director. For thirty years Schalk was to demonstrate his innate musicianship and love for the institution. Many of its brilliant productions during Austria's dark postwar years were due to his never-ending devotion to music and to Vienna.

After the last peacetime performance, of *Parsifal* on June 27, 1914, the opera was dark and silent for four months. It re-opened on October 18 with *Lohengrin* and, despite shortages and crises, continued to limp along during four years of war, privation, and defeat. Suddenly the limp became a strut. With the war lost, the monarchy dismembered, the emperor in exile, and hunger stalking the land, one man—Richard Strauss—filled the opera with his own brilliance. Strauss had come to Vienna in 1918 as guest conductor during a Strauss festival. Eager to restore the splendor of its opera, the new regime approached him. Strauss had always loved Vienna, and *Der Rosenkavalier* is his witness. To the astonishment of almost everybody he accepted codirectorship with Schalk in the impoverished city and set out to restore a still-remembered splendor.

As in Mahler's day, only under more trying circumstances, Strauss began to build a new repertoire on the foundation of the old one. *Fidelio*, *The Magic Flute*, and *Tristan* emerged side by side with Strauss' own *Rosenkavalier*, *Ariadne auf Naxos*, and *Die Frau ohne Schatten* (The Woman Without Shadow) and a number of works by Austrian composers. The most promising among them proved to be young Erich Wolfgang Korngold whose opera *Die tote Stadt* (The Dead City) received glowing notices. The state spared no expense. The long-dormant corps de ballet was rejuvenated with two Strauss ballets, *Josephslegende* and *Schlagobers* (Whipped Cream). A new Strauss ensemble emerged. Karl Alwin joined as musical director and brought his wife, Elisabeth Schumann, one of the world's greatest Lieder singers. The resonant baritone of Josef Manowarda was to elicit a "Com' e bello" (how beautiful) from hard-to-please Toscanini.

Then there was Alfred Jerger. There have been greater baritones than Jerger, but few were the artist he was with every fiber of his being. On one occasion when Verdi's *Otello* was to be given, the baritone took sick on the morning of the performance, and Jerger was called upon to sing Iago. Jerger had either never sung Iago or had not done so for many years. He made the last-minute assignment a personal triumph. Since he did not have time to study the role, he had an ornate stand put on stage in the background and the score placed on it. Such was his artistry that the score became part of his characterization. He made the turning of the pages, the turned back, a symbol of villainy, part of the sinister role he portrayed. So consummate was the interpretation that after a minute's surprise one noticed only the malevolent back, the secretive leafing, the sinister voice from the depth of the stage. Seldom was a singer accorded more rousing applause.

Maria Jeritza personified on stage everything that was sensuous: Carmen, Salome (which she sang superbly and danced clumsily), Tosca, Minnie in *The Girl of the Golden West*. Apropos *The Girl*— one day the State Opera received a letter from a Texan who had seen the performance. He praised the production but took exception to the English saddle that had been used, and a few days later the opera received a splendidly appointed western saddle from the opera-loving Texan.

When we think of Lotte Lehmann, the Marshallin in *Der Rosenkavalier* comes to mind first. Few remember that she also sang the role of the Rosenkavalier, Octavian, and only a dainty figurine of the Vienna porcelain works reminds us of Lehmann in that role. Her splendid Leonore in *Fidelio* was to bring her the ultimate triumph with Toscanini in Salzburg. Whether her voice was raised as Else or Sieglinde, whether she sang Turandot or Leonore or gave a Lieder recital with Walter at the piano, each evening with her was enthralling.

While Austria struggled to regain a place among the nations, virility returned to the music of Vienna. That the Viennese were outraged by the atonal creations of Schönberg and Berg was actually one of many encouraging signs. The opera blossomed as did the Philharmonic Orchestra. Vienna, of course, enjoys the unique distinction of having the Philharmonic double as the orchestra of the opera house which gives the State Opera the finest pit orchestra anywhere. It was too good to last. Inevitably some complained about the artistic extravagance of Strauss while the country struggled for survival. And two artists of the caliber of Strauss and Schalk were bound to develop honest artistic differences. The more frugal Schalk won, and Strauss, disgruntled, left.

Surprisingly, those who had feared the conservatism of Schalk found him open-minded toward contemporary composers, including Strauss. Thus Vienna enjoyed Strauss' *Intermezzo* with Lehmann, and Jeritza in *The Egyptian Helena*. Again a number of Austrian composers trod the boards into oblivion with only *Das Wunder der Heliane* (The Miracle of Heliane) leaving Korngold's impression. Indeed, one heard more moderns under Schalk than under Strauss, including *Oedipus Rex* by Stravinsky and Krenek's great success *Jonny spielt auf* (Johnny Plays) with Jerger. His spectacular leap onto the top of the piano was as eagerly discussed as his portrayal of Jonny which took Vienna by storm. So widespread became *Jonny*'s popularity that the Austrian tobacco administration named a new cigaret after him. Schalk made no secret of his personal dislike of *Jonny* but felt nonetheless that it merited performance, an excellent example of artistic integrity. There was no end to operatic innovation under the paradoxical Schalk. He brought out *Cardillac* by Hindemith and Ravel's *Magic Word*. And thanks to Franz Werfel's efforts and Schalk's interest in Verdi, Vienna heard *La Forza del Destino*, *Simone Boccanegra*, and *Don Carlos*. Puccini's *Turandot* had two premieres. One with the established stars Lehmann and Slezak, and a second with two new voices, temperamental Maria Nemeth and Jan Kiepura, whose lavish natural tenor quickly made him the darling of Vienna. Nor was the Philharmonic Orchestra neglected, and Stravinsky's *Sacre du Printemps* shared the repertoire with Bruckner.

Weingartner, who had remained as director of the Philharmonic when he left the opera, was now leaving the orchestra, disgruntled at having been passed over in favor of Richard Strauss for the Philharmonic's first South American tour. Furtwängler was invited to assume both posts but decided to lead only the Philharmonic. It was then that Strauss again made his influence felt. In urgent messages to the Vienna operatic powers that be, he recommended his friend and disciple Clemens Krauss: "The decisive moment has arrived . . . If you refuse 'the other' will inevitably take over." "The other"—Weingartner. Echoing Mahler's feelings, Strauss considered him a musical reactionary.

Clemens Krauss was chosen although he was not the drawing card the times demanded. He was a "modern" interpreter, a brilliant technician with excellent control. Tall, slender, with sleek black hair and sideburns, he cut a handsome figure, and a couplet was soon repeated in which a bevy of Viennese society ladies pleads "Ach nehmen's den schönen Clemens" (Oh please espouse the handsome Krauss—very free translation). But one innovation immediately endeared Krauss to the Viennese: a New Year's concert devoted exclusively to the music of the Johann Strauss family.

Two chamber ensembles stand out among the many-faceted musical activities of Vienna's inter-war years. Rudolf Kolisch, the founder and first violinist of the Kolisch Quartet, had injured his bowing arm in his youth, something that would have discouraged many a budding violinist. But he trained himself to bow with the left hand and achieved equal mastery. Such a sense of perfection pervaded the ensemble that eventually all compositions, even the excruciatingly difficult contemporary scores, were played from memory, an especially difficult task for the inner voices. Kolisch was drawn to the music of his time by his tie to Schönberg. After the death of his first wife, Schönberg married Rudolf Kolisch's sister in 1924. Kolisch's devotion to avant-garde music extended also to Berg and Webern, and his first performance of Berg's "Lyric Suite" was a major event. The Vienna highlight of the quartet came on September 19, 1927 when they premiered Schönberg's Third Quartet which had been sponsored by the generous American patron of music, Elizabeth Sprague Coolidge, who also arranged for the concert. It prompted Schönberg to call Mrs. Coolidge "the ideal patron" and the Kolisch Quartet "the ideal interpreters." Appropriately Schönberg's Fourth String Quartet was premiered ten years later by the same ensemble —in Los Angeles where composer and performers had found an artistic haven.

Felix Galimir, the leader of the other quartet, was the scion of an old Spanish family and looked the part: slender, dark complected, with eternal five o'clock shadow and the mark of the violinist, the chin scar. Whenever one entered the spacious Galimir apartment, one was assaulted by dissonance from all sides as Felix and his three talented sisters practiced their respective instruments in different rooms. These four young artists comprised the Galimir Quartet, one of the best chamber ensembles in the annals of music. Felix's youngest sister, Adrienne, married American violinist Louis Krasner who had commissioned Alban Berg's Violin Concerto and had premiered it in Vienna. The Galimir Quartet, which had already attained a large measure of European fame, was among the first to acquaint Vienna with the chamber music of Berg. At a private performance of a new string quartet by another Viennese composer, the Galimirs rendered the work with their customary polish. At the conclusion the beaming composer rushed over to Felix and shook his hand: "Masterly, masterly," he exclaimed, "not at all what I had in mind, but, I must confess, I like your version much better."

Any music lover who lived in Vienna between the wars has many memories: Of Bruno Walter recording Mahler's "Das Lied von der Erde," visibly annoyed with the enthusiastic applause which threatened to disrupt the public recording session. . . . Furtwängler conducting the annual performance of Beethoven's Ninth in memory of composer Otto Nikolai, the founder of the Philharmonic. With no other but Furtwängler did one ever have the actual impression of sparks flying from the baton. . . . *Fidelio* with Lotte Lehmann and Alfred Piccaver, under Schalk's baton. The only flaw was that the emaciated prisoner was portrayed by a singer leaning to portliness. . . . Victor de Sabata dancing Ravel's *Bolero* while conducting it. De Sabata always provided a show. When he conducted opera, his Italian temperament and elaborate motions diverted interest from the stage to the pit.

A comparison of conductors comes to mind: Toscanini, de Sabata, Walter, Krauss—each conducting Verdi's Requiem. De Sabata's conducting and mimicry were Mephistophelian. With his long, delicate fingers molding a phrase, face beaming in devilish glee, his Roman head, his entire body, swaying, writhing, he would convey the meaning of the music. Even in the concert hall he was a man of the stage.

To that towering operatic masterpiece of the church, Toscanini brought passion and in its "Dies Irae" (for which he demanded double skins on the timpani to sustain the crash), sheer terror. The impact of Toscanini on audience and players was remarkable. Some players swore that he actually hypnotized them during a performance. Toscanini seldom used scores; his phenomenal memory could dispense with them, and he was nearly blind. On the rare occasions when he did consult the printed page, his nose literally touched the paper. One rehearsal stands out. Even the Vienna Philharmonic had been unable to produce the demanded pianissimo despite the Italian invective showered on it by the maestro. Suddenly, in utter frustration, Toscanini whipped out a white handkerchief, raised it above his head, and let it flutter down. When one-hundred pairs of eyes, after having followed the drop of the filmy fabric in silent fascination, returned their gaze to the maestro, they were met by his outstretched arm pointing to it and one word: "Ecco." The desired pianissimo was forthcoming.

How different with Bruno Walter. When his disciple Maurice Abravanel once suggested to him that the thundering G-minor chords which burst open the "Dies Irae" could have been more forceful, Walter disagreed: "But I do not want physical force . . . I was searching for spiritual power." "Searching" remained the watchword of Walter's entire musical life. One stood in awe before Toscanini, but his command sometimes impressed as superhuman. We bowed before Furtwängler's grandeur of classic interpretation, but his air of Teutonic superiority was a gulf separating the interpreter from the man. No one felt that way about Walter. He was always grandly human. His music always sang. The splendor of his Bruckner, the dedication of his Mahler, the lofty charm and insight of his Mozart elated and warmed. This gentle man was incapable of the harsh reproach in which other conductors seem to delight. When a player's performance did not reach Walter's vision, he would turn his deep gaze on him and sigh gently: "I'm not happy with this."

It was possible to watch Clemens Krauss conduct the Verdi Requiem from a seat in the organ gallery of the Grossen Musikvereinssaal. It was the cheapest seat in the house, but it afforded the opportunity to face the conductor and watch him "work." Krauss would direct the Philharmonic, the opera chorus, and the soloists as a general would lead an army. Like a fencer he would stab with the baton for a precise cue. Krauss was always in command, never submerged by the excitement of the moment. "Always at the helm, never at the oars." But in the drama of the Requiem such a coolly objective approach tended to diminish its glories. One left with the knowledge of having observed a superb technician, but the visceral thrill was missing.

The Kaleidoscope of memory recalls other brilliant views: Weingartner conducting Brahms with the superb elegance of nineteenth-century tradition. Richard Strauss doing Beethoven in his no-nonsense approach. "Feel my armpit," he once urged Mahler, "completely dry; I hate conductors who perspire." How different with Walter. When Abravanel complimented him on a *Don Giovanni* performance, Walter shook his head, "No, it was bad. I don't need to change my shirt." Clemens Krauss, too, always finished drenched. After each selection or between acts, a man-servant in the wings immediately wrapped an ankle-length cape around the maestro.

Furtwängler invoking Mozart's *Magic Flute* at the Felsenreitschule in Salzburg. As the word implies, the locale originally was a riding academy. The "Felsen" (rock) gives it its unique flavor. One wall of the space now transformed into an open-air theatre is hewn out of solid rock. It is arranged in tiers of stone arcades through which the players enter and exit. To hear the Queen of the Night sing her aria of anxiety and revenge from those mysterious stone arches is an experience comparable only to opera among the ruins of the Baths of Caracalla in Rome. Clemens Holzmeister, the ingenious Austrian architect and stage designer, made use of those stone tiers to construct fantastic make-believe cities still remembered as "Faust City" and "Don Juan City."

The Kaleidoscope glitters: Evocative Backhaus' playing of the opening of Beethoven's Piano Concerto in G. . . . Horowitz rendering encore after encore with perspiration dripping from his face, while youngsters pressed against the stage like so many music-drunk sardines. . . . Emil von Sauer, who never denied the rumor that he was an illegitimate son of Franz Liszt and who wore his silvery hair shoulder-length as Liszt had. At his yearly "farewell" concerts, a doddering old man approached the piano and was transformed into a lion the moment he touched the keys. Bronislav Hubermann: One could observe him in the streets, his protruding lower lip in motion as if in silent conversation with his muse. What about Hubermann's violin enthralled the Viennese? It was the same warm human quality which endeared Walter to them and earned him the nickname "Bruno Walzer." Who would forget Hubermann and Casals playing the Brahms Double Concerto?

Music filled days and nights, minds, and often was the only thing to fill stomachs. People leaving the opera after a performance of *Samson and Delilah* would pass students already standing in line for standing room to hear Chaliapin the next night. An understanding opera official would distribute numbers in the morning to enable them to attend classes and return to their places in line at night. Chaliapin—contrary to all rules the mighty figure would strut and gesticulate on the concert stage, and the unadorned platform would become theatre as his hypnotic voice and personality transformed it.

Often it was the theatrical stunt, combined with artistry, which captivated. How horror-stricken everyone was when Jeritza, in the midst of an aria, tripped and fell down a flight of stairs—without missing a note. Or when a malevolent Scarpia threw her to the floor and she continued to sing, in prone position, thus setting an example for generations of Toscas. Who would not suffer with Gertrude Rünger as Amneris, writhing in despair, imploring the gods to spare her beloved, Rhadames, while he was being condemned to entombment.

Who would not wish to recall the Don Octavio of Richard Tauber, his voice a burnished blade of steel. Tauber was equally at home in grand opera and in the world of his friend Franz Lehar. At the premiere of *Das Land des Lächelns* (The Land of Smiles), he sang "Dein ist mein ganzes Herz" (Thine is my heart alone) seven times, his voice ranging from glorious fortissimo to a sigh floating through the vast theatre as we held our breath.

Indeed, the days were filled with memorable music. But night was falling.

XXIII

Götterdämmerung

Abandoned! No other expression can adequately describe Austria's position. The League of Nations, reduced to insignificance by its past inaction, again failed to take a stand.

In London Neville Chamberlain and Lord Halifax set greater store by the high-sounding sophisms of a German champagne salesman turned ambassador than the urgent dispatches of the British legation in Vienna and the reports of British correspondents.

On the critical day of Austria's rape, France was immobilized through lack of any government. The cabinet of Premier Chautemps had resigned and the cabinet of Leon Blum did not come into being until Austria had ceased to be.

Italy's Mussolini, the past protector of Austria's independence, who had sent four divisions to the Brenner Pass when Chancellor Dollfuss had been assassinated, suddenly let it be known that he "accepted the whole thing in a very friendly manner" and that the fate of "Austria would be immaterial to him."

President Eduard Beneš of Czechoslovakia was lulled into a false sense of security by Göring's soothing words to the Czech envoy in Berlin. He did not realize until too late that the *Anschluss* would inevitably toll the death knell for his country also.

The drama had unfolded in inexorable sequence. In 1933 German President Hindenburg had reluctantly called Adolf Hitler, the rabble-rousing former Austrian corporal, to power. Soon Nazi hatred began to spill its venom beyond German borders and Austria was the first to feel the poison sting. Demonstrations soon became overt, grew bolder by the day; Chancellor Engelbert Dollfuss was murdered by Nazi thugs, and Dr. Kurt Schuschnigg, his successor, could not stem the tide.

Meistersinger performances at the State Opera had to be removed from the repertoire because the phrase "Was deutsch und echt" (What's German and true) in Hans Sachs' aria became the signal for orgiastic Nazi demonstrations in the opera house. Through intimidation, subversion, and treachery, Austrian Nazis entered the government. The handwriting unfolded fiery on the wall but the Viennese hoped for a miracle and muddled along.

On Friday, February 12, 1938, Chancellor Schuschnigg was called, more precisely ordered, to Hitler's residence at Berchtesgaden. There he was subjected to long harangues by the screaming, raving dictator and returned to Vienna a dazed man.

Sunday, February 20: Bruno Walter led the Vienna Philharmonic in a program of Mendelssohn, Wellesz, and Bruckner. The caryatids of the venerable Musikverein Hall still shone in gilded splendor and Walter led serenely. But a mysterious paralysis had gripped the audience. After each selection the vast hall grew more empty. The voice of Hitler, ranting over public loudspeakers in the streets, drowned out the voice of music.

February 24: A last futile gesture of defiance by Schuschnigg: But as he pledged an Austrian plebiscite, 20,000 Nazis went on a rampage in Graz, trampling the Austrian flag into the dust and hoisting the swastika.

Friday, March 11: While Karl Alwin conducted the last opera performance, *Eugene Onegin* by Tchaikovsky, in free Austria, the mob went wild as the news of Chancellor Schuschnigg's resignation came over the loudspeakers. Brutal reality had finally displaced the ostrich dreams of the Viennese.

As Hitler's vanguard violated Austria's border, as the rejected, the repressed, the frustrated, the hopeful, the naive, the treacherous poured into the streets from their hiding places, Vienna, the musical capital of the world ceased to be.

While Hitler flaunted the *fait accompli* of the *Anschluss* before the world from the balcony of the Habsburg palace before the screaming Vienna multitudes, the exodus of the intellectual elite began: Werfel, Schönberg, Walter, Lehmann, Freud, Zemlinsky, Krenek, Toch, Alfred Einstein. Some left their beloved city because they were Jews, others because they could not bear to watch free spirit being yoked to the "New" Order's narrow, warped vision. The change affected all—writer, actor, journalist, musician, composer, scientist. Some resisted, some fled, some compromised. Richard Strauss remained and became an important member of the "Reichskultur-kammer." Ancient composer Hans Pfitzner remained, and so did young, promising conductor Herbert von Karajan. Clemens Krauss

had already left for Berlin and taken part of the Vienna opera
ensemble with him.

At first no occasion was missed to prove the solidarity between
Reich Germans and their "liberated brothers." Women waving swastika flags roamed the streets shouting hysterically: "Who is our
saviour, who is our redeemer," and the entire street would scream in
reply "Adolf Hitler!" followed by a triple "Sieg Heil." Mobile soup
kitchens appeared in the streets as evidence of Hitler's role as protector of the Aryan race, in itself a hollow mockery in view of the
heterogeneous population of Vienna. Next came the broken windows
of Jewish shops, black swastikas and the word "Jude" smeared on
their doors, the arrest of liberals in all walks of life, the endless stream
of ashen-faced men filing from police wagons into the Hotel Metro-
pole, headquarters of the Gestapo in Vienna. Gone was the proud
name "Österreich," replaced by the medieval term "Ostmark"— eastern march or eastern frontier. As distrust dawned and disillusionment
grew, the public embraces became more fervent. Der Führer and
his staff attended concerts and reciprocal guest appearances were arranged in Berlin and Vienna.

Great music was still heard. For its centennial celebration, the
Vienna Philharmonic offered a program reminiscent of its most
glorious days. The niches of Mendelssohn and Mahler stood empty,
however; their non-Aryan music, together with the "kultur-bol-
schewistisch" works of Hindemith, Stravinsky, and Schönberg, had
been added to the funeral pyre of great thoughts by free men. But
the decree ordering the destruction of their music was not carried
out by the Philharmonic; in typically Viennese fashion, the precious
scores were removed under the cover of night to the outskirts of
the city and hidden in wine cellars. The Vienna Philharmonic itself
was threatened by the concerted drive for centralization. A decree
providing for the disbanding of the orchestra and confiscation of its
assets was actually promulgated in Berlin. One man averted that
ignominious fate. At the risk of incurring disfavor in Berlin, Wilhelm
Furtwängler repeatedly spoke and acted on behalf of Vienna, ca-
joling, coercing, mediating, whenever political consideration threatened to snuff out the artistic flame of Vienna.

Amid such dearth of free expression, no occasion for music-making
was missed. Aside from the regular subscription concerts and the
centenary activities, Clemens Krauss, who had returned to Vienna,
instituted radio "Philharmonic Akademien" devoted to the lighter
classics. Even occasions of mourning served a musical purpose. When
Austria's famed composer Franz Schmidt (who had risen from Phil-

harmonic ranks) died in 1939, a memorial concert was devoted to his music. Concert tours were avidly promoted by Berlin authorities who wished to pose as protectors of art.

Not until Hitler invaded Poland did the European powers act. What could have been done without bloodshed when he occupied the Rhineland was now to be attempted at the cost of millions of lives and irreplaceable treasures. Hitler's "Blitz" rolled on: Holland, Belgium, France fell; England was bombed day and night. Paris had been declared an open city; Vienna was not so fortunate.

Music-making continued as air raids mounted and food stocks dwindled. In 1943 Berlin permitted the Vienna Philharmonic to travel to neutral Sweden. But the Swedes openly received them as Viennese, not as Germans. One concert was attended by the ambassadors of those countries with whom Germany was at war, to the embarrassment of Berlin. It was the last foreign tour under German overlordship. During those years of strain, Dr. Karl Böhm, significantly an Austrian, who had led the Vienna Opera for a number of years, was persuaded to take over a number of Philharmonic concerts. His was to be a long-term stabilizing influence and artistic inspiration.

But war took its toll in music also. While the 1942–43 season saw sixty-seven concerts, 1943–44 offered little more than thirty, and the bound program-notes for 1944–45 are lean indeed. The opera struggled valiantly under Böhm to maintain a modicum of artistic balance, and Orff's *Carmina Burana* and three new Strauss operas were heard as late as 1944. But time had run out for Vienna. The worst blow fell when American planes accidentally bombed the opera. "The Opera is burning"—the news spread from mouth to despairing mouth. Resentment over the bombing, even if accidental and in time of war, died slowly. When, shortly after the war, an American asked for directions to the opera, a Viennese snapped back, "You found it easily enough from the air!" Black Friday, June 30, 1944, saw the last performance in the opera house. Significantly it was *Götterdämmerung*, and it presaged the twilight of those false gods who had vowed to enforce their credo for a thousand years.

As the Russians approached the spas and resorts whose shaded walks Beethoven and Schubert had trod, music still went on. While the thunder of artillery could already be clearly heard in Vienna, Krauss conducted two Philharmonic concerts. Soon the actual siege of the city was on. Barbed-wire and anti-tank barricades blocked streets lined with the rubble of what once had been magnificent baroque palaces, and corpses of humans and animals littered the once charming boulevards. Vienna was caught in the cross-fire of advancing Russian and retreating German troops. One artistic center after another fell victim to a fanaticism which vowed to defend the city street by street and forced the helpless population to live in sewers, cellars, even in the catacambs of the ancient city. The voice of madness, screaming over loudspeakers on fateful Easter Monday, April 2, 1945, exhorted all able-bodied men to fight for values which by then had become meaningless. In the ensuing gun duel the Burg Theatre, the noblest theatre in the German-speaking world, was devastated, and St. Stefan's Cathedral, Vienna's geographic and spiritual center, set afire.

Answering an urgent call, the men and families of the Philharmonic had barely assembled at the Musikverein building when they were informed that it was considered unsafe and must be evacuated. Hurriedly they moved to the deep cellars of the Burg Theatre. There stage furniture which had once served make-believe kings and courtesans now bedded ordinary humans. Barely had the group settled in their new quarters when they were ordered out to make room for high-ranking Nazi officials. Through shell-pocked, deserted streets, the members of the Philharmonic and their families fled on foot to the cellars of the Fire Brigade "Am Hof," leaving behind all their meager possessions, including their priceless instruments. But there was to be an end even to Hitler's madness. The Russian troops pressed on, and although the retreating Germans continued to shell the city for a short time, the battle was over.

XXIV

The Phoenix

As the thunder of guns receded, Vienna raised its bloody head. A haggard humanity emerged from the grimy world below like the prisoner of *Fidelio*, blinking in the sun, happy to be alive, horrified by the carnage and destruction. The homeless roamed amid rubble, corpses, discarded German uniforms, burned out tanks, abandoned weapons. For many a famed landmark they looked in vain. The opera, the cathedral, the Burg Theatre were gutted shells. Monuments to human greatness and the spirit of man had been wiped out. The vast parks of Vienna with their massed lilacs, forsythia, and roses now served as graveyards for soldiers and civilians, German, Russian, Viennese alike.

The first thoughts of the Philharmonic men turned to their instruments. A chilling sight awaited them. The pipes had burst in the cellars of the Burg Theatre and many instruments seemed damaged beyond repair. But the will to make music overcame all obstacles. While occasional shells still burst over the smoldering city, the men returned to the Musikverein building. Priceless manuscripts and scores were retrieved from bank vaults and hiding places; men formed a human chain and, from hand to hand, the music was returned to its rightful place. Rehearsals began immediately under Clemens Krauss who had remained in the city. Miraculously, Vienna heard its first concert within weeks after the guns had been silenced.

No better tonic could have been prescribed for the battered Viennese. From make-shift hovels they came, over heaps of rubble two stories high, out of the ground they came like ants, all converging on the great Konzerthaus Saal, the only large auditorium left undamaged. As Krauss appeared among the men he knew so well to conduct Beethoven's Third (Leonore) Overture, Schubert's "Unfinished" Symphony, and Tchaikovsky's Fifth Symphony, there welled up tears of joy and shouts of jubilation.

Soon the music hatred had banished—of Mahler, Mendelssohn, Stravinsky, Hindemith—followed in joyful succession. New men made their appearance. Josef Krips' energy, scholarship, and devotion made him equally important to the opera and the Philharmonic, and

Karl Böhm made himself more and more felt. And there were, of course, the great leaders of a past, Furtwängler, Knappertsbusch, and Krauss.

Slowly, the Philharmonic rose toward its former eminence. It reached a new high point in its memorable reunion with Bruno Walter in Edinburgh in September 1947. No other conductor had been so close to Vienna as Walter. It had been the place of his greatest triumphs, his happiest hours. The artists of the Vienna Philharmonic had been his inspired tools to shape his inspired interpretations. If one had expected cool reserve from the man who had been forced to flee before a wave of human degradation, one was mistaken. The meeting of Walter and the orchestra was emotionally and musically inspired, the tour a triumph. Walter's parting words were scarcely an exaggeration: "Do you know what has happened these weeks? What you have achieved? You have made history."

The rebirth of the State Opera lagged behind that of the Philharmonic. Thanks to the determination of Alfred Jerger, however, only five days after the first Philharmonic concert the first opera production was staged. Some credit is due the commander of the Soviet troops in Vienna, also a music lover—of sorts: About the middle of April 1945, Jerger was called before the commander. A well-fed man in general's uniform received him amicably and asked in broken German: "You director of Vienna Opera?" Jerger replied that he was the acting director. Satisfied and smiling the general continued: "I command you to play opera on First of May."

> I was horrified. This Russian general commanded me to perform an opera within fourteen days and all I had was a fraction of an ensemble, no decorations or costumes. I tried to explain . . . He listened, smiling peacefully, but then repeated "But I order you to play on First of May. And if you do not play then (he made a significant gesture by crossing his wrists) . . . Siberia." I was deeply disturbed, but then I gritted my teeth and set to work. We found a large hand cart and . . . went from storage depot to storage depot and dragged from the bombed-out ruins dust-covered scenery and torn costumes . . . Meanwhile an ensemble rehearsed at the Volksoper under the direction of Kapellmeister Krips and, lo and behold, on May 1, 1945 we actually presented a first-class artistic and vocal performance of *The Marriage of Figaro* with only scenery and costumes leaving much to be desired.

Soon the Volksoper proved inadequate and a second home had to be found for the homeless State Opera. The choice fell on the Theatre an der Wien, Vienna's grand old lady among theatres. There

Fidelio had been premiered 140 years earlier, and Beethoven had personally conducted his Fifth and Pastorale Symphonies and heard his Violin Concerto and G-major Piano Concerto performed for the first time. There Mozart and Johann Strauss and Franz Lehar had triumphed. There, on October 6, 1945 *Fidelio* reopened the famed old house as a second temporary opera house. (The building was condemned in 1955 and was to be razed in 1960, but the city administration decided to restore the historical theatre. It was reopened in May 28, 1962 in the presence of the Austrian President and government and invited guests with a program of Mozart, Beethoven, and Schubert.)

Artistic difficulties also beset the opera. Star ensembles such as Vienna had once boasted were things of the past. A spirit of restlessness had turned the great performers into nomads, equally at home in and equally detached from Vienna, Milan, Berlin, London, or New York. But Vienna had retained an important edge: its emphasis on ensemble. From its earliest beginnings, the chorus had been of high caliber, even incidental roles had been carried by fine voices, and the Philharmonic was in the pit.

The city which had twice repulsed the Turks and kept Europe Christian, the city from which the powerful Counter Reformation began, turned its first efforts to rebuilding its religious shrine. Although people continued to live in make-shift shelters, the cathedral rose again in medieval splendor. Forever gone were the magnificent stained glass windows, the gothic pews, the baroque choir stalls where Haydn and Schubert had sung, but the vaulted ceilings, the tiled roof, were restored with unerring craftsmanship. The state of Austria and Vienna, however, was still precarious: There was the four-power occupation and shortages of housing, clothing, and food. And the famed opera house still stood gutted, a mute symbol of the triumph of sword over lyre.

The home of the Philharmonic, the Musikvereinssaal, had been restored to its classic elegance and reopened with a festival concert on September 16, 1945. Inevitably thoughts turned to the restoration of the opera house. Under the approving eye of an artistically-inclined administration it was decided to build, within the still-standing facade, a monument to Vienna's past greatness and current perseverance and a symbol of its faith in the future. The result, at a cost of $10 million, the most modern operatic stage in the world. On its multiple stages and in its seven hundred rooms, several operas can be staged and rehearsed at the same time. The gilt interior is a happy blend of the traditional and contemporary.

Hand in hand with the rebuilding of stone went the re-creation of spirit. Karl Böhm, now a director of world renown, an opera expert, and, above all, an Austrian steeped in Vienna's musical tradition, began to shape the inaugural program. Beethoven's *Fidelio*, that story of victory over oppression, was to open the rebuilt edifice 150 years, to the day, after its premiere. With Böhm at the helm and Anton Dermota singing Florestan, the cast would mix the finest voices of past and present.

To follow *Fidelio*, Mozart's *Don Giovanni*. The role of the Italian roué was to be sung in German by an American with an English name, born in Canada of Russian-American parents—George London. Where should the inaugural program go from Mozart? The choice was Hofmannsthal's fable, *Die Frau ohne Schatten*, lavishly set to music by Richard Strauss. The choice was obvious because Strauss had brought the opera to Vienna with him in 1919. Another bond was Karl Böhm who had served his apprenticeship under Strauss.

The next selection was Verdi's *Aida*; at the time of the destruction of the house, it had been presented almost six hundred times—a record surpassed only by *Lohengrin*. Raphael Kubelik, a Vienna favorite, was to conduct, with George London portraying Amonasro.

Next Richard Wagner and *Die Meistersinger von Nürnberg*. Hans Sachs was to be sung by Paul Schöffler, perhaps the best portrayer of the role in his time.

Those who hoped for *Der Rosenkavalier* would not be disappointed. In his first letter to Strauss on the opera, Hofmannsthal, the librettist, left no doubt as to time and place: "Vienna under Maria Theresia." Viennese the work always remained, with its greatest interpreters coming from the city. Knappertsbusch would preside over what was to be the highpoint of the festival. The indelible memories of Lotte Lehmann and Richard Mayr were to be rekindled by Maria Reining and Kurt Böhm.

At that point the Vienna Opera had to prove that it was more than a musical museum. It had to serve as a laboratory for testing the masterpieces of the present and the future. Thus Alban Berg's *Wozzeck*, that often praised but seldom performed masterwork of our time was a "must." Actually the 1955 production was not new. Krauss had introduced the work in Vienna in 1930, and it had been given a new production in Salzburg in 1951. It was the Salzburg version which Vienna would hear under Böhm.

If *Wozzeck* was a signpost for the future, the ballet evening which would follow pointed in both directions. Ballet at the Vienna Opera has a long, fondly remembered and ofter neglected history. Fanny Elssler, the daughter of Haydn's valet, was Vienna's first great ballerina. But the Viennese seldom treated ballet as an art apart. To them it was the frosting on the cake, the whipped cream on the coffee. Richard Strauss apparently expressed that attitude when he named his own ballet *Schlagobers* (Whipped Cream). The revitalized Corps de Ballet intended to prove its versatility by presenting the tried and successful, *Giselle* by Adam, and the new and bold, Boris Blacher's *Othello*, especially composed in honor of the occasion.

Finally the question was how to conclude a festival of highpoints without lapsing into anticlimax. "Austria's Inauguration," which was to open with Beethoven, would end with Beethoven. The Philharmonic Orchestra would take the stage to close the festival with Beethoven's Ninth "Choral" Symphony. "Wir betreten, feuertrunken / Himmlische, Dein Heiligtum." (Drunk with fire, heaven advancing / Goddess, to thy shrine we come.) Schiller's youthfully exuberant words in the titanic setting of Beethoven were to acquire a new meaning in the new edifice.

Walter was to conduct. Once before, shortly after World War II, he had led Beethoven's opus in the rebuilt Musikvereinssaal when the opera house was still a rubble-strewn shell. Now he would re-create it again in the proud edifice, would exercise his deep insight on the superb instrument of the Philharmonic. Beethoven's testament to humanity and Bruckner's Te Deum, Austria's hymn of thankful praise, were to close one of the greatest musical events of our time.

Ten productions: seven operas, two ballets, one symphony, to be given on the same stage within nine days. The seven hundred rooms of the building hummed with feverish activity. Finally the day was at hand. The opera house was ready, and so was Vienna. And the world was listening. Over 26,000 reservations had been requested for 1,658 seats. Half the people who filled the house on that evening had come from outside Austria's borders. The day, November 5, 1955, was doubly auspicious because only a few days earlier all foreign troops had left Austrian soil. Joyful as that exodus had been, it was to be eclipsed by the event of the evening.

The horseshoe of the opera hall was humming with a festive crowd. The United States was represented by Secretary of State John Foster Dulles, Ambassador Clare Booth Luce, and Assistant Secretary of State Carl McCardle. Composer Dimitri Shostakovich was Russia's musical ambassador. But the guests inside the gilt hall were only a small part of the listening crowd in attendance. Outside, before the floodlit, flag-draped opera house and before huge loudspeakers, stood 30,000 Viennese in rapt anticipation. No streetcar bell, no automobile horn, no airplane drone disrupted the prayerful silence.

Inside the houselights dimmed and Karl Böhm raised his baton. A breathless silence settled over the vast house. As Beethoven's opening *Fidelio* chords shattered the silence, there was a moment of stunned unbelief, then unashamed tears. Vienna's most precious jewel in her crown of music was glittering again in a myriad facets. At that moment, unseen but felt by all, there was a beating of wings as the Phoenix rose renewed from its own ashes, as life itself was renewed in the city of music on the Danube.

BIBLIOGRAPHY AND INDEX

Bibliography

General Reference Works

Adler, Guido. *Handbuch der Musikgeschichte*. Berlin, 1930.

Bukofzer, Manfred D. *Music in the Baroque Era*. New York, 1947.

Einstein, Alfred. *A History of Music*. Leiden, 1934.

———. *Music in the Romantic Era*. New York, 1947.

Ferguson, Donald. *A History of Musical Thought*. New York, 1935.

Grove, George. *Dictionary of Music and Musicians*. New York, 1954.

Jewish Encyclopaedia Handbook. New York, 1952–55.

Lang, Paul Henry. *Music in Western Civilization*. New York, 1941.

Riemann, Hugo. *Musiklexikon*. Leipzig, 1929.

Salazar, Adolfo. *Music in Our Time*. New York, 1946.

Slonimsky, Nicolas. *Music Since 1900*. New York, 1938.

Specialized Works

Abert, Hermann. *W. A. Mozart*. Leipzig, 1955. A revised and enlarged edition of Otto Jahn's *Mozart*.

Abraham, Gerald (ed.) *The Music of Schubert*. New York: W. W. Norton, 1947.

Adler, Guido. *Gustav Mahler*. Vienna: Universal Edition, 1916.

———. *Musikalische Werke der Kaiser Ferdinand III, Leopold I, Joseph I*. Vienna, 1892.

Anderson, Emily. *Letters of Mozart to his Family*. New York: Macmillan, 1938.

Armstrong, T. H. *Strauss Tone Poems*. London: Oxford Univ. Press, 1931.

Auer, Max. *Anton Bruckner: sein Leben und Werk*. Vienna: Musikwissenschaftlicher Verlag, 1934.

Bates, Ralph. *Franz Schubert*. New York: D. Appleton-Century, 1934.

Baumgartner, Bernhard. *Mozart*. Berlin and Zurich: Atlantis Verlag, 1940.

Berger, A. "Berg, Schönberg and Krasner," *Saturday Review*, Apr. 24, 1954.

Berges, Ruth. "Mahler and the Great God Pan," *Musical Courier*, Jan. 1960.

Beyes, Ruth. "The Tragic Star of Hugo Wolf," *Musical Courier*, Mar. 1960.

Biancolli, Louis (ed.). *The Mozart Handbook*. New York: Grosset & Dunlap, 1962.

Blom, Eric. *Mozart*. New York: Farrar, Strauss and Cudahy, 1935.

———. *Richard Strauss: Der Rosenkavalier*. London: Oxford Univ. Press, 1930.

Burk, John N. *Clara Schumann*. New York: Random House, 1940.

Cooper, Martin. *Gluck*. London: Oxford Univ. Press, 1935.

Copland, Aaron. *Music and Imagination*. Cambridge, Mass.: Harvard Univ. Press, 1952.

Da Ponte, Lorenzo. *Memoirs*. New York: J. B. Lippincott Co., 1929.

Davenport, Marcia. *Mozart*. New York: Charles Scribner's Sons, 1932.

Decsey, Ernst von. *Bruckner: Versuch eines Lebens*. Berlin: Schuster & Loeffler, 1920.

———. *Franz Lehar*. Munich: Drei Masken Verlag, 1930.

———. *Hugo Wolf*. Berlin: Schuster & Loeffler, 1919.

———. "Jazz in Vienna (Jonny Spielt Auf)," *Living Age*, Mar. 1928.

———. *Johann Strauss*. Stuttgart: Deutsche Verlags-Anstalt, 1922.

Deutsch, Otto Erich. *Franz Schubert: die Dokumente seines Lebens*. Berlin: G. Müller, 1920.

Downes, Olin. "Berg's Wozzeck," *New York Times*, Apr. 14, 1951.

———. "Electra in 1952," *New York Times*, Aug. 25, 1952.

———. Symphonic Masterpieces. New York: Tudor Publishing Co., 1943.

Einstein, Alfred. *Gluck*. New York: Farrar, Strauss and Cudahy, 1931.

———. *Mozart: His Character, His Work*. London: Oxford Univ. Press, 1945.

Engel, Gabriel. *The Life of Bruckner*. New York: Roerich Museum, 1931.

———. *Gustav Mahler: Song Symphonist*. New York: Bruckner Society, 1932.

Ewen, David and Frederic. *Musical Vienna*. New York: McGraw-Hill, 1939.

Finck, Henry T. *Richard Strauss*. Boston: Little, Brown & Co., 1917.

Frost, H. F. *Schubert*. New York: Scribner & Welford, 1881.

Fuller-Maitland, J. A. *Schumann*. New York: Scribner & Welford, 1884.

Furtwängler, Wilhelm. *Johannes Brahms, Anton Bruckner*. Leipzig: Reclams Universal Bibliothek, 1942.

Geiringer, Karl. *Brahms: His Life and Work*. Boston: Houghton Mifflin Co., 1936.

———. *Haydn: A Creative Life in Music*. New York: W. W. Norton & Co., 1946.

Girdlestone, Cuthbert. *Mozart and His Piano Concertos*. New York: Dover Publications, 1958.

Goldberg, Albert. "Bruno Walter: Poet of Conductors." *New York Times*, Aug. 9, 1956.

Goldsmith, Margaret. *Maria Theresia of Austria*. London: A. Barker, 1936.

Graf, Max. *From Beethoven to Shostakovitch*. New York: Philosophical Library, 1947.

——. *Legend of a Musical City: The Story of Vienna*. New York: Philosophical Library, 1945.

——. *Modern Music*. New York: Philosophical Library, 1946.

——. "Strauss–Hoffmannsthal Letters," *Musical America*, Feb. 1953.

Gregor, Josef. *Richard Strauss der Meister der Oper*. Munich: R. Piper, 1939.

Grove, George. *Beethoven and His Nine Symphonies*. London: Novello & Co., Ltd., 1886.

Grünwald, Max. *The Jews of Vienna*. Philadelphia: The Jewish Publication Society of America, 1936.

Gutmann, Albert. *Aus dem Wiener Musikleben*. Vienna: Hofmusikalienhandlung A. G. Gutmann, 1914.

Haas, Robert Maria. *Anton Bruckner*. Potsdam: Akademische Verlagsgesselschaft 1934.

Hadamowsky, Franz and Heinz Otte. *Die Wiener Operette*. Vienna: Bellaria Verlag, 1948.

Hadden, J. Cuthbert. *Haydn*. New York: Pellegrini & Cudahy, 1905.

Hanslick, Eduard. *Aus dem Concertsaal*. Vienna: W. Braumüller, 1870.

——. *Aus meinem Leben*. Berlin: Allgemeiner Verein für deutsche Literatur, 1894.

——. *Geschichte des Concertwesens in Wien*. Vienna: W. Braumüller, 1869–70.

——. *Vom musikalisch Schönen*. Leipzig: Johann Ambrosius Barth, 1885.

Herriot, Edouard. *The Life and Times of Beethoven*. New York: Macmillan, 1935.

Hodeir, André. *Music Since Debussy: A Contemporary View of Music*. New York: Grove Press, 1961.

Howard, John Tasker & J. Lyons. *Modern Music*. New York: Thomas Crowell, 1957.

Hughes, Gervase. *Composers of Operetta*. New York: St. Martins Press, Inc., 1962.

Hughes, Rosemary. *Haydn*. London: J. M. Dent & Sons, Ltd., 1950.

Huneker, James Gibbons. *Ivory, Apes and Peacocks*. New York: Sagamor Press, 1957.

Jacob, H. E. *Johann Strauss, Father and Son*. New York: The Greystone Press, Inc., 1939.

Janetschek, Ottokar. *Emperor Franz Josef*. London: T. Werner Laurie Ltd., 1953.

Kalbeck, Max. *Johannes Brahms*. Berlin: Deutsche Brahms-Gesellschaft, 1908.

Kelly, Michael. *Reminiscences*. New York: Collins and Hannay, 1826.

Kenyon, Max. *Mozart in Salzburg*. London: Putnam & Co. Ltd., 1952.

Kobald, Karl. *Alt–Wiener Musikstätten*. Zurich: Amaltheaverlag, 1919.

——. *Franz Schubert and His Times*. New York: A. A. Knopf, 1928.

——. *Johann Strauss*. Vienna: Österreichischer Bundesverlag, 1925.

──────. *Josef Haydn: das Bild seines Lebens und seiner Zeit*. Vienna: H. Epstein, 1932.

Kolodin, Irving (ed.). *The Composer as Listener*. New York: Horizon Press, 1958.

Kralik, Heinrich. *Das grosse Orchester*. Vienna: W. Frick, 1952.

──────. *Wiener Staatsoper*. Vienna: Bundestheaterverwaltung, 1955.

Krenek, Ernst. *Gustav Mahler*. New York: The Greystone Press, 1941.

──────. "Is 12-Tone Technic on the Decline?" *Musical Quarterly*, Oct. 1953.

Lang, Oskar. *Anton Bruckner: Wesen und Bedeutung*. Munich: Beiderstein, 1947.

Lange, Fritz. *Joseph Lanner und Johann Strauss*. Leipzig: Breitkopf & Härtel, 1919.

Lansdale, Maria H. *Vienna and the Viennese*. Philadelphia: John C. Winston Co., 1902.

Leibowitz, René. *Schönberg and His School*. New York: Philosophical Library, 1949.

Levetus, A. S. *Imperial Vienna*. New York: John Love Co., 1905.

Liess, Andreas. *Wiener Barockmusik*. Vienna: Ludwig Doblinger, 1946.

Maecklenburg, A. "Hugo Wolf and Anton Bruckner," *Musical Quarterly*, Jul. 1938.

Mahler, Alma. *Gustav Mahler: Memories and Letters*. New York: The Viking Press, 1946.

Marken, Leonard. "Portrait of Berg," *New York Times,* Mar. 3, 1952.

Marliave, Joseph de. *Beethoven's Quartets*. New York: Dover Publications, Inc., 1961.

Mendel, A. "Anton Bruckner," *The Nation*, Nov. 18, 1931.

Mitchell, Donald. *Gustav Mahler: The Early Years*. London: Rockliff, 1958.

Mittag, Erwin. *Aus der Geschichte der Wiener Philharmoniker*. Vienna: Gerlach & Wiedling, 1950.

Moscheles, Ignace. *The Life of Beethoven*. Boston: Oliver Ditson & Co., 1841.

Nettl, Paul. *The Book of Musical Documents*. New York: Philosophical Library, 1948.

──────. *Forgotten Musicians*. New York: Philosophical Library, 1951.

──────. *Mozart and Freemasonry*. New York: Philosophical Library, 1957.

──────. *Das Wiener Lied im Zeitalter des Barock*. Vienna: Dr. R. Pass, 1934.

Newlin, Dika. *Bruckner, Mahler, Schönberg*. New York: Kings Crown Press, 1947.

Newman, Ernest. *Gluck and the Opera*. London: Dobell, 1895.

──────. *The Life of Richard Wagner*. New York: Alfred A. Knopf, 1949.

Niemann, Walter. *Brahms*. New York: Alfred A. Knopf, 1929.

Paumgartner, Bernhard. *Mozart*. Zurich: Atlantis Verlag, 1945.

Peyser, Herbert F. *Richard Strauss*. New York: Philharmonic–Symphony Society, 1952.

Pleasants, Henry. "Alban Berg's Retrospect in Vienna," *New York Times*, Jun. 20, 1954.

———. "Fresh Insight into the Mind of Rich. Strauss," *New York Times*, Sep. 8, 1954.

———. (ed.). *Vienna's Golden Years of Music*. New York: Simon & Schuster, 1950.

Pohl, Karl F. *Joseph Haydn*. Berlin: A. Sasso Nachfolger, 1927.

Redlich, Hans F. *Bruckner and Mahler*. New York: Farrar, Strauss & Cudahy, 1955.

Redlich, Joseph. *Emperor Franz Josef of Austria*. New York: Macmillan, 1929.

Reich, Willi. *Alban Berg*. Vienna: H. Reichner, 1937.

———. "A Guide to Wozzeck," *Musical Quarterly*, Jan. 1952.

Robertson, Alex. *Chamber Music*. Harmondsworth, Middlesex: Penguin Books Ltd., 1957.

Rolland, Romain. *Beethoven the Creator*. New York: Harper & Brothers, 1929.

———. *Goethe and Beethoven*. New York: Harper & Brothers, 1931.

St. Foix, George de. *Mozart's Symphonies*. New York: Alfred A. Knopf, 1949.

Schauffler, Robert H. *Beethoven: The Man who freed Music*. New York: Tudor Publication Co., 1947.

———. *Florestan: The Life of Robert Schumann*. New York: Henry Holt & Co., 1945.

———. *Franz Schubert: The Ariel of Music*. New York: G. P. Putnam's Sons, 1949.

Schloss, E. H. "Mozart's Librettist (da Ponte)," *New York Times,* Mar. 27, 1955.

Schönberg, A. "My Evolution," *Musical Quarterly*, Oct. 1952.

———. *Style and Idea*. New York: Philosophical Library, 1950.

Schönberg, H. "A Genius Reappraised (A. Berg)," *New York Times*, Sep. 13, 1959.

———. "Lulu, Berg's Freudian Opera," *New York Times*, Sep. 28, 1952.

Schumann, Robert. *Gesammelte Schriften über Music und Musiker*. Leipzig: Philipp Reclam Jr., 1888.

Sedgwick, Henry D. *Vienna*. Indianapolis and New York: The Bobbs-Merrill Co., 1939.

Selden-Goth, G. "Schönberg's Life: A Struggle Shown in Letters," *Musical Courier*, Apr. 1960.

Specht, Richard. *Gustav Mahler*. Berlin: Schuster & Loeffler, 1913.

———. *Johann Strauss*. Berlin: Marquardt, 1909.

———. *Richard Strauss und sein Werk*. Leipzig: E. P. Tal, 1921.

———. *Das Wiener Operntheater*. Vienna: P. Knepler, 1919.

Stefan, Paul. *Arnold Schönberg*. Vienna: Zeitkunst Verlag, 1924.

———. *Bruno Walter*. Vienna: H. Reichner, 1936.

———. *Gustav Mahler*. New York: Schirmer, 1913.

———. *Neue Musik und Wien*. Leipzig: E. P. Tal & Co., 1921.

———. *Die Wiener Oper*. Vienna: Wila Verlag, 1932.

Steichen, Dana. *Beethoven's Beloved.* New York: Doubleday & Co., 1959.

Strauss, Eduard. *Erinnerungen.* Vienna: F. Deuticke, 1906.

Strauss, Johann. *Johann Strauss schreibt Briefe . . . mitgeteilt von Adela S.* Berlin: Verlag für Kulturpolitik, 1926.

Stuckenschmidt, H. *Arnold Schönberg.* New York: Grove Press, Inc., 1959.

Taubman, H. "Berg's Wozzeck," *New York Times,* Mar. 7, 1959.

———. "Die Frau ohne Schatten," *New York Times,* Sep. 21, 1959.

———. "The Modern Music of Mozart," *New York Times,* Jan. 22, 1956.

———. "Thanks to Walter," *New York Times,* Mar. 18, 1956.

———. "Unfamiliar Mozart," *New York Times,* Jun. 24, 1956.

Teetgen, Ada B. *The Waltz Kings of Old Vienna.* London: Jenkins, 1939.

Thayer, Alexander W. *The Life of Ludwig van Beethoven.* Ed. by E. Forbes. Princeton, New Jersey: Princeton University Press, 1964.

Trojan, Felix. *Das Theater an der Wien.* Vienna: Wila Verlag, 1923.

Trollope, Frances. *Vienna and the Austrians.* London: P. Bentley, 1838.

Tschuppik, Karl. *Maria Theresia.* Amsterdam: A. de Lange, 1934.

Turner, W. J. *Beethoven: The Search for Reality.* London: Dent, 1927.

———. *Mozart.* New York: Doubleday & Co., 1956.

Walter, Bruno. *Gustav Mahler.* New York: The Greystone Press, 1941.

———. *Theme and Variations.* New York: Alfred A. Knopf, 1946.

Weigl, Bruno. *Die Geschichte des Walzers.* Langensalza: H Beyer & Söhne, 1910.

Weingartner, Felix. *The Symphony Writers Since Beethoven.* London: Reeves, 1925.

Wellesz, Egon. "Anton Bruckner and the Process of Musical Creation," *Musical Quarterly,* Jul. 1938.

———. *Arnold Schönberg.* New York: Dutton, 1925.

Wolff, Werner. *Anton Bruckner, Rustic Genius.* New York: Dutton, 1942.

Yates, P. "Arnold Schönberg, Apostle of Atonality," *New York Times,* Sep. 11, 1949.

Index

Abravanel, Maurice, 231, 232
"Ach, du lieber Augustin," 17, 213
Adam, Adolphe, 243
Adler, Guido, 214, 215, 220
Alarcón, Don Pedro de, 188
d'Albert, Eugene, 126, 188, 226
Albertina (Gallerie), 7
Albert of Saxony, Duke, 7
Albrecht of Bavaria, 11
Albrechtsberger, Johann Georg, 58
Altenberg, Peter, 113, 197, 210, 222
Alwin, Karl, 227, 235
Anschluss, 3, 234, 235
Anti-Semitism in Vienna, 109, 110
Apollosaal, 132, 133, 138
Arco, Count Georg Anton Felix, 35, 38, 45
Aspern, Napoleon defeated at, 6, 133
Atonality, 214
Auernhammer, Josepha, 45
Auersperg, Princess, 94
Augustin, Mark, 17
Augustins, Church of, 106

Bach, Johann Sebastian: 9, 42, 105, 118, 119, 127, 180, 220; *Well-tempered Clavichord*, 14; *Well-tempered Clavier*, 42; B-minor Mass, 119; Chorale in Berg Violin Concerto, 223
Backhändel, 5
Backhaus, Wilhelm, 232
Bahr, Hermann, 114, 161, 183, 184, 197, 210, 213
Bahr-Mildenburg, Anna, 197
Baillet von Latour, Count, 97
Balzac, Honore de, 141
Barbi, Alice, 125
Barnum, P. T., 105

Bartok, Bela: 218; explains the "Tone Row," 214
Bastille, 128
Bäuerly, Adolf, 131
Bauernfeld, Eduard von, 87, 89, 91, 129
Bayreuth, 164, 178, 185
Beaumarchais, Pierre de, 44
Beethoven, Johann, 72
Beethoven, Ludwig van: vii, 14, 34, 38, 45, 48, 53, 54, 55, 74, 75, 77, 79, 84, 85, 87, 90, 105, 110, 113, 118, 122, 136, 138, 140, 141, 146, 147, 156, 164, 167, 173, 178, 179, 187, 192, 193, 194, 198, 201, 212, 213, 218, 220, 231, 237; *Fidelio*, 3, 58, 62, 68, 76, 78, 196, 199, 227, 230, 239, 241, 244; life and work, 57–73; plays for Mozart, 57; and Hadyn, 57, 60; symphonies, 58, 60, 61, 62, 65, 67, 68, 71, 72, 75, 127, 230, 241, 243; trios, 59, 66, 68; "Heiligenstadt" Testament, 60; overtures, 60, 62, 66, 67, 71, 81, 239; quartets, 61, 63, 73, 91; sonatas, 61, 62, 63, 65; deafness, 62, 68, 72; concertos, 63, 232, 241; appearance, 65, 70; "Immortal Beloved," 66; and Goethe, 66; humor, 67; financial embarrassment, 67; *Missa Solemnis*, 71, 119; funeral, 88
Bekker, Paul, 213
Bellini, Vincenzo, 189
Belvedere Palace, 20, 21, 182
Benatzky, Ralph, 107, 131
Beneš, Eduard, 234
Berchtold, Count Leopold von, 205–7 *passim*
Berg, Alban, 213–15, 218, 220–23 *passim*, 228–30 *passim*

253